IMAGES
of America
HARRISON

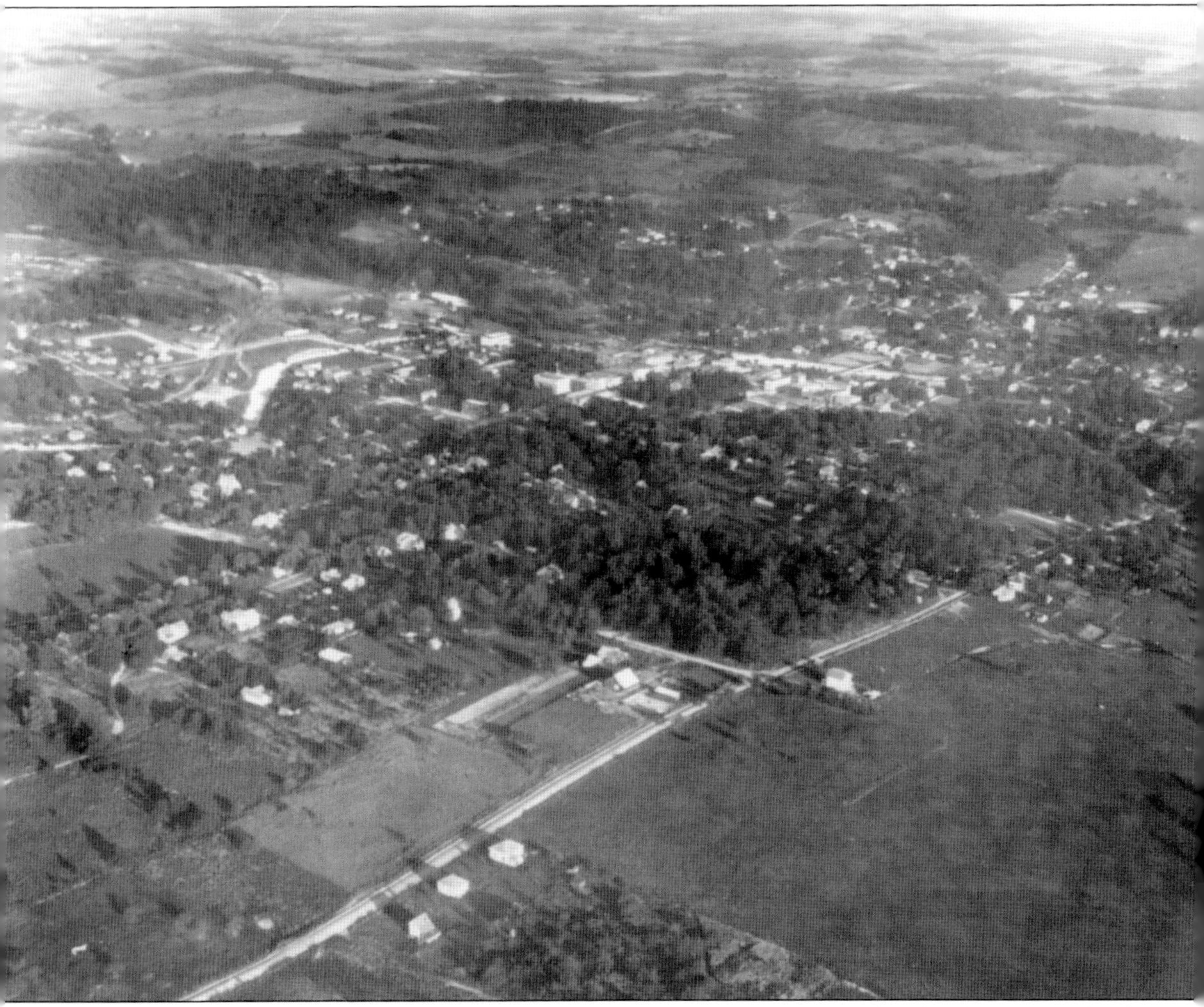

AERIAL VIEW OF HARRISON, JULY 4, 1927. This photograph was most likely taken by Earl Rowland, the famous airman from Harrison. Rowland, a pioneer aviator and test pilot for Cessna Aircraft, was the first pilot to land at what is now Boone County Airport in Harrison in 1921. During his illustrious career, Rowland won the Cross-Continent Air Race and many other competitions. (Courtesy of Boone County Library.)

On the Cover: **RAILROAD CAR SHOP, 1928.** Workers for the Missouri & North Arkansas Railroad had recently been enjoying the eight-hour workday; nonetheless, workers did unionize and strike. The most significant wage strike occurred in 1921 and divided the community. Vandalism and intimidation were rampant, and the railroad remained shut down for eight months. There was a violent citizens' uprising, which included a lynching. (Courtesy of Boone County Library.)

IMAGES
of America

HARRISON

Nate Jordon

ARCADIA
PUBLISHING

ISBN 978-1-4671-1431-8

Published by Arcadia Publishing
Charleston, South Carolina

Printed in the United States of America

Library of Congress Control Number: 2015932171

For all general information, please contact Arcadia Publishing:
Telephone 843-853-2070
Fax 843-853-0044
E-mail sales@arcadiapublishing.com
For customer service and orders:
Toll-Free 1-888-313-2665

Visit us on the Internet at www.arcadiapublishing.com

To all of the good citizens of Harrison, Arkansas, who value their cherished history, and to the memories of the courageous lives of the people whose images are featured in this book.

Contents

ACKNOWLEDGMENTS

Over the decades, many citizens have donated photographs to the Boone County Library for the preservation of a visual history of Harrison and the surrounding area. This book would not have been possible without the generous contributions of these people. The Boone County Library archives these photographs as well as newspapers and rare local histories. These were an invaluable resource for the completion of this book. The staff members and volunteers who maintain these collections were very helpful to me and this project, and they have earned my gratitude. Unless otherwise noted, all images in this book were kindly provided by the Boone County Library.

A special thank-you is due to Tina Farmer, genealogist with Boone County Library, for her generous cooperation in helping me research the images contained here.

Another special thank-you is due to Marcille Lawrence and First Christian Church for their assistance in researching the history of Harrison.

A warm thank-you is also due to the citizens of Harrison, who met with me to help research the history of this city and its people. I would also like to thank the *Harrison Daily Times*, the Rotary Club of Harrison, Arkansas, Patty Methvin with the Harrison Regional Chamber of Commerce, and Carolyn Cline with Cline Berry Farm for promoting the history of Harrison, this book, and its author.

Finally, I wish to thank my editor at Arcadia Publishing, Jesse Darland, for his patience, guidance, and oversight.

Introduction

Nestled in the heart of the Ozarks of north-central Arkansas, Harrison is a small city that embodies an intriguing history within the state. Inhabitants had a hardscrabble existence for much of its early history, challenged by wars, outlaws, poverty, and nature itself. It represented a dichotomy in this landscape of unlimited beauty, producing a people who have a close relationship with the environment and their neighbors.

The first inhabitants of the area lived in the caves and bluffs along the rivers. The Osage, a branch of the Sioux, was the main tribe in the Ozarks. One of their larger villages is thought to have been to the east of the present site of Harrison. The Shawnee, Quapaw, and Caddo were also in the area.

Some historians contend that the first white men to explore the area were some 40 followers of Hernando De Soto who camped at an Indian village on the White River at the mouth of Bear Creek. It is also probable that the first white men were French hunters and trappers who followed the course of the White River. What is known is that the Arkansas Territory was under the control of Catholic countries, France and Spain, until the Louisiana Purchase in 1803. After that date, many people came to the area seeking a place to settle. Among the first were frontier people, or mountain men, who hunted and trapped for their subsistence.

Dubuque, the earliest village in the area, was a cluster of cabins built around the home of Joseph Coker, who settled there in 1814. His homestead was located not far from the present site of the Lead Hill Boat Dock; the land is now under the waters of Bull Shoals Lake.

The Cherokee arrived in the area around 1816. They could not get along with the Osage, and this hostility erupted into a full-scale tribal war in the Ozarks. By the 1830s, both tribes were removed to Oklahoma.

In the early 1830s, only a few hunters, trappers, and settlers had made their way up the White River and scattered to take up residence among the surrounding hills. Brothers William and Peter Beller were among the first to settle near what is now Harrison. The real wave of settlers started in the 1840s, due in part to improved military roads originally built to remove Native Americans east to Indian Territory.

Pitifully poor by the standards of the day, settlers came seeking unsurveyed government land on which to homestead. Few of them had enough money to buy land, and fewer still were wealthy enough to own slaves. Not many wagons carried luxuries, like dishes, tools, cutlery, or furniture, but almost every wagon carried a large iron pot, and almost every settler held a Kentucky rifle. The pot was used for cooking food, heating water, making soap, and washing clothes. The rifle provided meat for the table.

After crossing the humid delta lands in the eastern part of the region, and faced with crossing the Indian Territory to the west, many weary families decided they had gone far enough in their search for a homestead and decided to stay in the Ozarks. The landscape was soon dotted with cabins, most of them having only one room heated by a fireplace. Bear oil burning in bowls and gourds provided lighting. What little furniture they had was made by hand.

In 1840, Joseph Burkett settled near what is now downtown Harrison. In 1855, James Stiffler arrived, homesteading near the spring that continues to bear his name.

In the late 1850s, rumors of civil war began to travel around the Ozarks. Slavery was a major issue nationwide, but in this area it was not much of a concern. Most mountaineers would never become wealthy enough to own slaves. Over the years, a few wealthy families moved into the area, but there were never many in proportion to the total population. Faced with a daily struggle for survival, most people in this area did not consider slavery to be an issue worth fighting over. Most settlers had worked very hard to manage and improve their homes and land to farm with some profit. Having come to the frontier running down a dream, it looked like their dreams were about to come true. These fiercely independent people wanted, above all else, to be left alone to pursue their lives on their own terms. Then, the war came.

It is one of the great ironies of the Civil War that these frontier people, who did not want to fight and did not want to leave the Union, suffered more from the effects of the war than the people of almost any other part of the country. Families were torn apart by a division of sympathies, with sons fighting on both sides. Some men attempted to hide out in the Ozarks, hoping the war would pass them by.

Hill folks soon discovered they were fighting two wars. One war, perhaps the most serious for local people, was waged against the hated bushwhackers, who fought solely for their own gain. Skirmishes between armies and bushwhackers were common.

Life in the Ozarks became a nightmare. Soldiers from both armies were sent out to forage for cattle, chickens, food, and horses. Homes were burned, innocent civilians were murdered, livestock and food were seized, and the land was pillaged. By the end of the war, only two houses were left standing within miles of today's Harrison.

Residents who hoped the end of the war would mean a return to normal living were doomed. They faced a period of terrible want and the greatest time of lawlessness in American history. Until the men made their way home from the war, there were few guns and no ammunition. Any food that had not been hidden had been stolen or destroyed. Families hunted squirrel, possum, and other small animals with stones and clubs. Boiled weeds provided nourishment during the summer months. Salt was leached from the floors of burned-out smokehouses. Even after the men returned, it took some time for the land to be restored and for crops to be planted. People managed to survive by resourcefulness and by sharing what little they had with their neighbors.

"It was in an era of defiance, discord, and bitter hatred that Boone County and Harrison were born," wrote local attorney and historian Ralph Rea in his book *Boone County and Its People*. There were political struggles among former Confederates, carpetbaggers, Republicans, and Democrats. It was during this turbulent Reconstruction period that James Townsend Hopper, better known as "Town," was elected Arkansas state senator. He introduced a bill creating Boone County on April 9, 1869.

There are two versions of how the county got its name. Many people believed it was meant to be called Boon. They based their claim on a letter written by Senator Hopper. In it, he wrote that the "natural and beautiful views created by a wild and romantic scenery suggested the name Boon." Others claimed the county was named after Daniel Boone, pointing out that the act creating the county did spell it with an "e." The edition of the *Arkansas Gazette* published the day the act passed stated the county was named after Daniel Boone.

Senator Hopper was a controversial figure due to his years of service as a Union recruiter for northwest Arkansas. Some people with Confederate sympathies claimed his job masked bushwhacking activities by him and his men. Others scoffed at the idea and held Hopper in the highest regard.

Town Hopper was a close friend of Henry W. Fick, Harrison's founding father. Fick, an attorney and Union officer from New York, arrived in 1863, purchased the Stiffler property, and built a store. He was a staunch Republican and had the distinction of being Harrison's first real political boss. Despite his Union service and the fact that he was a close friend of the unpopular Reconstruction governor Powell Clayton, Fick counted many former Confederates among his friends, including his brother-in-law James O. Nicholson, who helped him run his store. Together with a small group of likeminded Republicans and Union veterans, including D.B. Jernigan, W.W. Jernigan, Town Hopper, Gillum Hopper, and Fick's son-in-law Isaac Moore, they established a powerful political clique.

Fick used his political influence to have a town built around his store. A temporary county seat was established there, in what was then known as Jackson Township, until an election could be held to choose county officers, who would then determine the location of the county seat as nearest as possible to the center of Boone County.

Marcus LaRue Harrison, chief engineer for the Pacific & Great Eastern Railroad, was in the vicinity with a survey crew when Fick asked Harrison to survey a town on the banks of nearby Crooked Creek. Harrison, a brigadier general in the Union army, may have already been familiar with the area. He had led the 1st Arkansas Cavalry Volunteers, praised for being the finest Union counter-guerrilla unit in the state, across northwest Arkansas on a counterinsurgency campaign from 1863 to 1865. Harrison agreed to survey a townsite. Fick named the town in Harrison's honor on February 7, 1870.

Also in February 1870, legislation passed appropriating $13,000 for a two-story brick courthouse to be built in the center of the town square. Once completed, the courthouse quickly became a community center as well as the seat of local government. People gathered there for social events, programs, and church services. A bandstand was erected in the courtyard. The Harrison Town Band played there on weekends and special occasions. A replica of the original bandstand resides on the courtyard square to this day and is still used to stage musical performances.

At the time Harrison was being established, Fick focused his efforts on establishing the town as the county seat. His plans were met with resistance from citizens of nearby Bellefonte. Residents of the town, located three miles east of Harrison and heavily populated by former Confederates, wanted their town to be named county seat. According to *Boone County and Its People*, "Most of the former Confederates were pulling for Bellefonte, because it was definitely a community that had favored the southern cause. On the other hand, Harrison had been fathered by former Union soldiers and carpetbaggers, and it was openly called, 'a Carpetbagger's town.' " However, Fick persuaded several former Confederates who lived in and around Harrison that the value of their properties would rise with the fortunes of the town. The resulting dispute almost ended in a shoot-out before someone suggested an election. When the election was held to determine the county seat, Fick's town emerged victorious by two votes. The news set off a wild celebration. Guns and anvils were fired, the band played, and a huge bonfire was built on top of Woodland Heights for the benefit of the people of Bellefonte.

Nonetheless, many county residents were unhappy with Harrison being chosen as the county seat. A petition for a special election was circulated, and enough signatures were obtained for an election to be called. Emotions ran high between the two sides, and several fights took place. A rumor started that forces from Bellefonte were marching on Harrison. Residents promptly armed themselves with guns, sticks, and rocks and went to the top of Harrison Hill, where they waited through the night. Fortunately, bloodshed was avoided when the insurgents from Bellefonte failed to arrive. Harrison was incorporated six years later, on March 1, 1876, and received its charter in 1878.

Fick also decided Harrison needed a weekly newspaper. In an effort to bolster Republicanism and consolidate his considerable influence over the town, he invited newspaper publisher Thomas Newman to move to the Arkansas Ozarks.

Newman, a native of England, arrived in Philadelphia as a boy but soon moved westward. Initially working as a railroad engineer, he quickly became involved in the abolitionist movement and moved to Kansas, where he published an abolitionist newspaper. During the Civil War, he moved to St. Louis and quickly signed up for service with the 9th Regiment of the Enrolled Missouri Militia. After the war, he returned to St. Louis, but he did not stay long, quickly accepting Fick's invitation. Once in Harrison, Newman began publishing the *Boone County Advocate* in 1870. It ran until 1876, when the *Harrison Daily Times* replaced it. Though Newman was a strong abolitionist and Union man, he had Democratic principles and became the first mayor of Harrison.

The office of the *Harrison Daily Times* was built in 1876 and remains located on the north side of the town square at 109 West Rush Avenue. While the building retains its original look, the facade has been updated several times, and the interior has been completely remodeled. The *Harrison Daily Times* continues to be the local newspaper. Run as a family business by the Dunlap and Christenson families for several generations, it is presently owned by Community Publishers, Inc.

The mid-1880s saw the construction of five buildings on the Harrison square in the 100 block of North Willow Street and seven buildings on the south side of the square along the 100 block of West Stephenson Street. In the mid- and late 1890s, thirteen buildings were constructed, and they remain today. The buildings erected prior to 1900 were made of native stone but later were dressed in brick veneer.

The railroad came to Harrison in 1901, and it had a profound impact on the community. The first St. Louis & North Arkansas locomotive arrived on March 22, 1901, at 9:15 a.m. In 1912, the Missouri & North Arkansas decided to relocate its offices here. The City of Harrison raised $25,000 for the construction of railroad offices located above Coffman Brothers Drugstore, presently Sam Alexander's Pharmacy. Eventually, all of the railroad shops were moved to Harrison, but plagued by misfortune, the railroad was abandoned in 1960.

In 1903, work began on the Federal Building at 201 North Main Street. It was completed in 1905. It served as the post office from 1906 to 1965. It was constructed at an original cost of $78,000, with a total floor space in excess of 20,000 square feet. This three-story brick building with Classical Revival features is an imposing landmark in the downtown area. Now owned by Boone County, it houses county- and state-funded offices and courtrooms. Though the post office and other federal offices have been relocated, the old courtroom is still in use. Cow tracks are still present in the west sidewalk.

The original Boone County Courthouse was burned out on July 4, 1908. The cause of the fire remains controversial. One story blamed it on an accident involving a fireworks display that was conducted from the roof of the building. Another report claimed the fire was set by someone trying to destroy evidence in a court case. Whatever the cause, the new courthouse was built in 1909 and continues to house many county offices and to store county records. It has two courtrooms on the top floor.

The ambitious design of the town square, with broad streets and a spacious design, has enabled the downtown area to continue to accommodate over 140 years of growth and change while retaining its original character. The Boone County Courthouse Square is registered as a historic district, and many of the buildings on and near the square have been listed in the National Register of Historic Places, the official list of the nation's historic places worthy of preservation. The neighborhoods and business districts convey the atmosphere of the old days when visitors come to walk or drive the streets and alleyways running through the middle of the blocks.

One

The Town Square

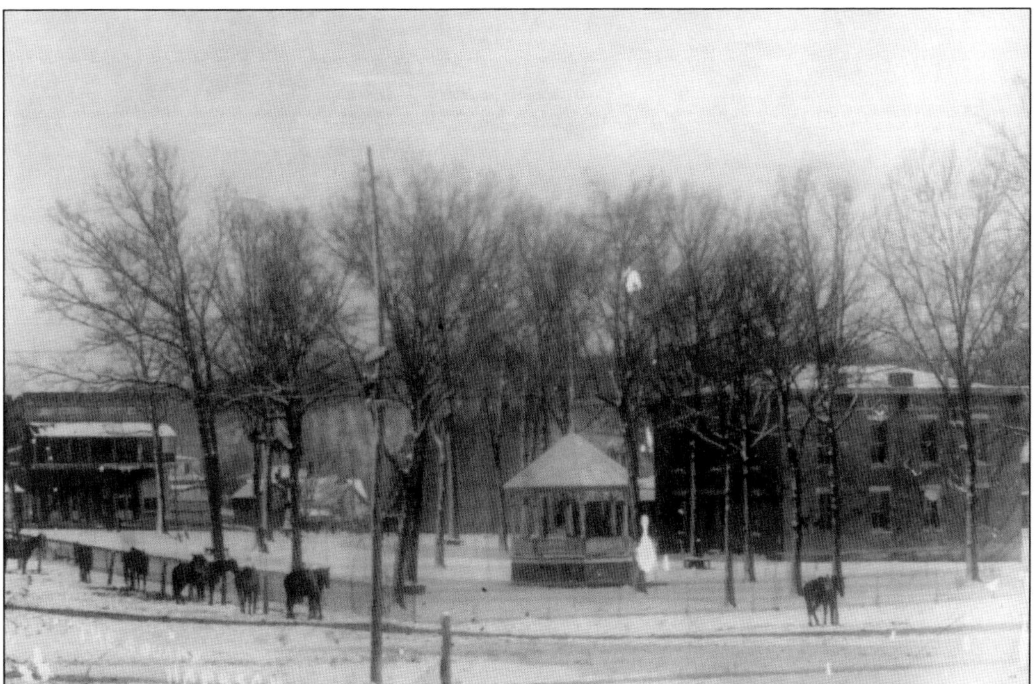

Northwest Corner of Town Square, 1890s. This photograph looks southeast from the northwest corner of the town square. The Speer Hotel can be seen on the east side of the square. On the courthouse square, the original bandstand can be seen, as well as the original Boone County Courthouse, built in the 1870s. There is snow on the ground, and horses are tied to hitching posts.

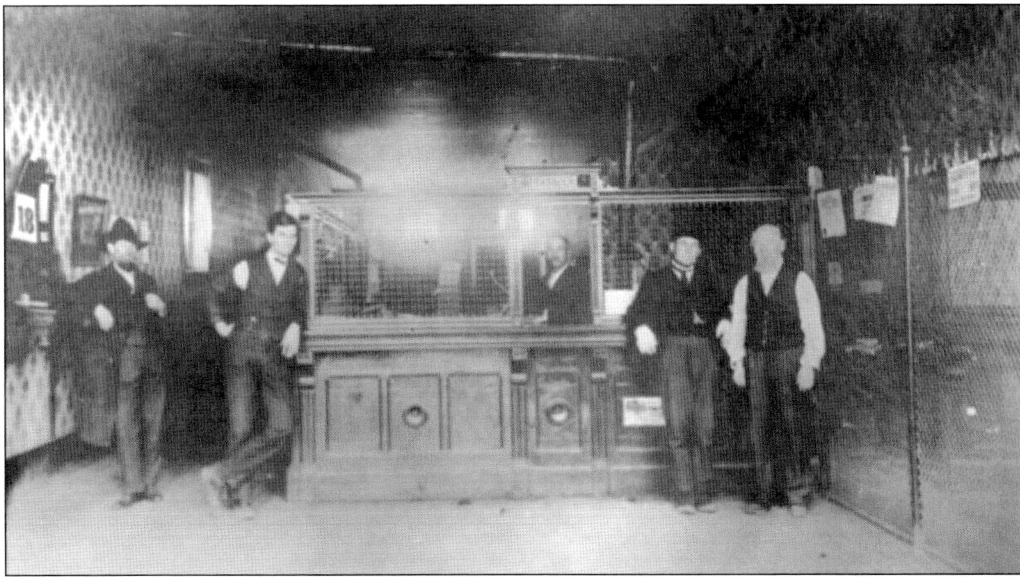

BANK ON TOWN SQUARE, 1890s. One of the most enduring myths of the American frontier is that of bank robberies and bandits. The fact is that bank robberies were rare at this time. Thieves would have a difficult time robbing banks built around the center of town, with entryways facing the town square. As well, most citizens were armed, presenting a very real threat to potential criminals.

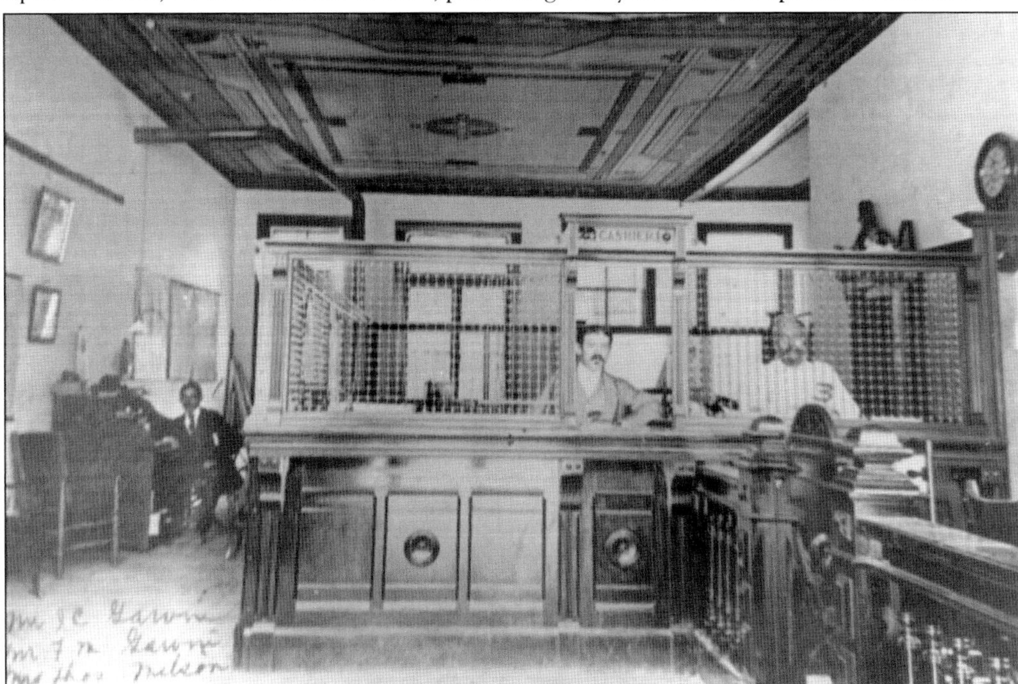

BANK OF HARRISON, 1894. Creating a record of good business sense and reliability were just two of several requirements for a frontier banker. Another involved the appearance of the establishment and its employees. Note the ornate wood of the service desk and the ceiling, as well as the fine dress of the workers. These bank employees are, from left to right, I.C. Garvin, F.N. Garvin, and Thomas Nelson.

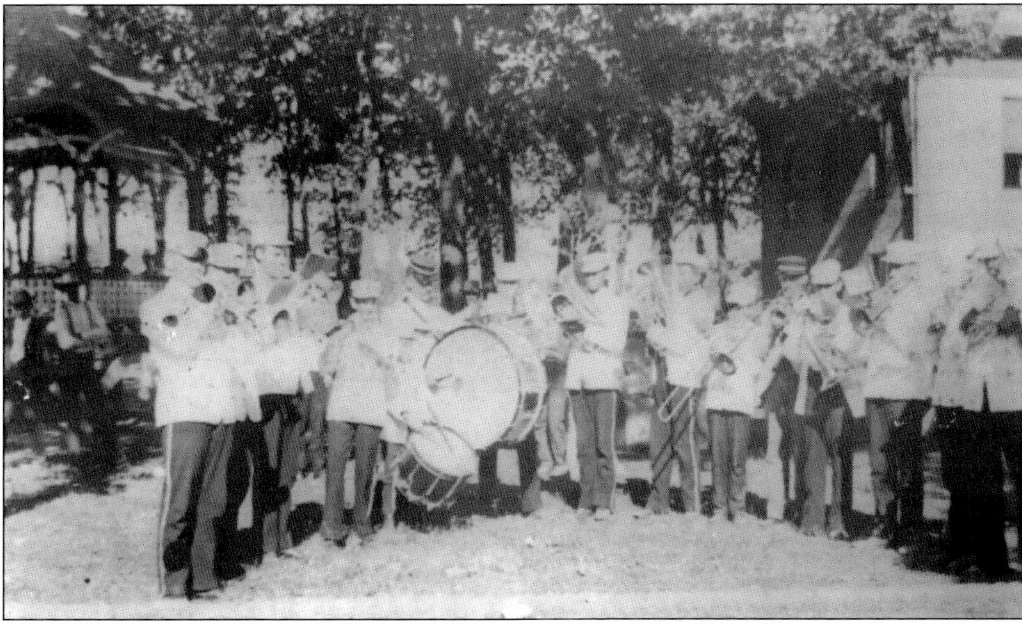

Harrison Silver Cornet Band, 1895–1900. Here, the Harrison band is seen playing on the northwest corner of the Boone County Courthouse Square. The members are in front of the bandstand, which can be seen to the left. The original courthouse is on the right. Featuring 14 musicians, the band played for parades and other special community events.

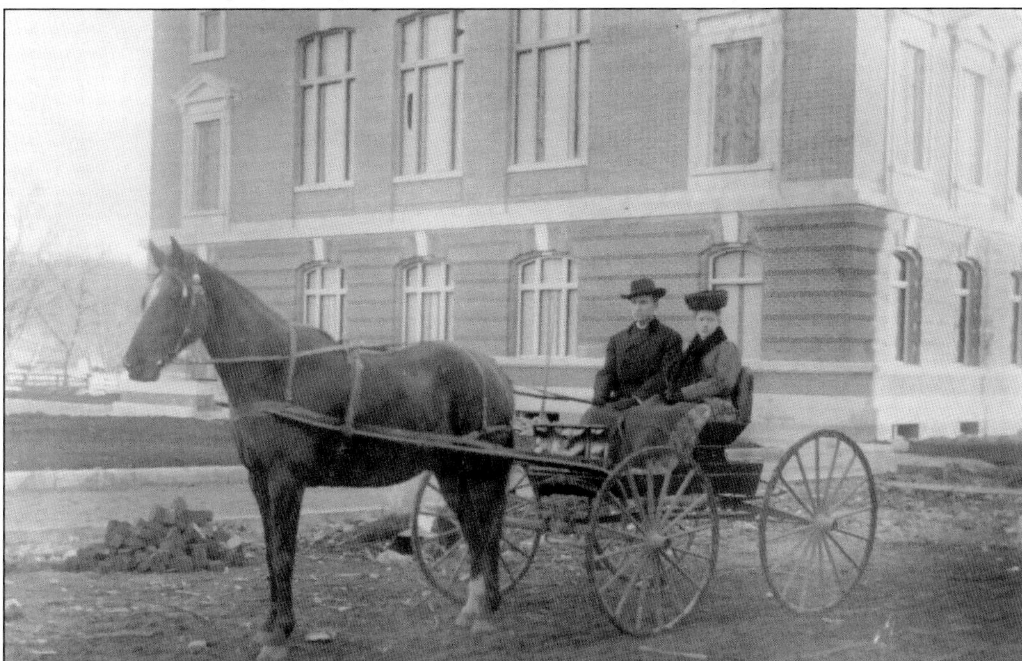

Couple in Horse Buggy, 1906. Will and Rose Henry ride in their buggy on North Main Street in front of the Federal Building. Construction on the building began in 1903 and was completed in 1905. Here, glass has yet to be installed in the windows. Bricks from the project are still on the ground, and the sidewalk is being paved. Cow tracks are still present in the west sidewalk.

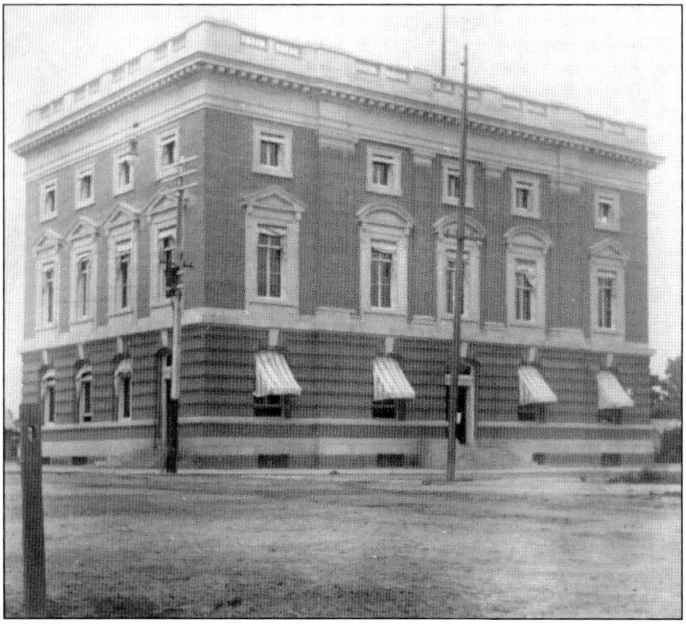

Federal Building, Early 1900s. Located at 201 North Main Street, the Federal Building was constructed at an original cost of $78,000. The three-story brick building continues to be an imposing landmark in the downtown area. It is now owned by Boone County and houses county- and state-funded offices and courtrooms.

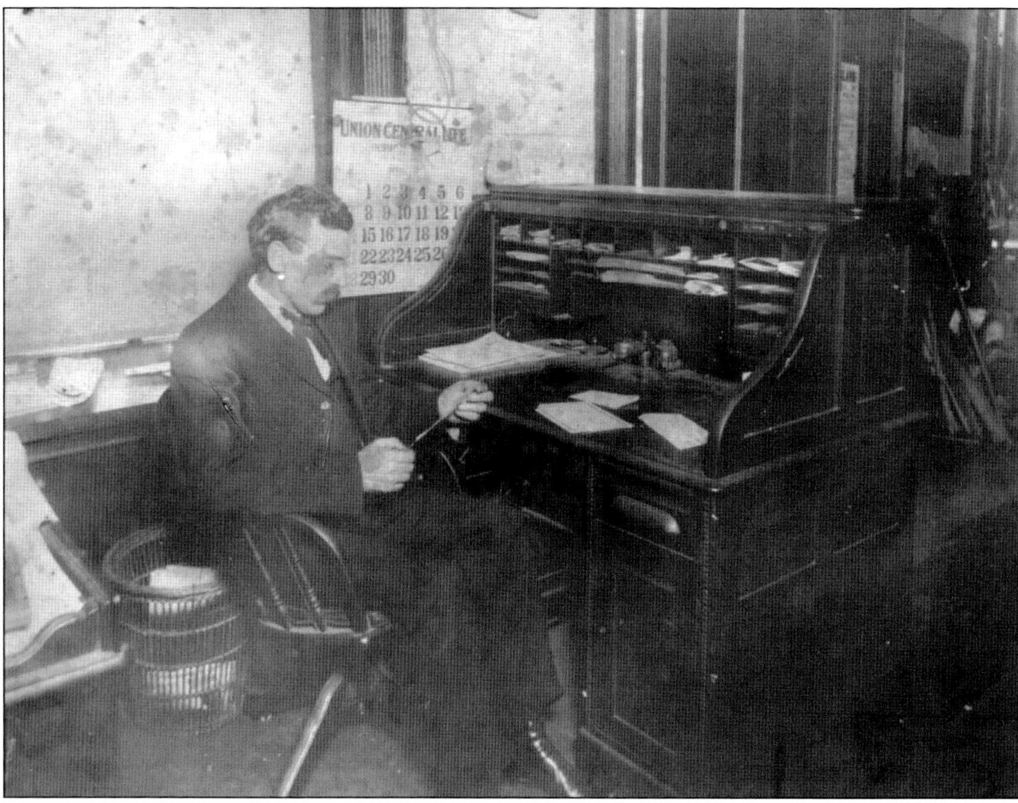

State Land Commissioner, 1906. Lafayette Lee Coffman sits at his desk inside the Federal Building. The office of the commissioner of state lands was created in 1868 by the Arkansas General Assembly to manage immigration and state lands. Born in Arkansas in 1857, Coffman was state land commissioner from 1906 to 1910. He passed away in 1940.

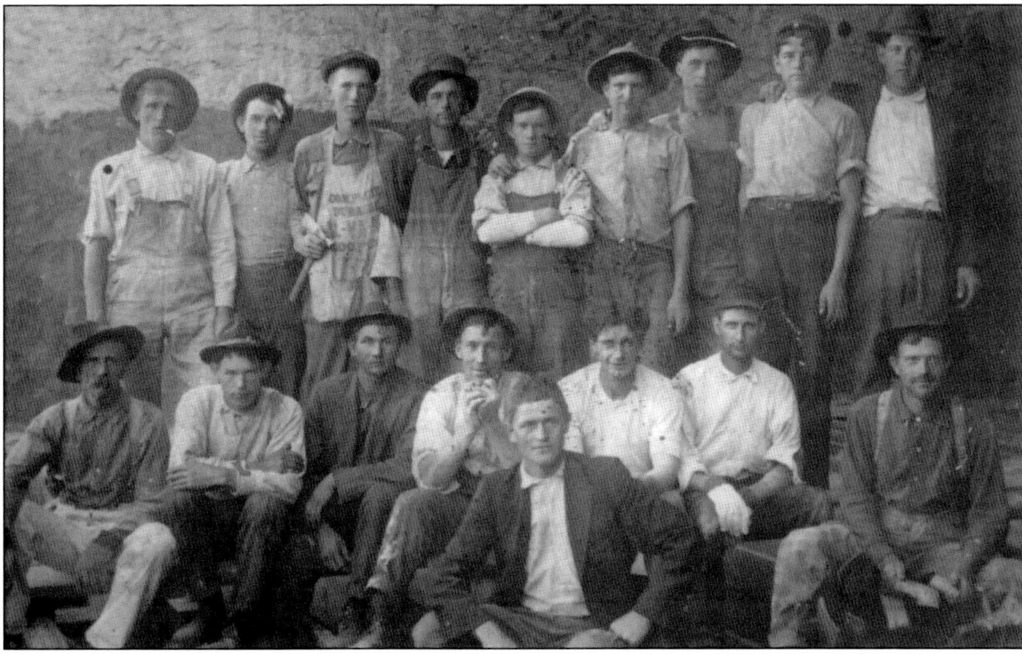

Courthouse Construction Crew, 1909. The original Boone County Courthouse went up in flames on July 4, 1908. Controversy continues to this day as to the cause of the fire and whether it was an accident or arson. The new courthouse was erected in 1909 and continues to house many county offices, including two courtrooms on the top floor.

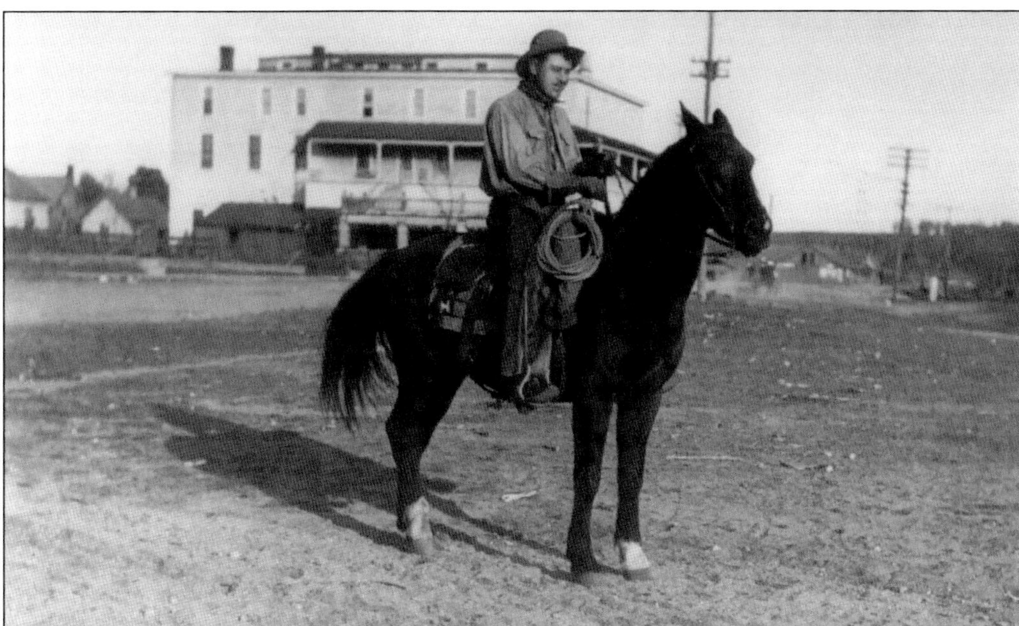

Man on Horse, Early 1900s. Visible behind this unidentified man and his steed is the Southern Hotel, located on the southeast corner of the Harrison town square. Though electricity has reached the area, as evidenced by the power lines in the background, the roads are still unpaved. Harrison's population at this time was over 1,600.

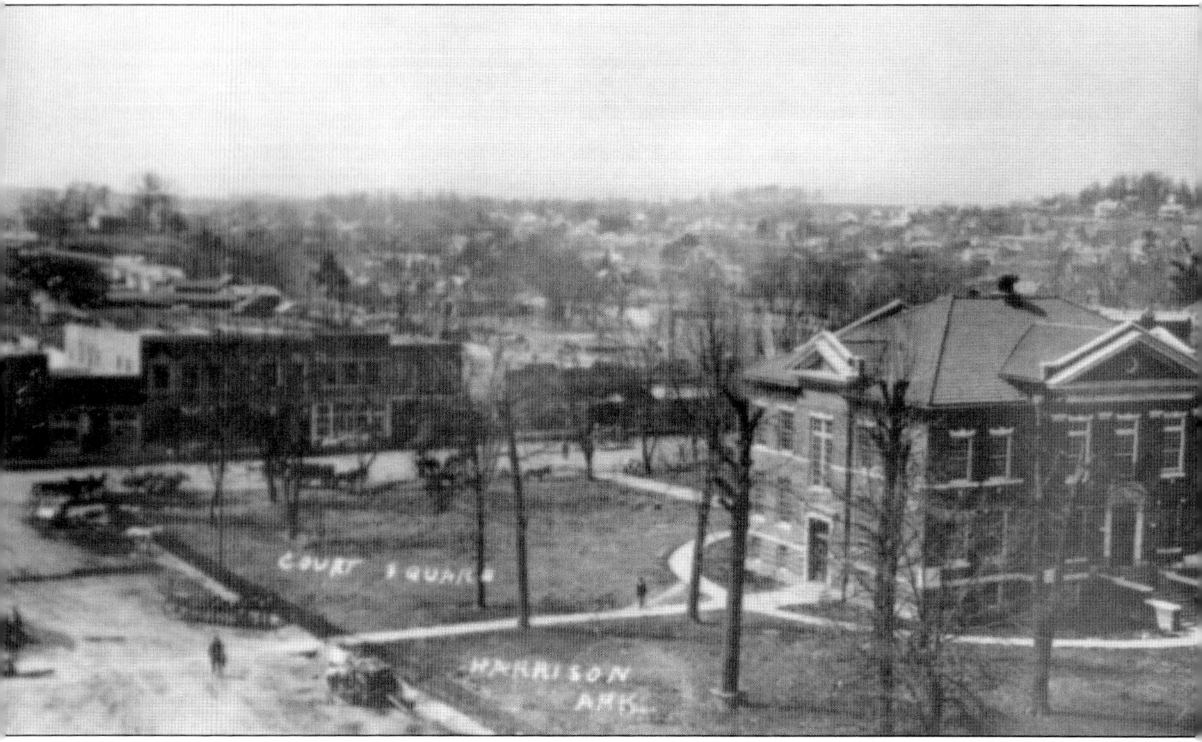

HARRISON TOWN SQUARE, 1910. With the completion of the new Boone County Courthouse, the town square received a new look. The ambitious design of the square, with broad streets and wide spaces, has enabled the downtown area to continue to accommodate over 140 years of growth

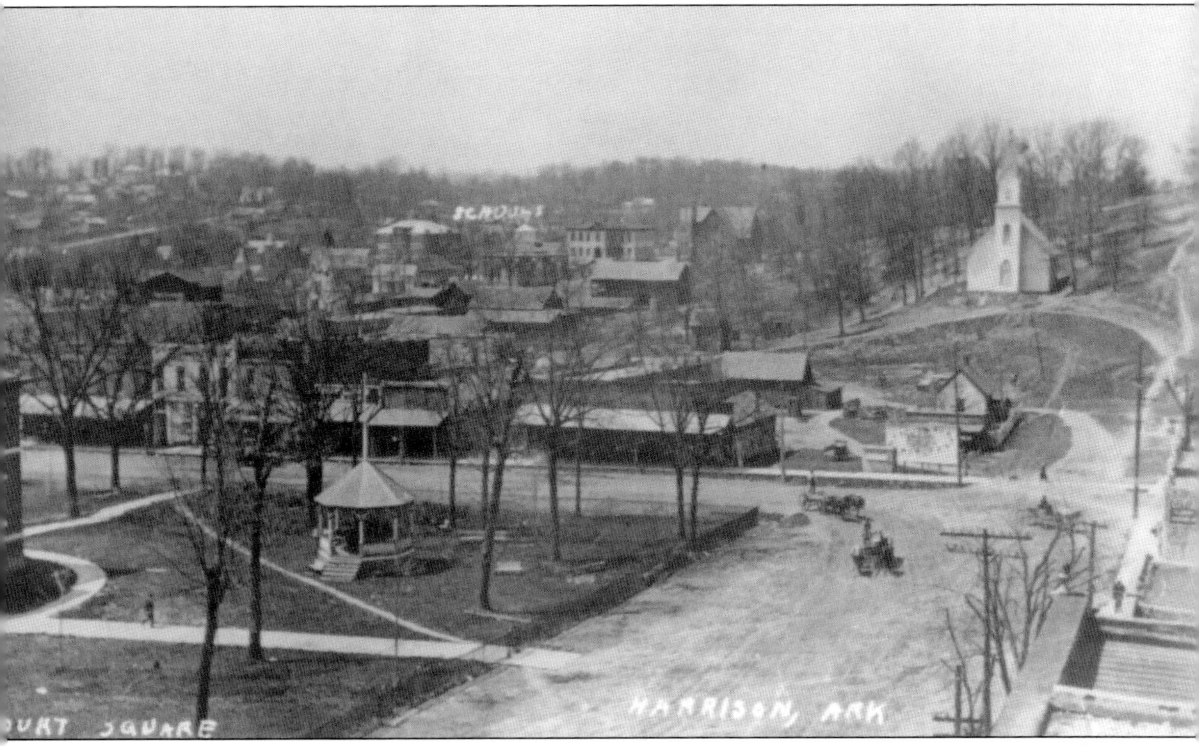

and change while retaining its original character. The Harrison Courthouse Square is registered as a historic district, and many of the buildings on and near the square have been listed in the National Register of Historic Places.

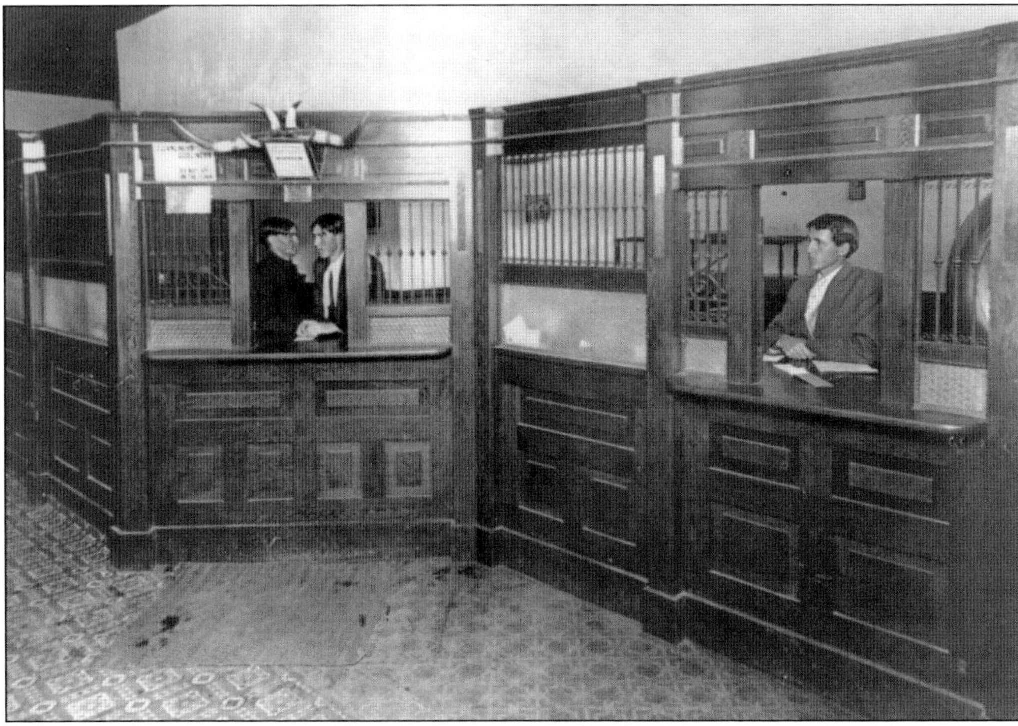

BANK CLERKS, EARLY 1900S. Though banks and their employees needed to present an appearance of success, it may not have mattered to some of their customers. In this bank, a small sign has been placed next to the bullhorns above the tellers at left, and it reads, "Cleanliness is Next to Godliness—Do Not Spit on Floor." Note the tobacco juice stains on the rug covering the stained floor.

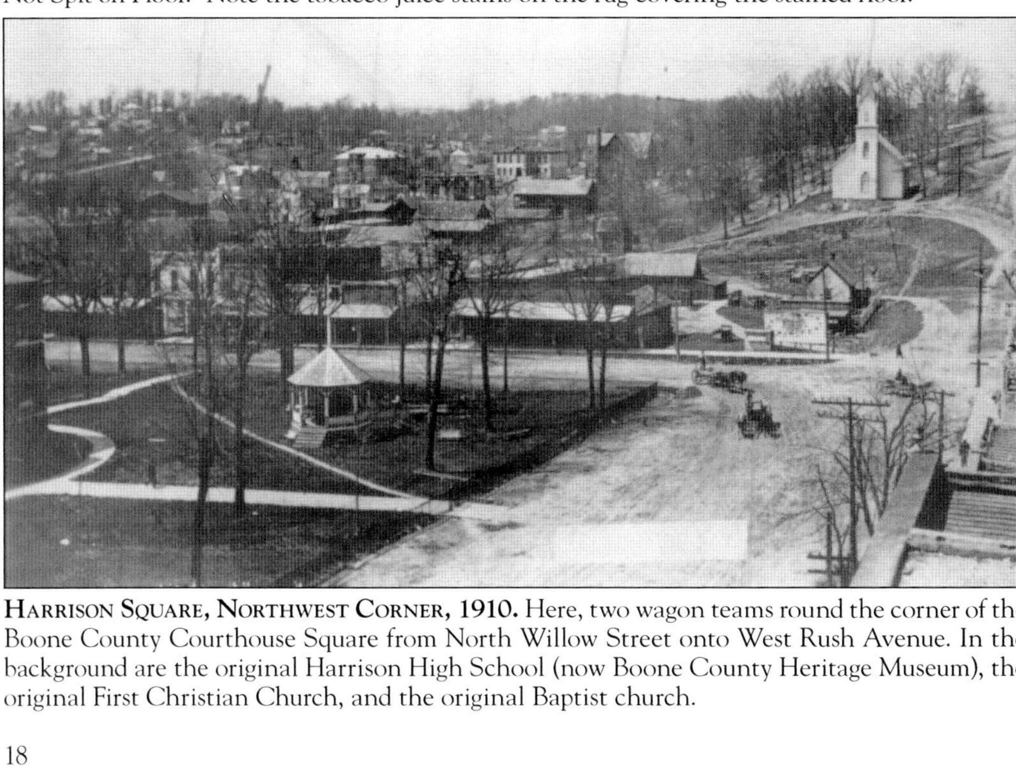

HARRISON SQUARE, NORTHWEST CORNER, 1910. Here, two wagon teams round the corner of the Boone County Courthouse Square from North Willow Street onto West Rush Avenue. In the background are the original Harrison High School (now Boone County Heritage Museum), the original First Christian Church, and the original Baptist church.

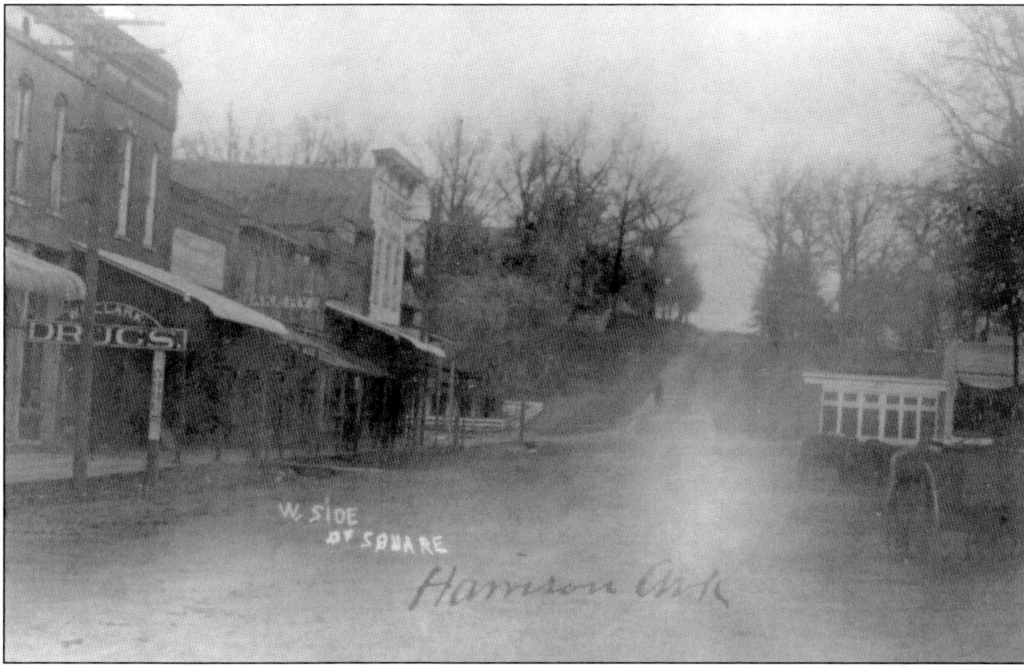

TOWN SQUARE, WEST SIDE, 1910. Looking north up North Willow Street from the west side of the square, the stores have an elevated sidewalk constructed of wood planks. Today, shoe stores, clothing boutiques, a church, law offices, and other businesses occupy this side of the square.

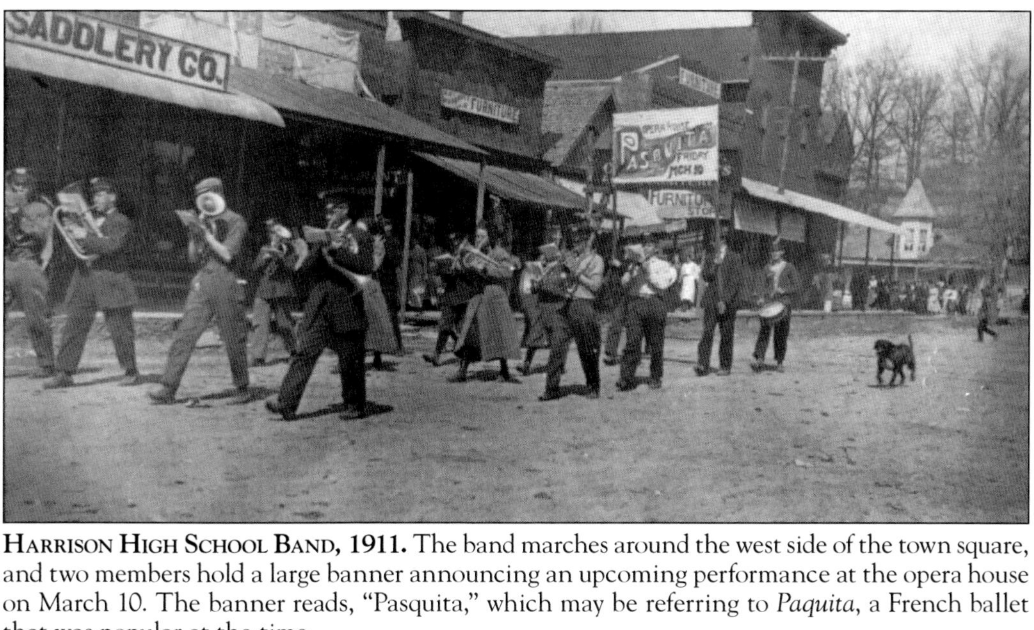

HARRISON HIGH SCHOOL BAND, 1911. The band marches around the west side of the town square, and two members hold a large banner announcing an upcoming performance at the opera house on March 10. The banner reads, "Pasquita," which may be referring to *Paquita*, a French ballet that was popular at the time.

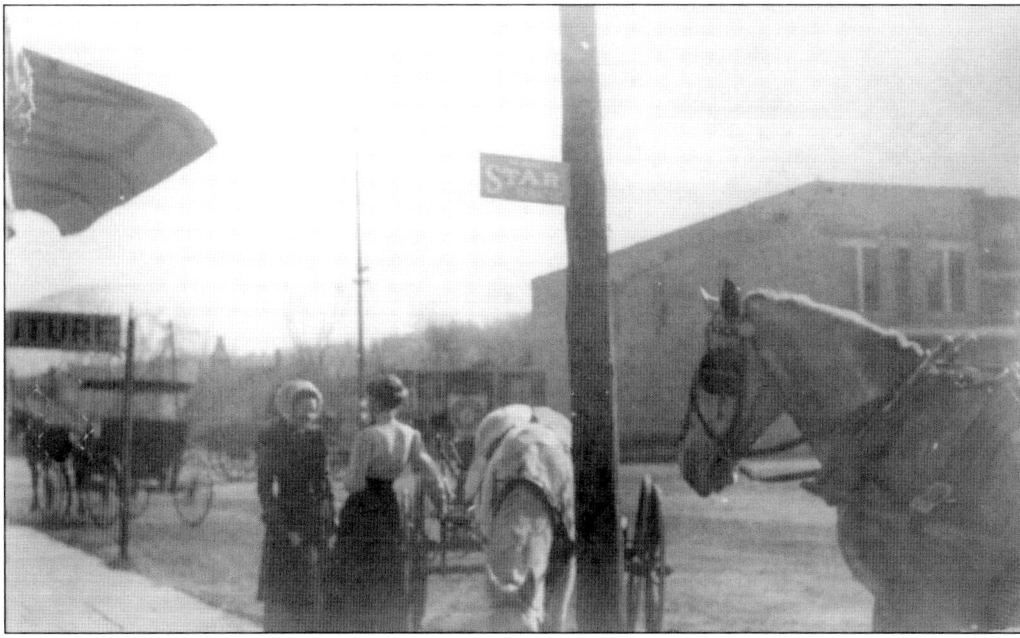

WOMEN ON TOWN SQUARE. Several horses and buggies can be seen in this photograph. The town square was the center of activity for the community. Many residents came there to socialize, catch up on local news, do their shopping, and get informed on social events, church services, and other activities.

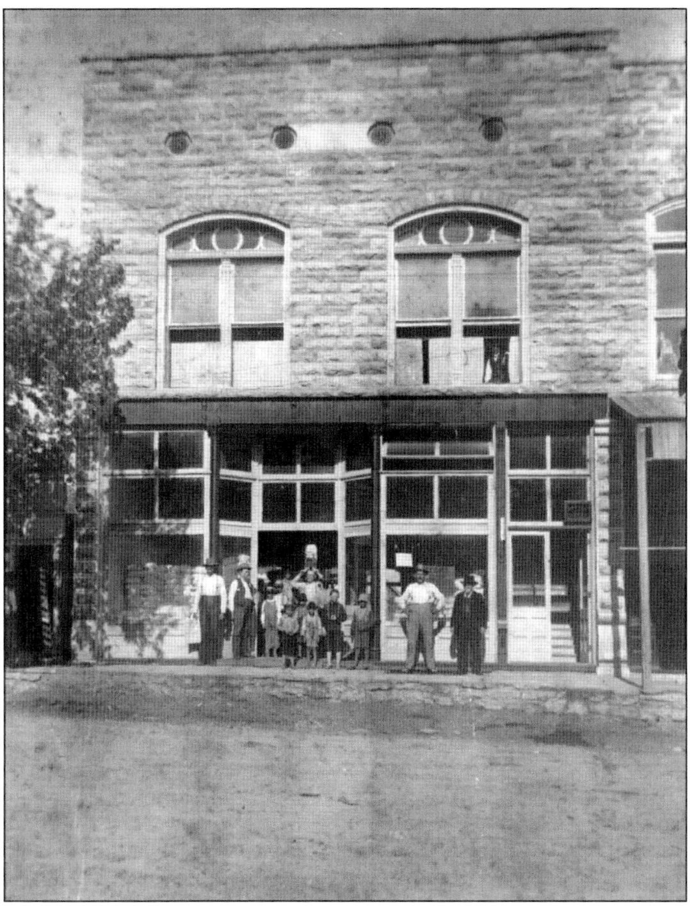

KIRBY BUILDING. Erected in 1913, the Kirby Building is located at 123 North Main Street. Its architectural classification is early-20th-century Vernacular Commercial, with Classical and Spanish Revival features. It stands directly across the street from the courthouse, claiming a proud place for itself on the town square. It was certified in the National Register of Historic Places on March 26, 1999.

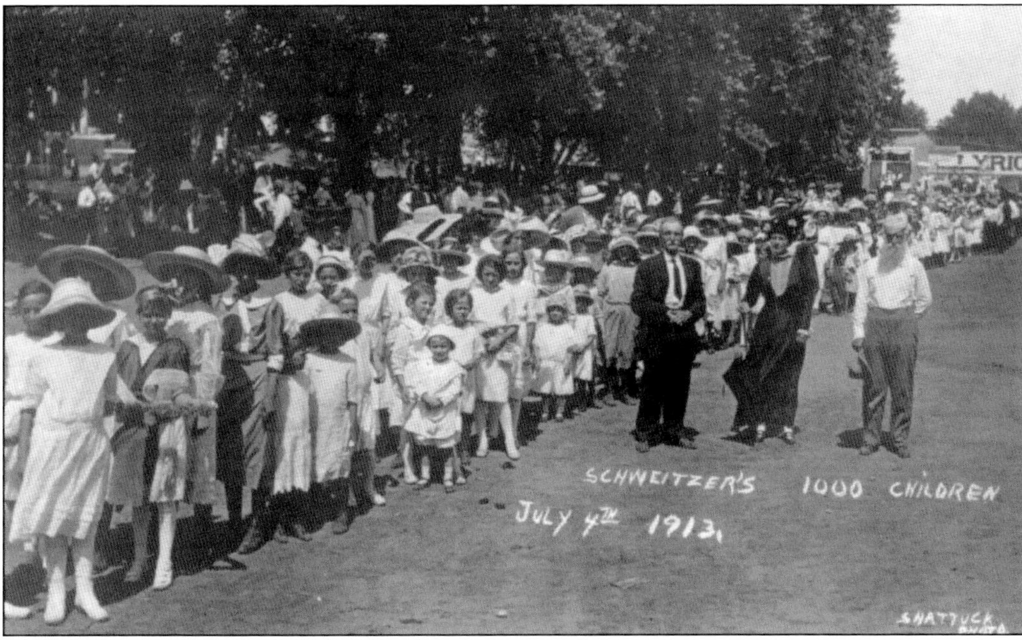

SCHWEITZER CHILDREN, JULY 4, 1913. Featured here are L.H. Schweitzer and his wife, Mae H. Schweitzer, with their 1,000 children. Standing to the left of Mrs. Schweitzer is Mr. Williford. The story goes that the Schweitzers had all of these descendants, though the story has yet to be substantiated; nonetheless, they are gathered here around the courthouse square on Independence Day.

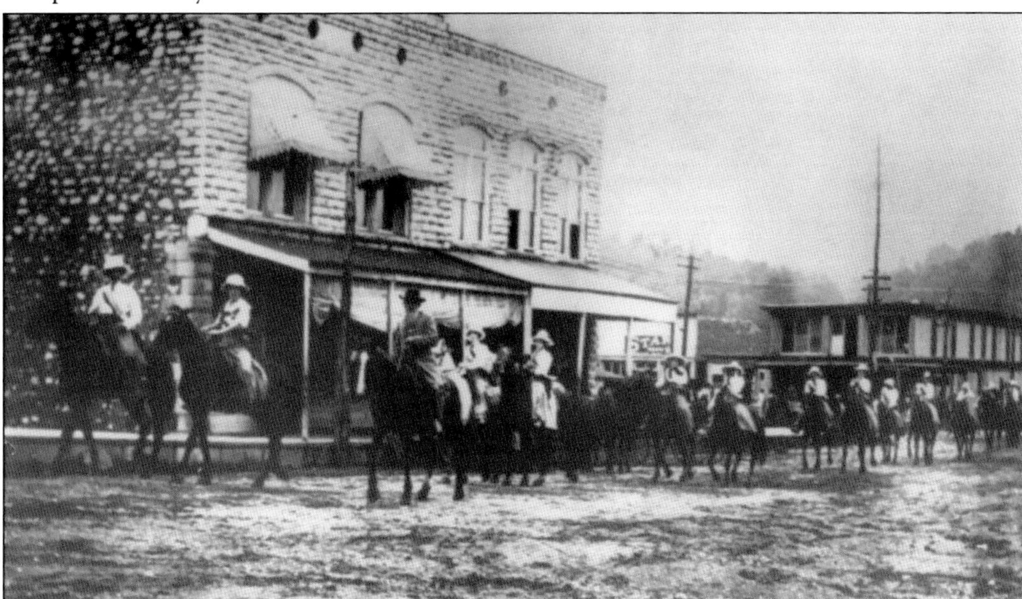

PARADE ON SQUARE. Members of the United Daughters of the Confederacy ride in a parade on the northeast corner of the town square. The parade was celebrating soldiers of the Civil War. The Daughters of the Confederacy was formed to fulfill many objectives, one being "to honor the memory of those who served and those who fell in the service of the Confederate States of America."

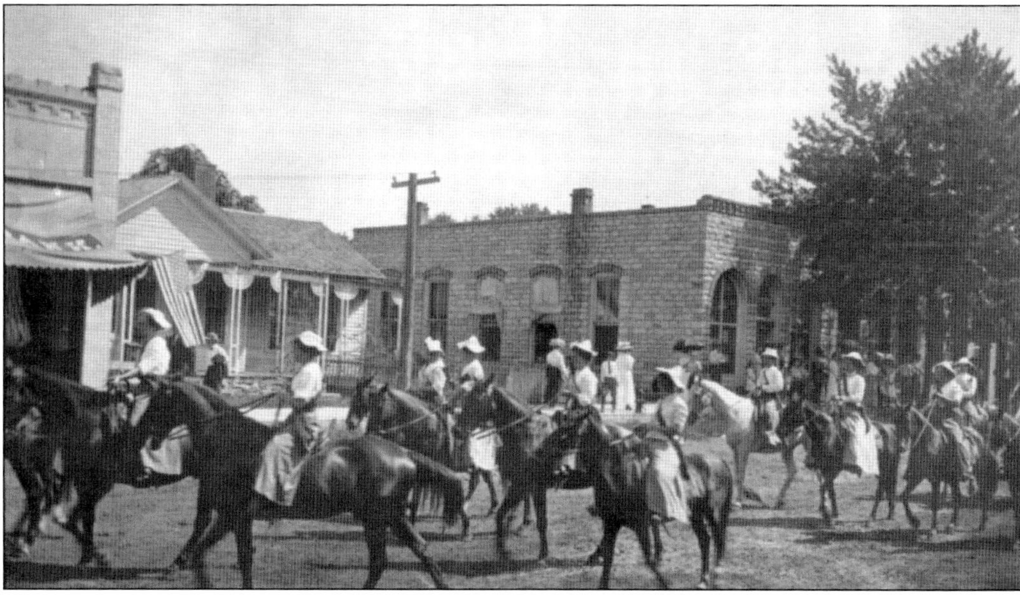

DAUGHTERS OF THE CONFEDERACY. In the background is the office building of the *Harrison Daily Times*. Built in 1876, the office remains located on the north side of the town square at 109 West Rush Avenue. While the building retains its original look, the facade has been updated several times. Next to it is a house that was later demolished to make way for the Lyric Theater.

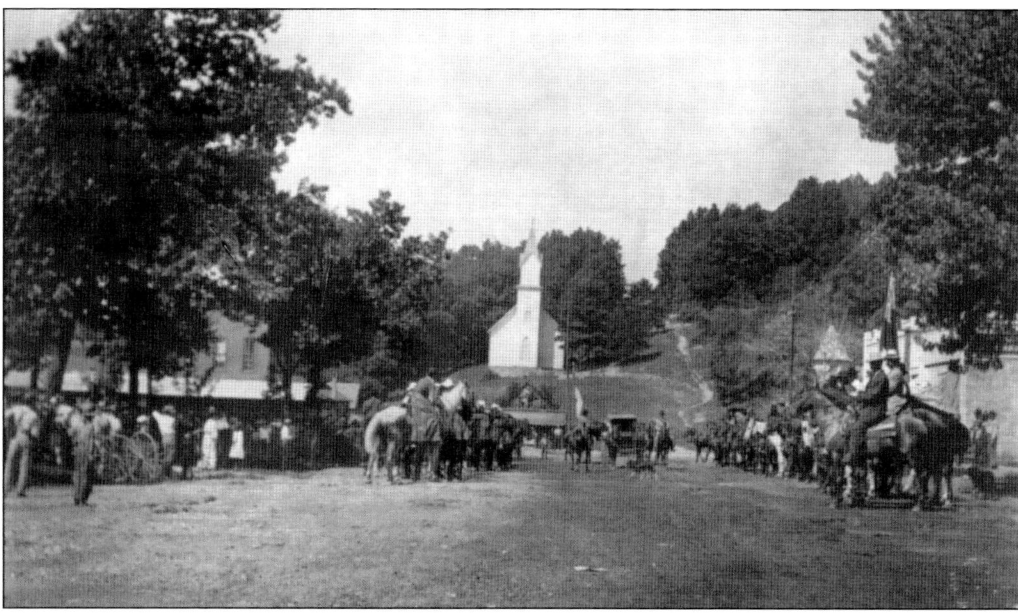

OLD SOLDIERS PARADE. The buggy in the center of the photograph, coming up West Rush Avenue, contains Gen. Edmund Kirby Smith. Following the Union capture of Vicksburg and Port Hudson and the closing of the Mississippi River, Smith was essentially cut off from the Confederate capital at Richmond and had to command a virtually independent area of the Confederacy. The area, which included Arkansas, became known as "Kirby Smithdom."

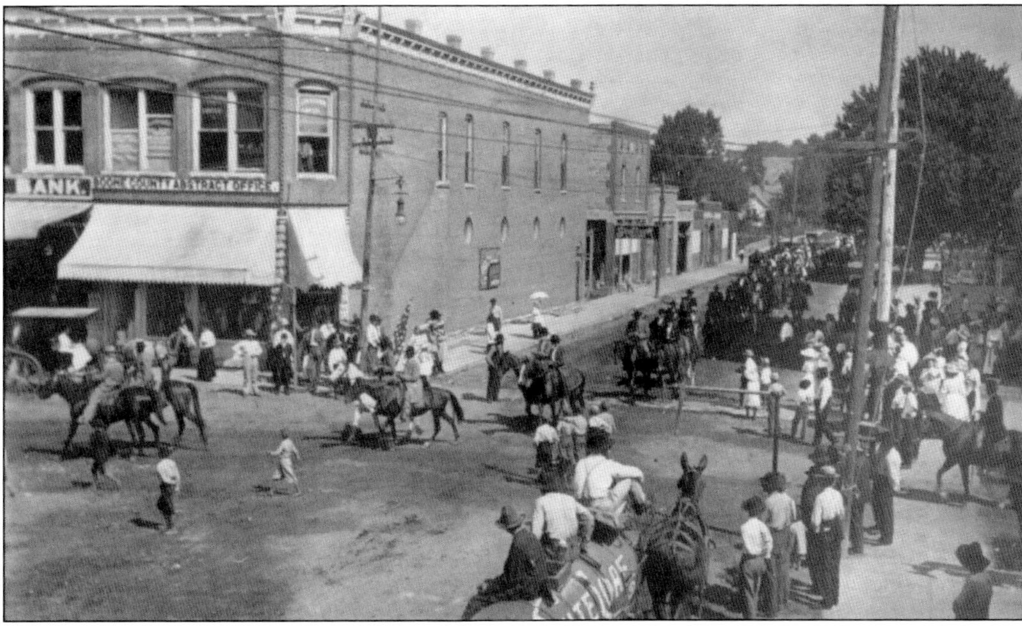

PARADE ON TOWN SQUARE. The Old Soldiers Parade rounds the corner of the Boone County Abstract Office. The Boone County Abstract Company was founded by George Cotton in 1886 to provide reliable records for the real estate industry in the county. Parades were a source of community entertainment and were always well attended. Heroic war veterans, community leaders, and politicians could be seen riding through the streets.

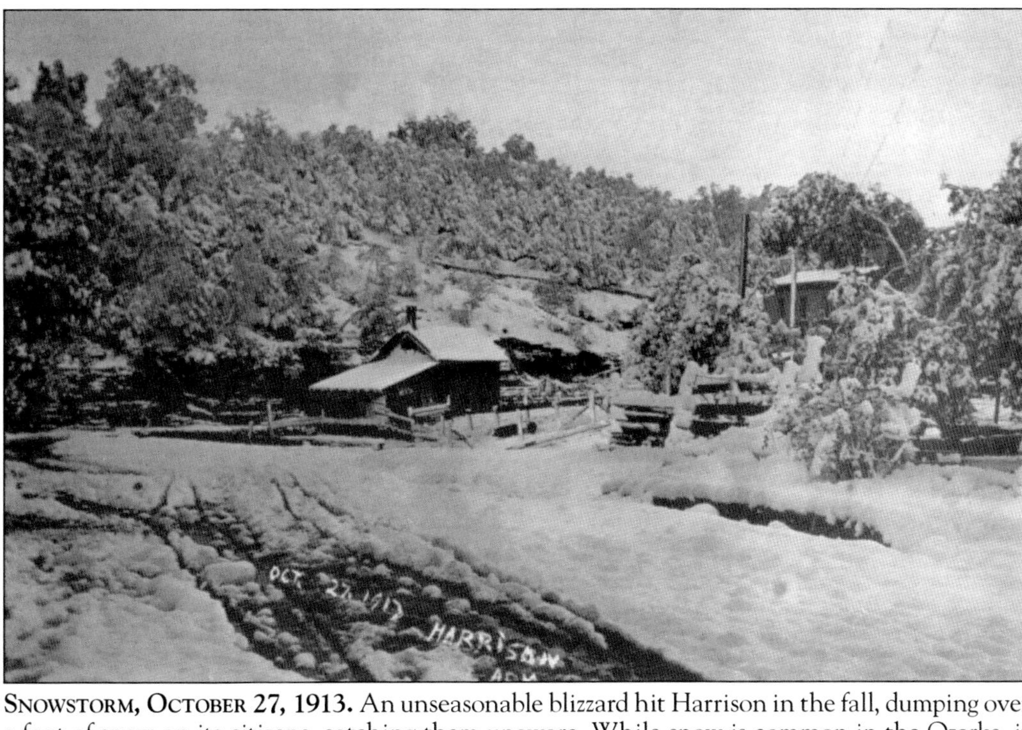

SNOWSTORM, OCTOBER 27, 1913. An unseasonable blizzard hit Harrison in the fall, dumping over a foot of snow on its citizens, catching them unaware. While snow is common in the Ozarks, it usually falls in the winter. This photograph looks southwest, toward the Baptist church.

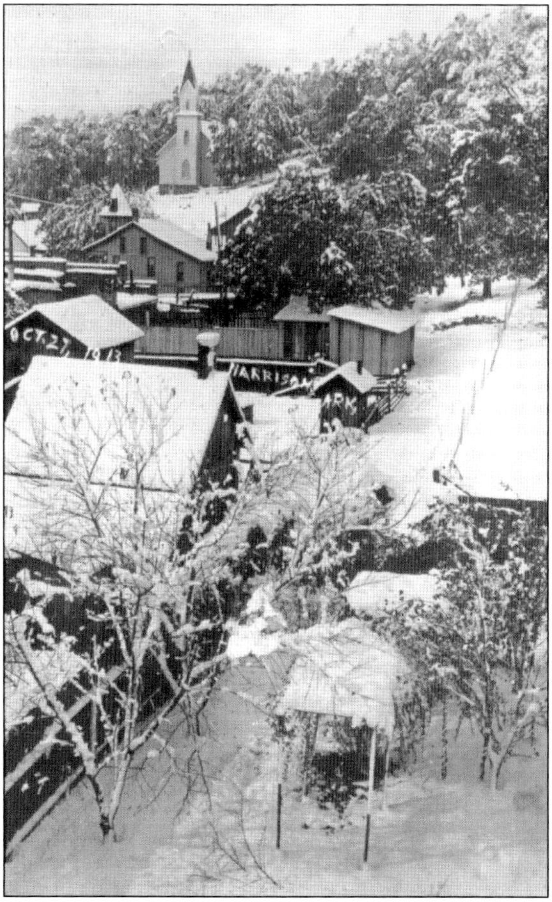

WINTER STORM, 1913. The photograph on the left looks west along the alley of West Rush Avenue on October 27, 1913. In the background is the Baptist church. Below, the Boone County Courthouse is seen from the corner of West Stephenson Avenue. Tree branches around the courthouse square are bent and broken from the weight of the snow. In winter, this area of Arkansas averages a little over six inches of snow. On this date, over a foot of snow was dumped on Harrison residents. Arkansans are resilient folks, and the majority had the skills to weather this storm safely.

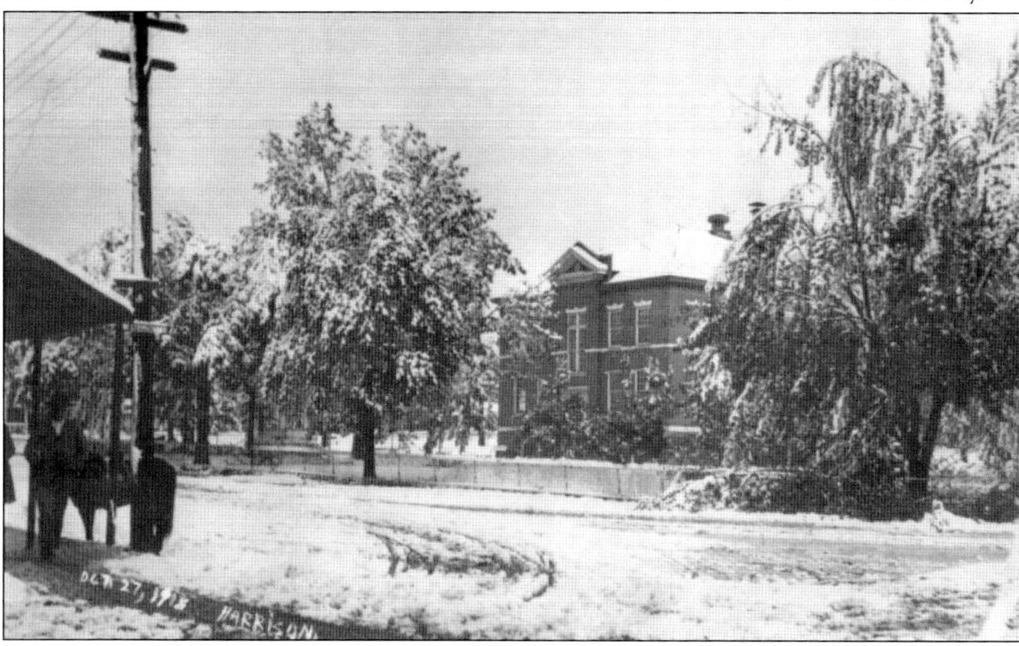

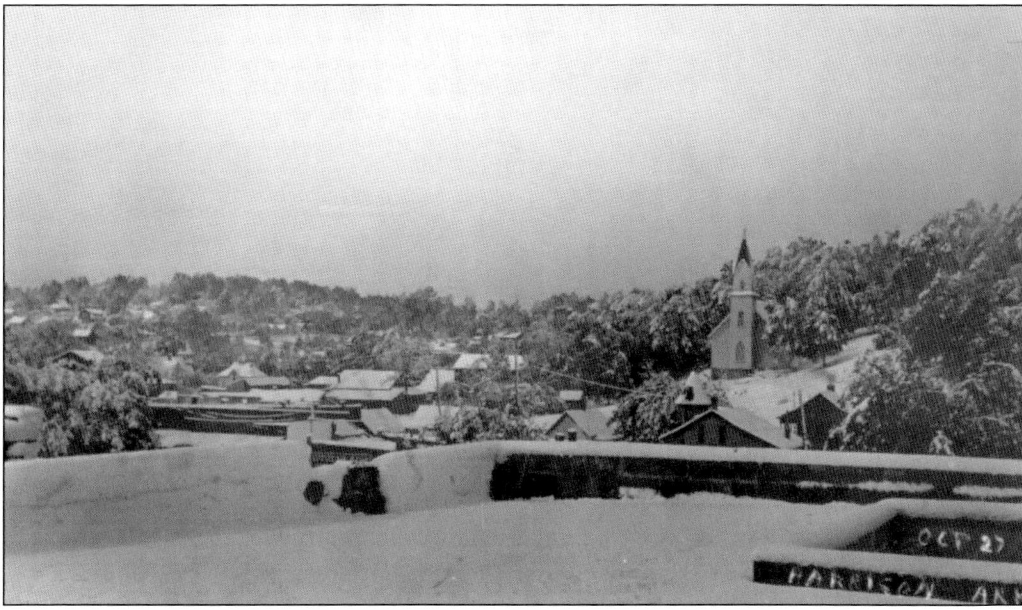

Blizzard of 1913. The photograph above shows Crooked Creek Bluff in the southwest part of town. The photograph below, taken on West Rush Avenue, looks toward North Main Street. The Boone County Courthouse is clearly seen on the far right. The Federal Building is at the far left on the street corner. Harrison residents were no strangers to natural disasters. The area experienced floods, tornadoes, and earthquakes. Though electricity was in the area at the time, most residents did not have it in their homes, so losing power was not a major concern. People relied on wood to heat their homes and oil or kerosene lamps to light the interiors. Many homes also had water pumps or wells at this time, so accessing water for survival was also not a major concern.

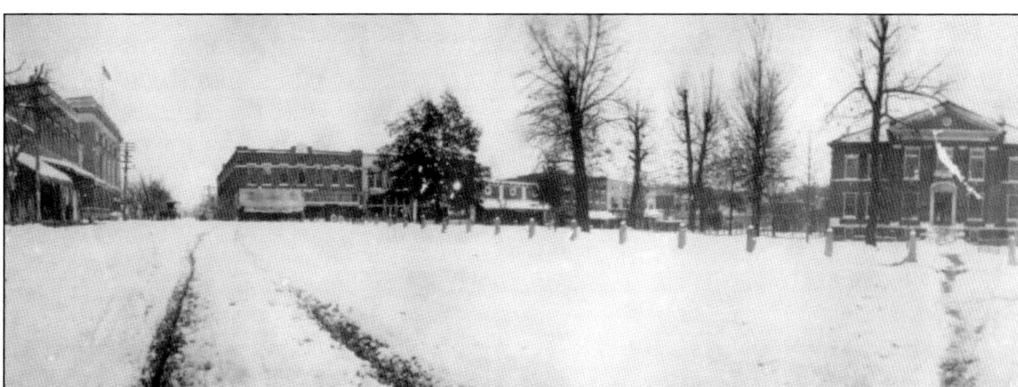

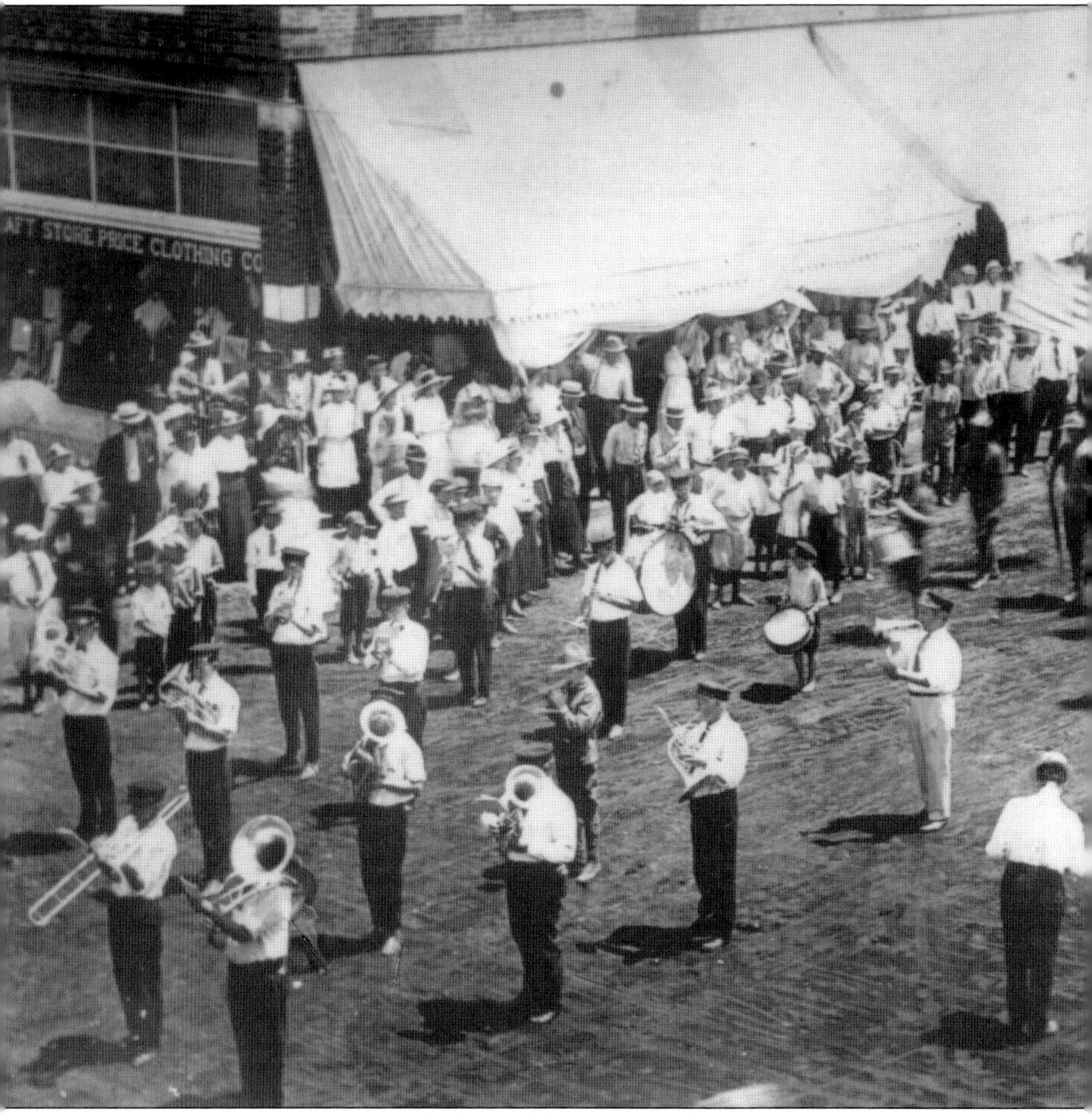

PARADE ON SQUARE, 1914. On the back of this photograph, the following is written: "WW I contingent leaving for France." World War I began on July 28, 1914. Before entering the war, the United States remained neutral, though it was an important supplier of raw materials and capital to Britain and other Allied powers. When the United States entered the war, it officially

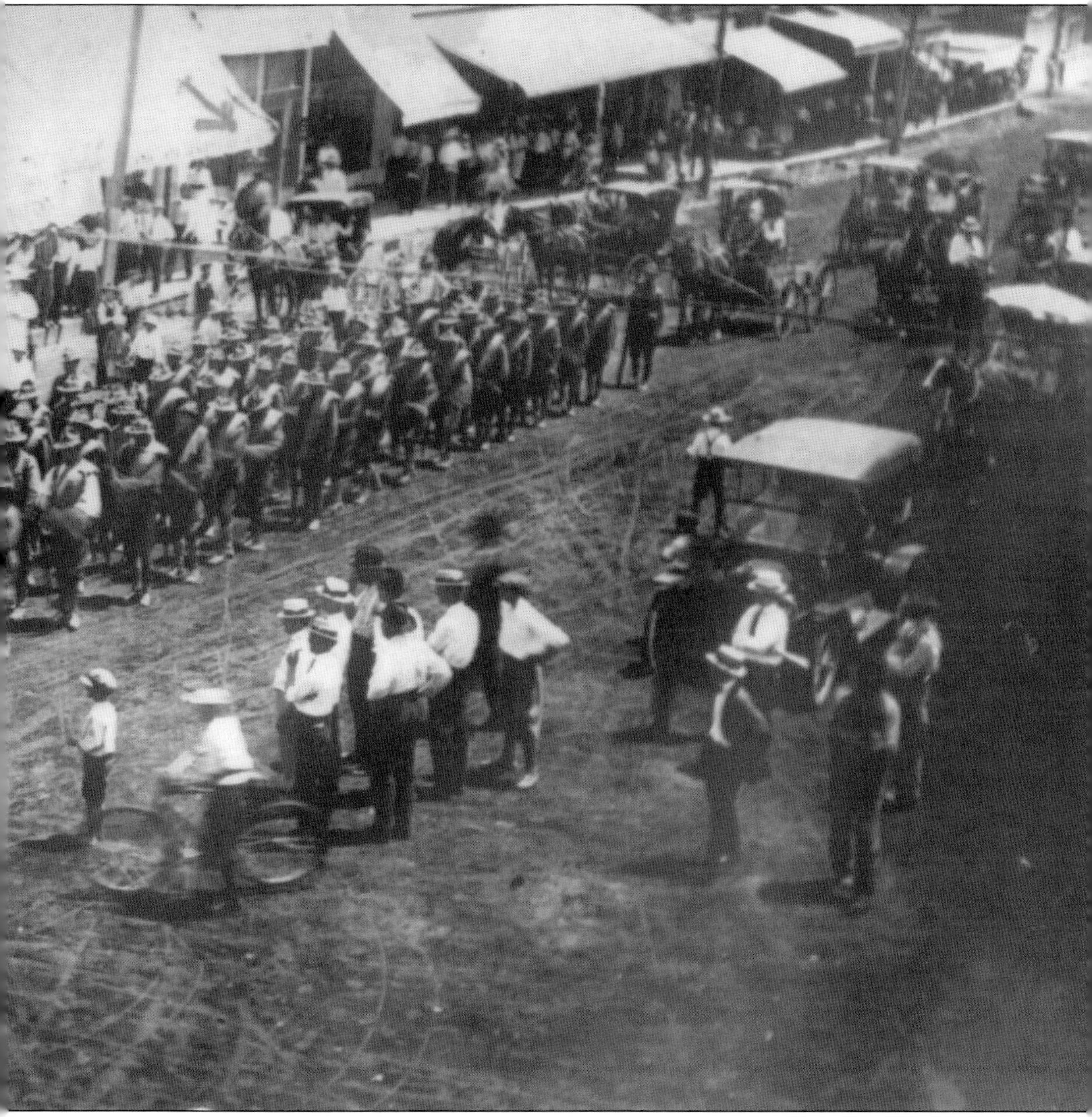

remained independent and did not join the Allied powers. During the war, the nation mobilized over four million military personnel and suffered 110,000 casualties. This period saw a dramatic expansion of the federal government in an effort to harness the war effort, and the US military increased significantly in an effort to bring reform and democracy to the world.

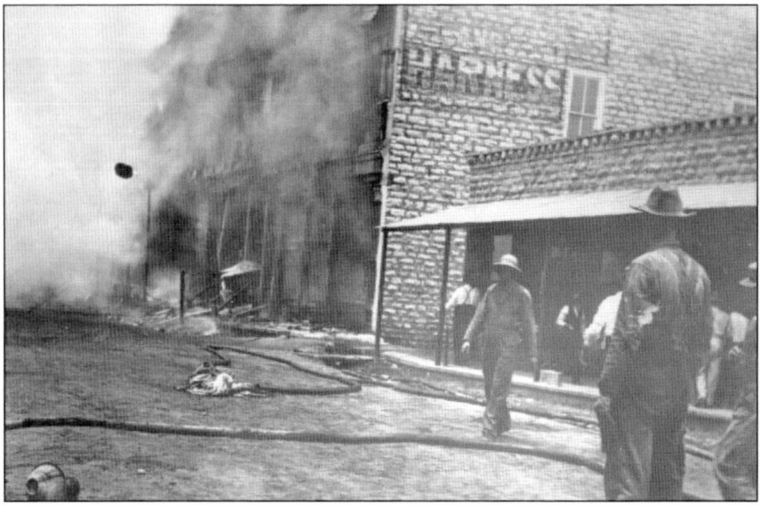

Town Square Fire. Because of fires like this one, which could destroy entire city blocks and neighborhoods, wooden structures began to be torn down, and brick buildings were erected in their place. Many of the structures on the Harrison square were redressed with brick to prevent fires.

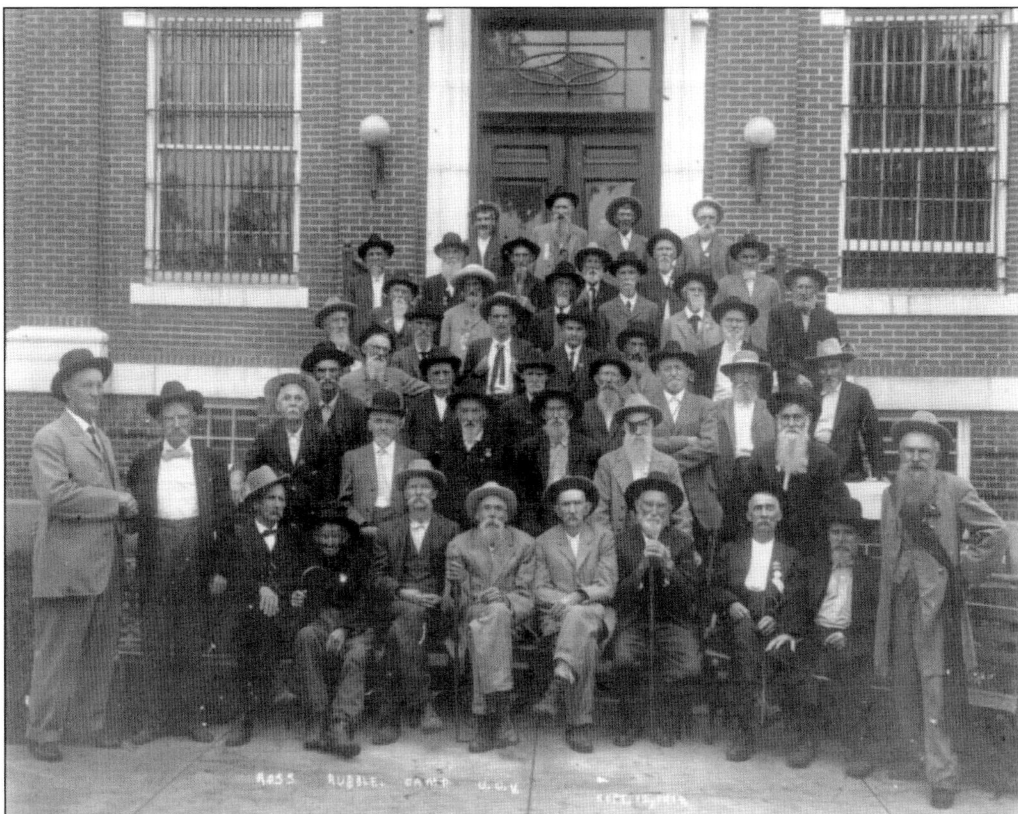

Confederate Veterans Reunion, September 12, 1914. The United Confederate Veterans was an association of former Confederate soldiers and sailors, founded on June 10, 1889 in New Orleans, Louisiana. The organization grew rapidly in the 1890s, culminating in 1,555 camps. Its purpose was to foster "social, literary, historical, and benevolent" results. Membership peaked in 1904, following which veterans began to die off rather rapidly. These veterans are posing in front of the courthouse.

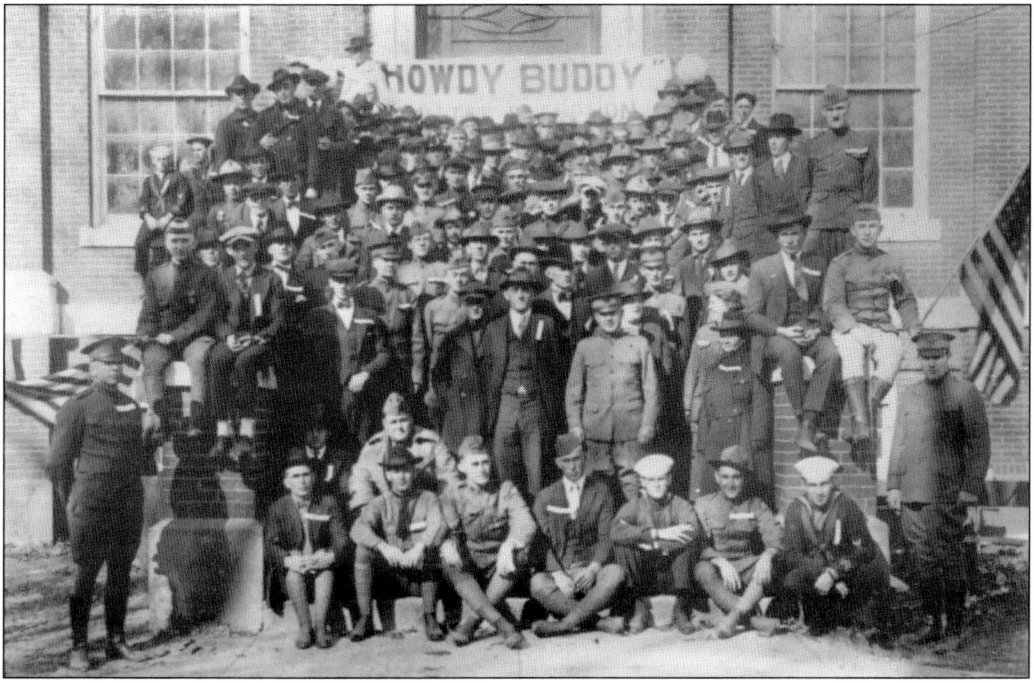

World War I Servicemen, 1918. US military veterans pose outside the Boone County Courthouse at the close of World War I. The only persons identified in this photograph are in the front row. Shown are, from left to right, Cpt. George McKinney, unidentified, William Jennings Bryan "J.B." Holt, two unidentified persons, Ford Maggard, two unidentified men, and Cpt. Troy Coffman.

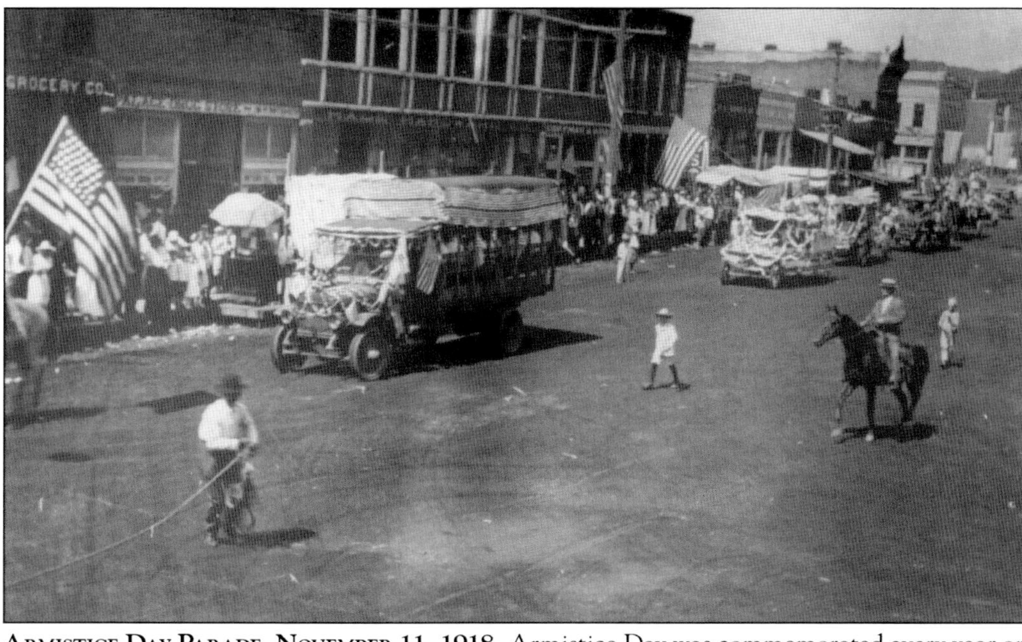

Armistice Day Parade, November 11, 1918. Armistice Day was commemorated every year on November 11 to mark the treaty signed between the Allies and Germany at Compiègne, France. The holiday marked the cessation of hostilities on the Western Front in World War I. The armistice took effect on the 11th hour of the 11th day of the 11th month of 1918.

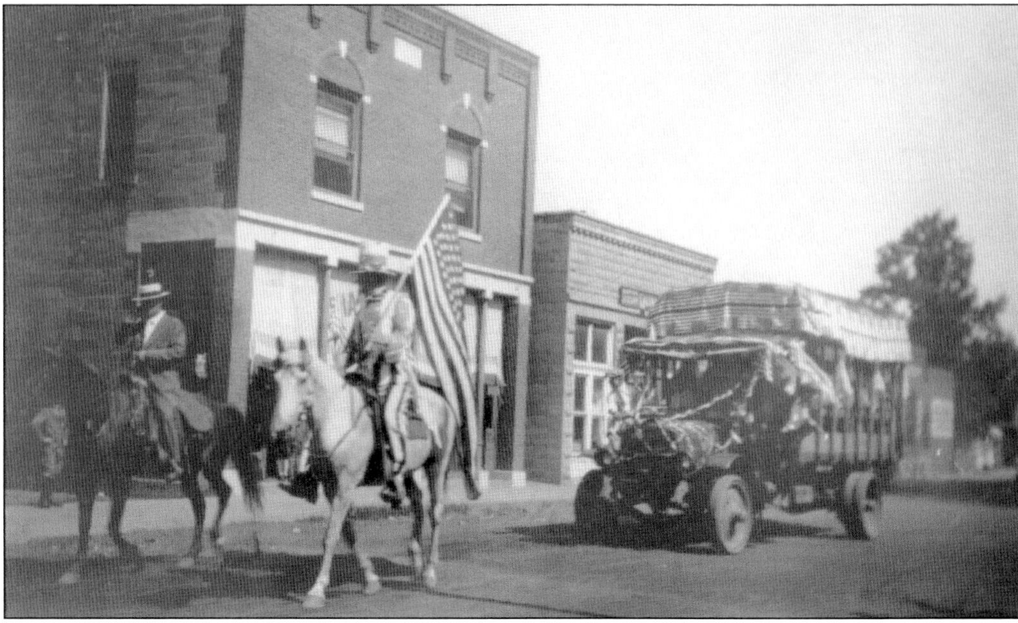

ARMISTICE DAY PARADE, 1918. November 11 was declared a national holiday in many Allied nations to memorialize members of the armed forces who were killed during World War I. Most countries changed the name of the holiday after World War II to honor veterans of that and subsequent conflicts. The United States chose the name Veterans Day to honor all military veterans, living and dead, including those participating in other conflicts.

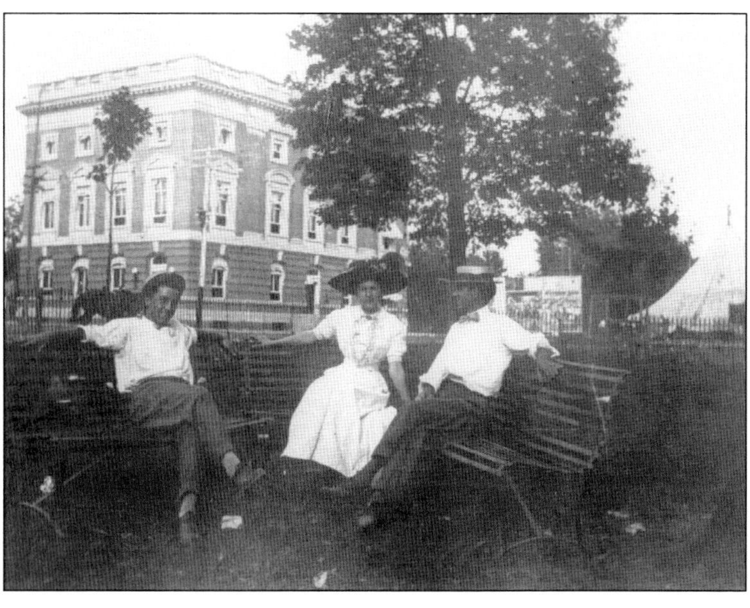

FAMILY AND FEDERAL BUILDING, 1918. Celebrating Armistice Day festivities, a family relaxes on benches near the town square. The Federal Building can be seen in the background. Harrison's infrastructure was improving at this time, as new industries arrived in the area. Consequently, the local residency was growing, with a population nearing 5,000.

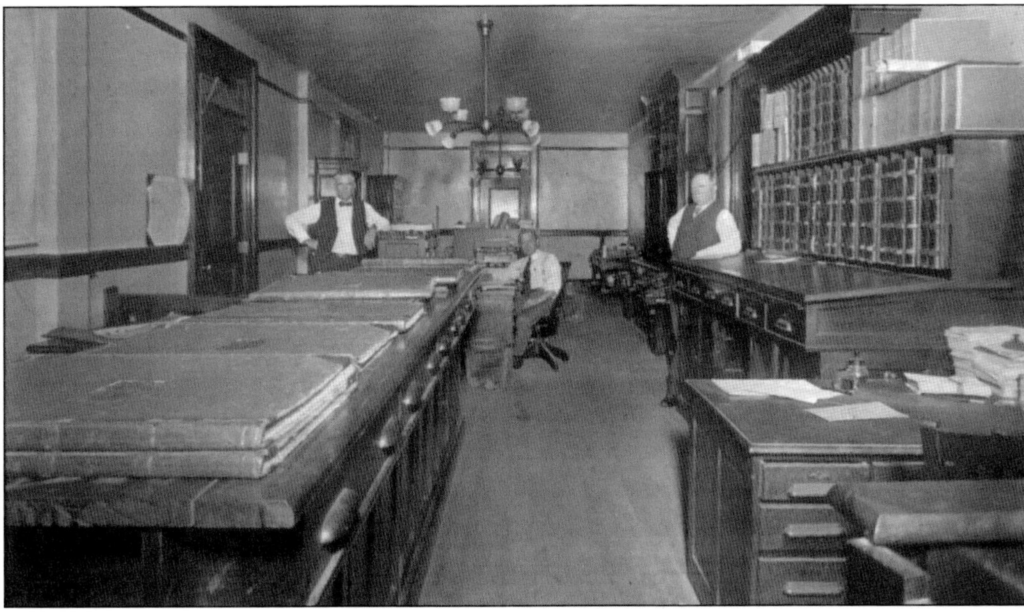

US Land Office, Early 1920s. Located in the Federal Building, the US Land Office was an independent agency of the government responsible for public-domain lands. Placed within the Department of the Interior in 1849, it later became the Bureau of Land Management. The office oversaw the surveying, platting, and sale of public lands in the western United States and administered the Homestead Act.

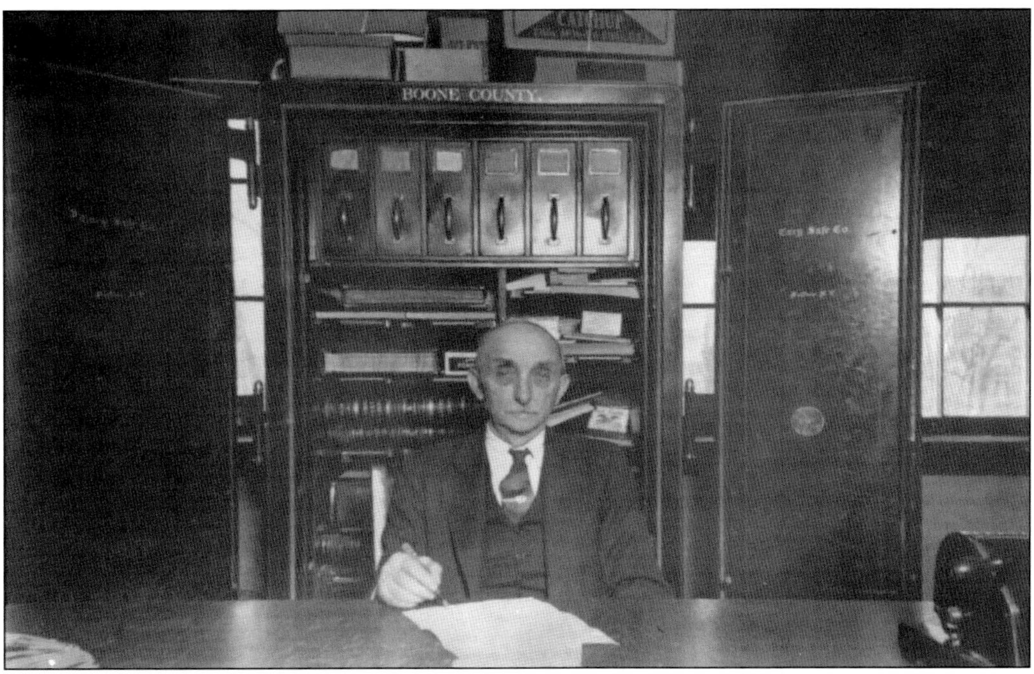

Wesley Wood Hudson. Hudson served as Boone County treasurer (1933–1939). Here, he sits at his desk in the treasurer's office. As a child, he and his family suffered greatly during the Civil War. Despite the hardships he experienced, Hudson grew to be a kind-hearted, generous man to his family and community and became a well-respected figure in local business and politics.

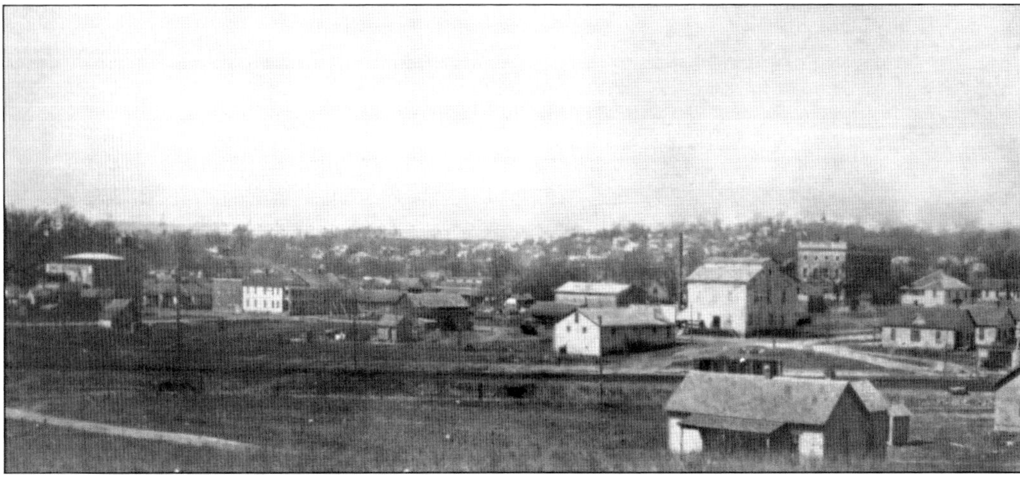

VIEW FROM EAGLE HEIGHTS. This photograph provides a southwesterly view of Harrison, showing an elevated perspective of the city's early days. The Federal Building (right) dominates the center of town as it continues to do in modern times. Though many changes have occurred over the years, Harrison retains its original character.

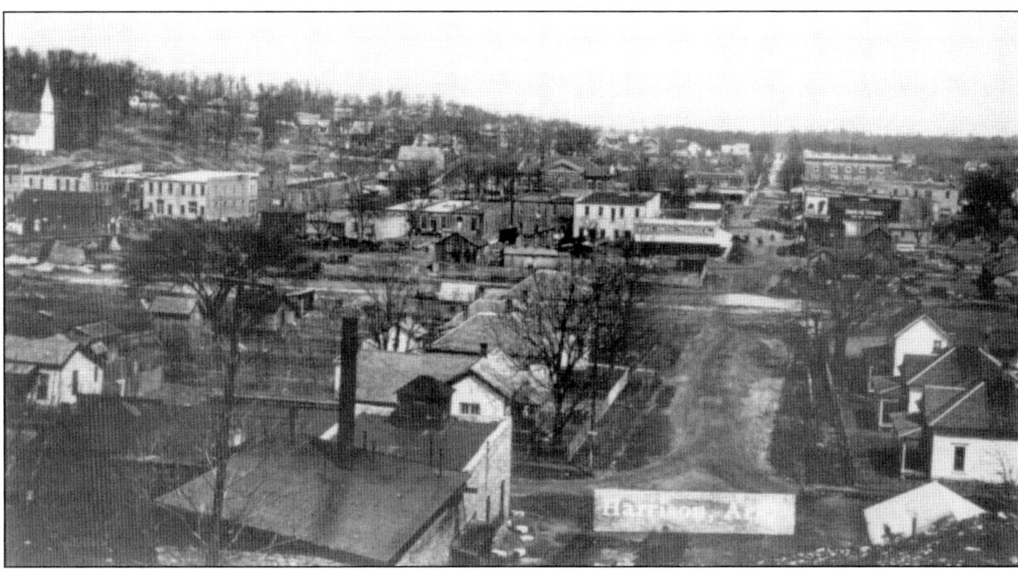

HARRISON, AFTER 1910. This elevated photograph looks north from Woodland Heights Hill up North Main Street. The Boone County Courthouse can be seen at top center, and the Federal Building is to the right of it. When tourists come to visit the historic district and surrounding neighborhoods, they are graced with the same old-time atmosphere.

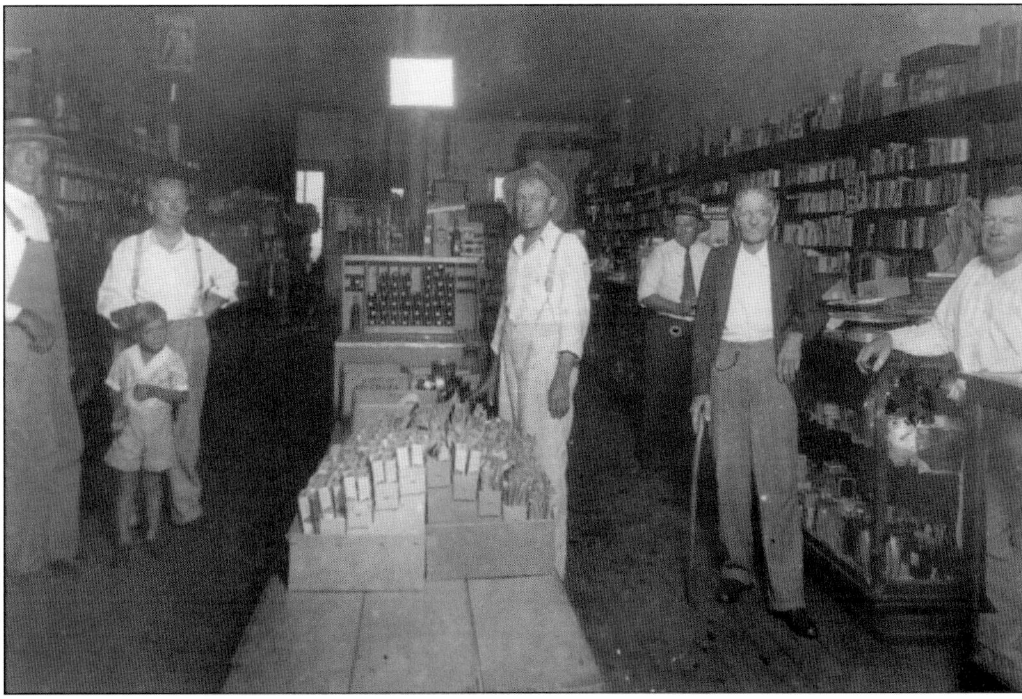

Coffman Kirby Drug Store. William Walter Coffman opened this drugstore with a Mr. Watkins in 1901. After Watkins moved on to another venture, Leander Bender Kirby became Coffman's partner. Coffman eventually bought out Kirby and then ran the store with his son Raymond until his death.

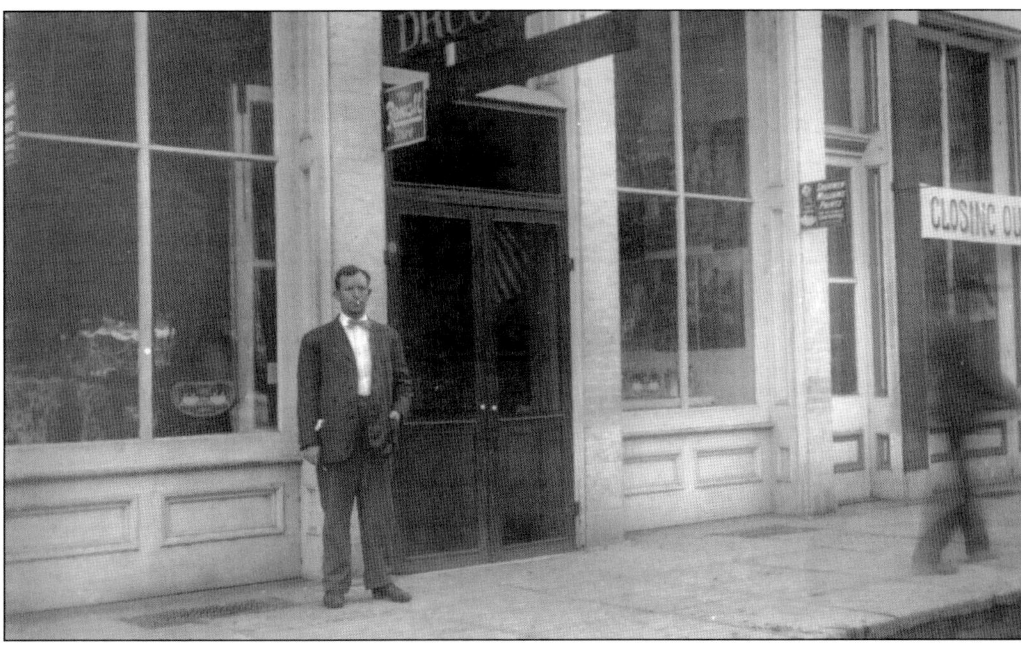

William Walter Coffman. Coffman stands outside the drugstore he owned on the south side of the town square. He operated this store and pharmacy with his son for several decades. After Coffman died, his son Raymond and Raymond's wife, Bertha, operated the store until 1972.

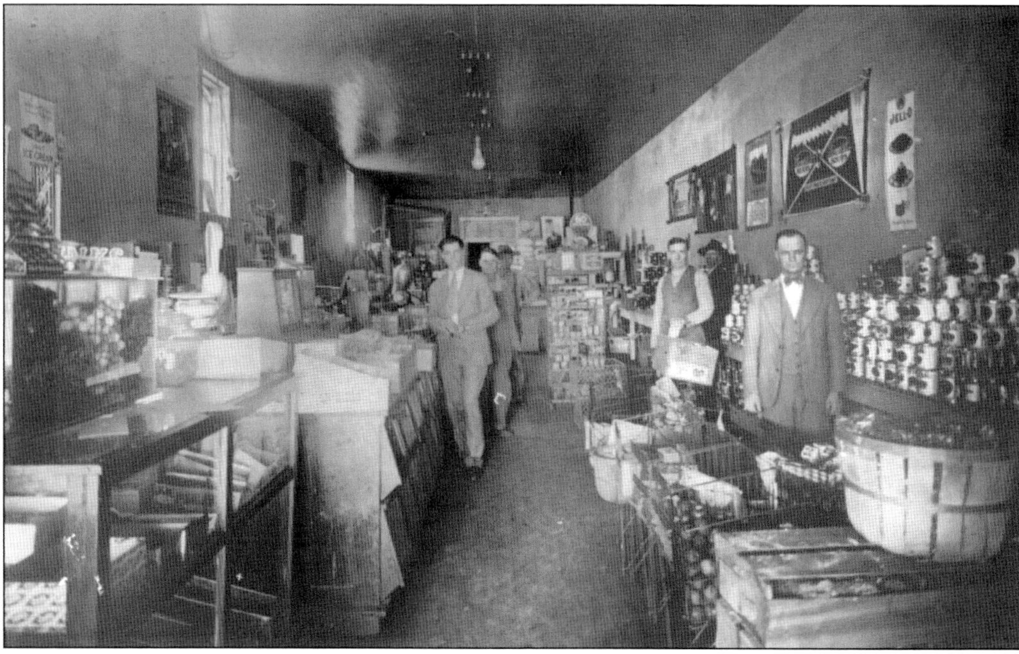

Hudson's Grocery, 1920s. Hudson's Grocery opened its doors on the Harrison square in 1920. In this photograph, a variety of objects can be seen. An advertisement for beans is on the wall at right. A pound of bacon cost approximately 50¢, chicken was selling for about 40¢ a pound, and coffee could be had for around 50¢ a pound.

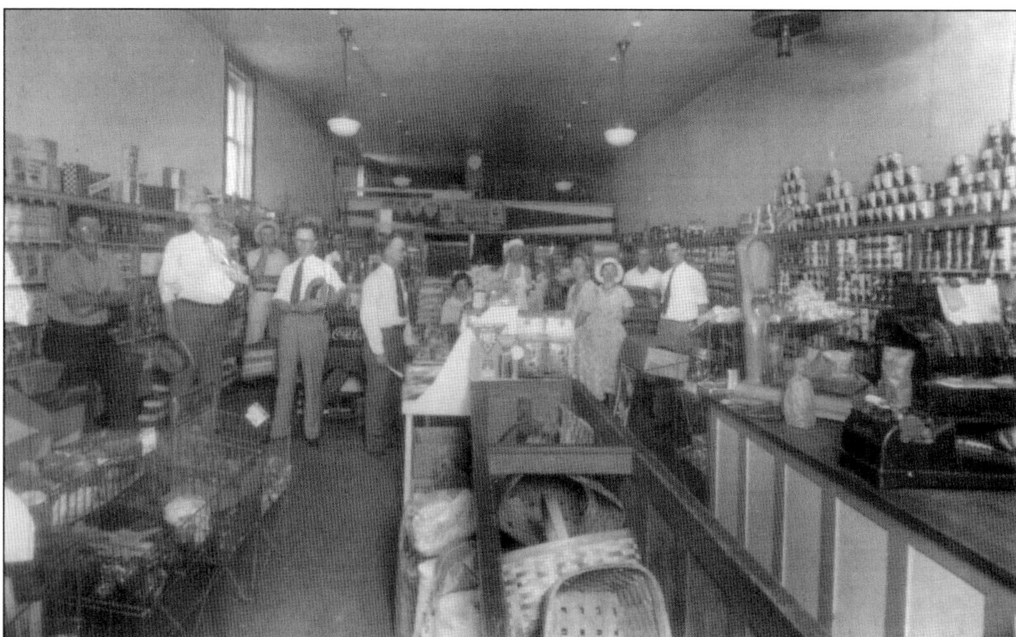

Hudson's Grocery, 1930s. At this time, a dozen eggs cost about 18¢, a loaf of white bread around 10¢, and bacon approximately 38¢ a pound. Here, several unidentified patrons are seen inside Hudson's Grocery, which remains in operation to this day. Renamed Hudson's Supermarket, it is located not far from the historic town square.

Two

Industry and Business

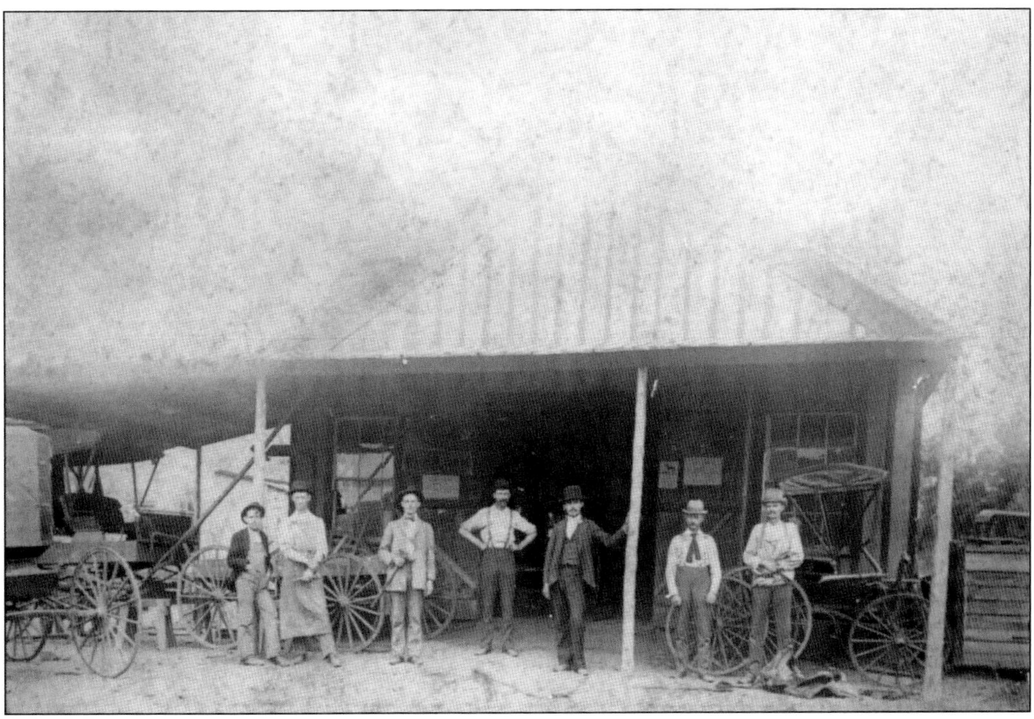

Wagon Manufacturer, 1888. This is the West Central Avenue entrance, or rear entrance, to the Bower Brothers Wagon Manufacturing Company, established in Harrison in 1888 by George Bower and sons William, Frank, and Herbert. They manufactured wagons, buggies, and surreys. Posing here are, from left to right, an unidentified boy, Herbert Bower, Fred Green, Bas Parker, Willie Bower, Frank Bower, and Knox Gibson.

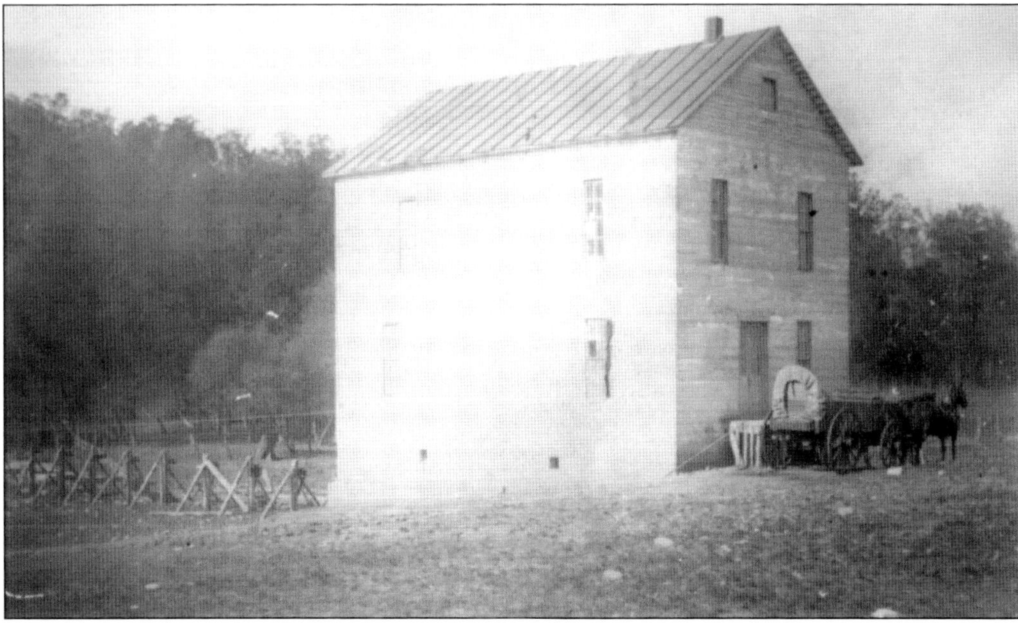

PHOENIX MILL, LATE 1890S. This mill, located on Crooked Creek, was the third at this location. The first was the Crandall Mill, which burned down. The second and third mills were built by A.D. Basore and his sons. The second washed away in the 1894 flood with Basore and two sons in it; they survived. The third mill was built farther from the creek to escape future floods.

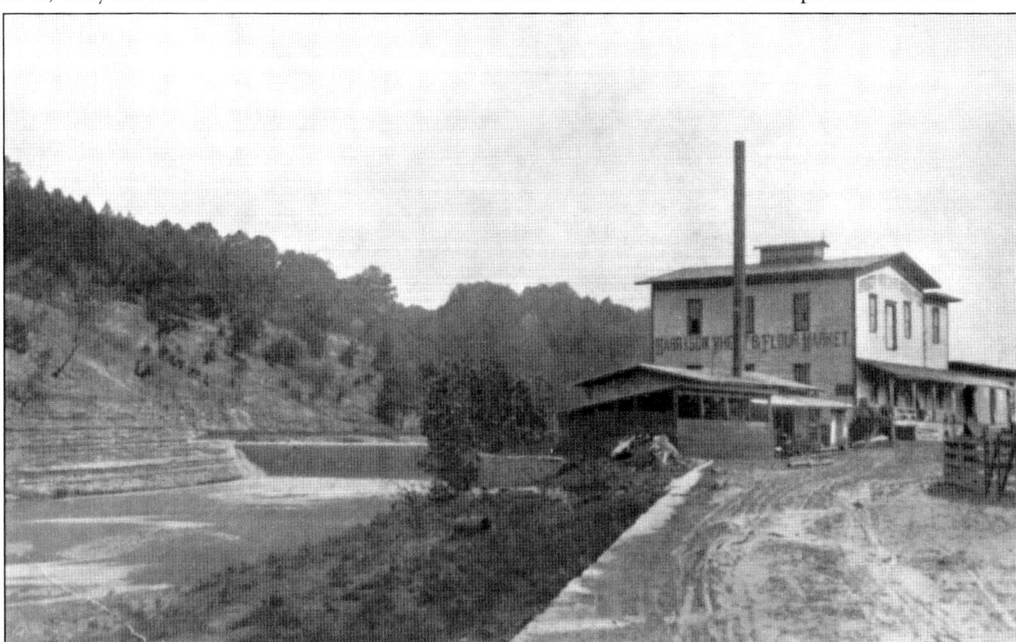

JERSEY ROLLER MILL. Roller mills were an important feature in frontier life. They used cylindrical rollers, either in opposing pairs or against flat plates, to grind various materials such as grain, ore, and gravel. This is the Jersey Roller Mill, operated by Charles W. Czech from 1894 to 1915. It processed wheat and flour and was located on Crooked Creek at today's site of the parking lot for Harrison Junior High School.

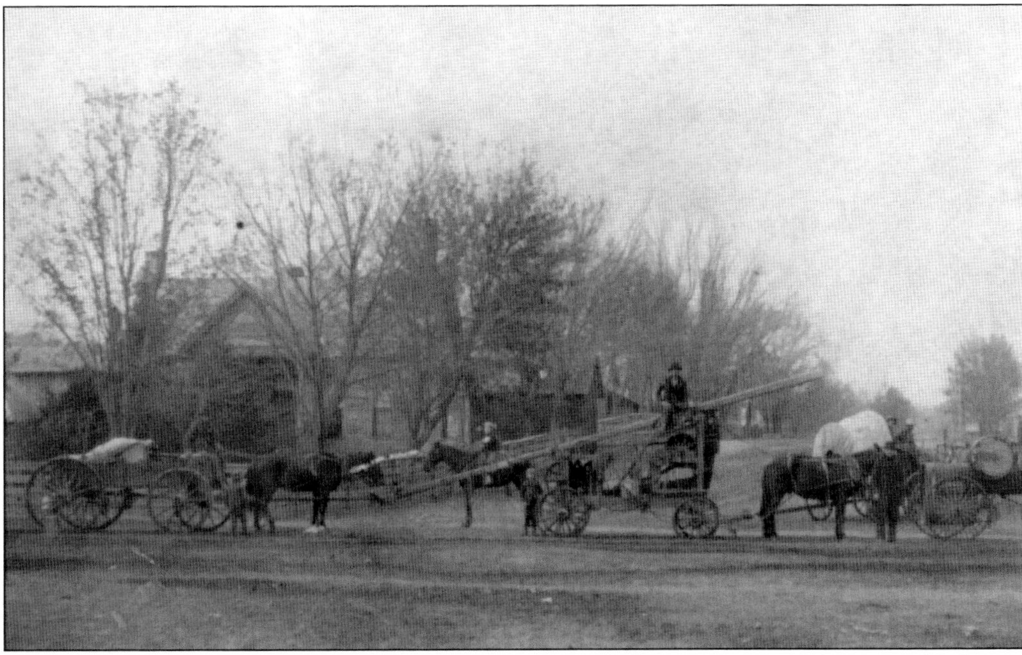

WATER WELL DRILLING CREW, 1900. In some respects, drilling for water in this area of Arkansas has never been difficult, as water tables can be tapped at short depths. The only persons identified in this photograph are Warden Brown, seated on the wagon at the far left, and Tom Plymate, on the pole of the portable drilling rig. Brown and Plymate were partners in a well-drilling business.

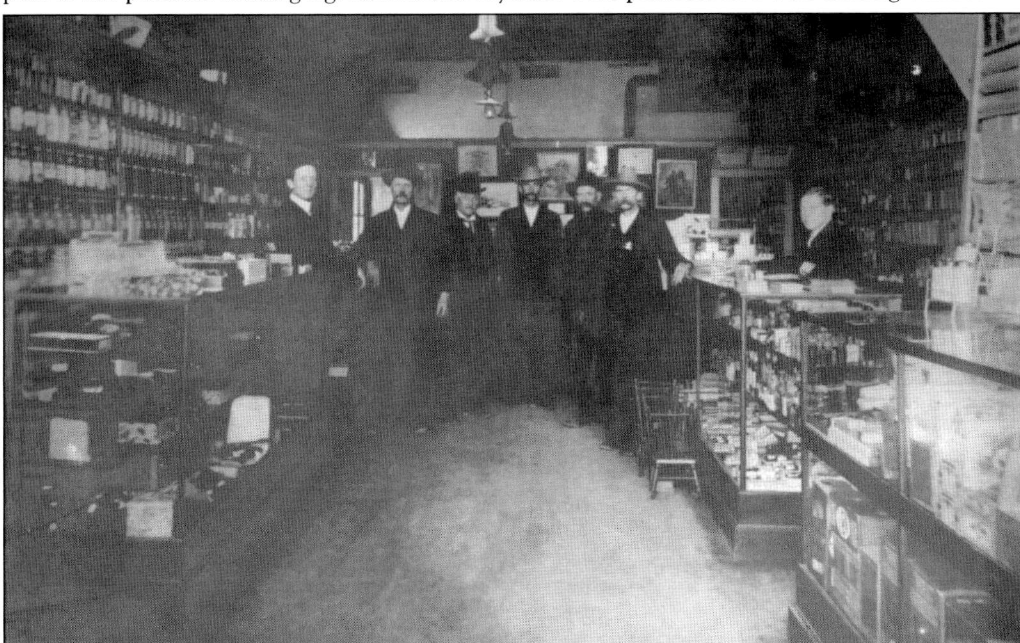

SAFER DRUG STORE, EARLY 1900S. Pharmacists at this time fulfilled the role of apothecary, the historical name for a medical professional who formulated and dispensed medical materials to physicians, surgeons, and patients. They also prepared drug products and chemicals for medicinal use. Leander Bender Kirby was the pharmacist for this drugstore.

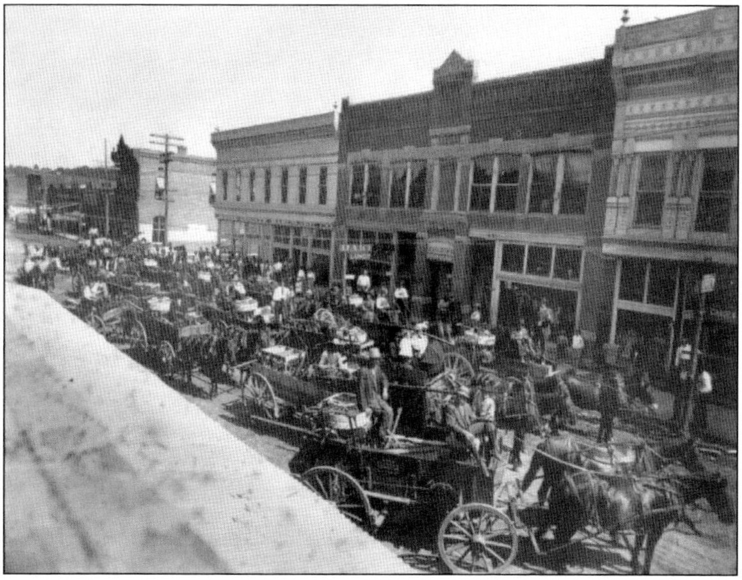

Street Scene on Square. These teams of horse wagons on the town square are loaded with equipment for threshing and harvesting machines. They were either delivering the equipment to the railroad for transport, or they had just picked them up from the railroad. At this time, threshing with horsepower was the most common feature in Arkansas agriculture.

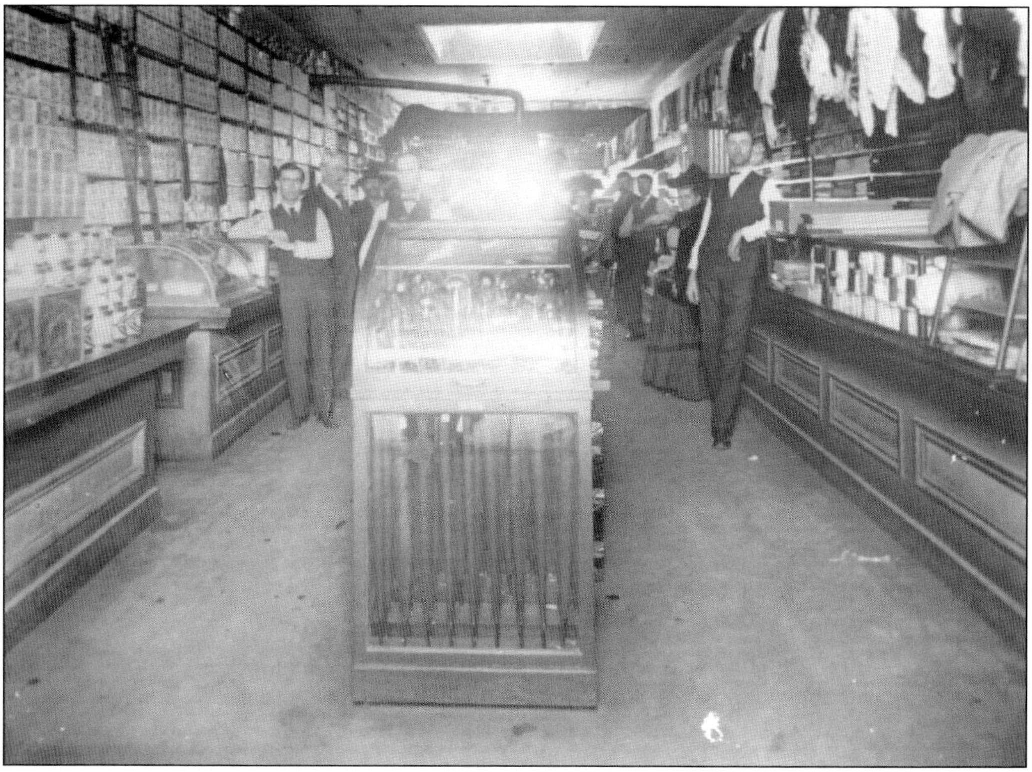

Walter's Store, 1904. This store sold men's and women's clothing items, including shoes and accessories. It also sold sewing fabrics, a common feature in most clothing stores at the time. The wood and glass case in the center foreground contains umbrellas. Fashion during this period, in European and European-influenced countries, followed the Victorian ideal.

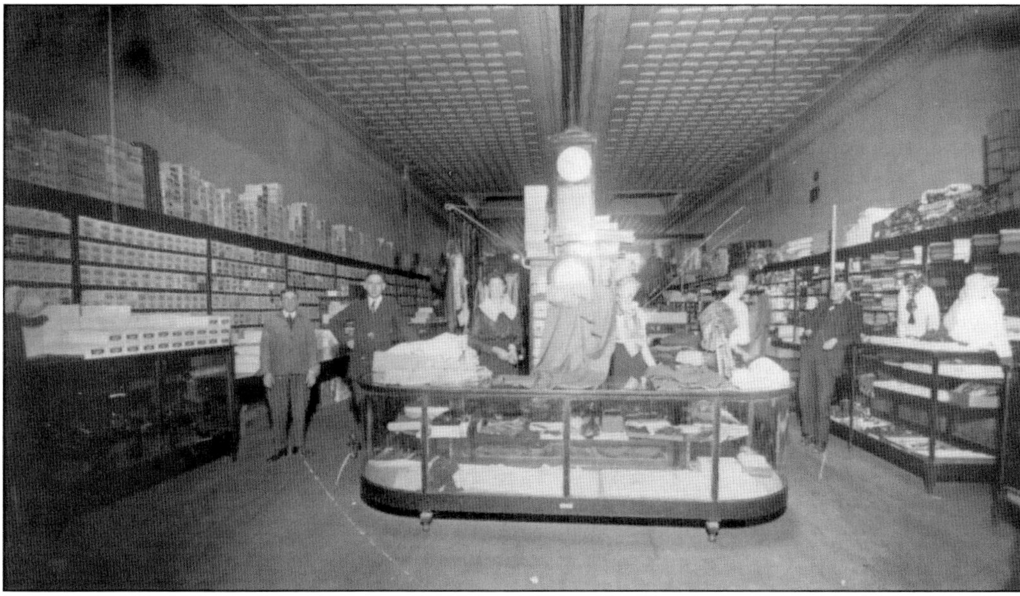

Fair Store, 1904. This is another store that sold men's and women's clothing, as well as shoes and sewing materials. Custom sewing was the common way one's clothing was manufactured at this time. It was not until 1907 that clothing was increasingly factory made and sold in large, fixed-price department stores, so small stores like this one remained a common feature in this area of Arkansas for a long time.

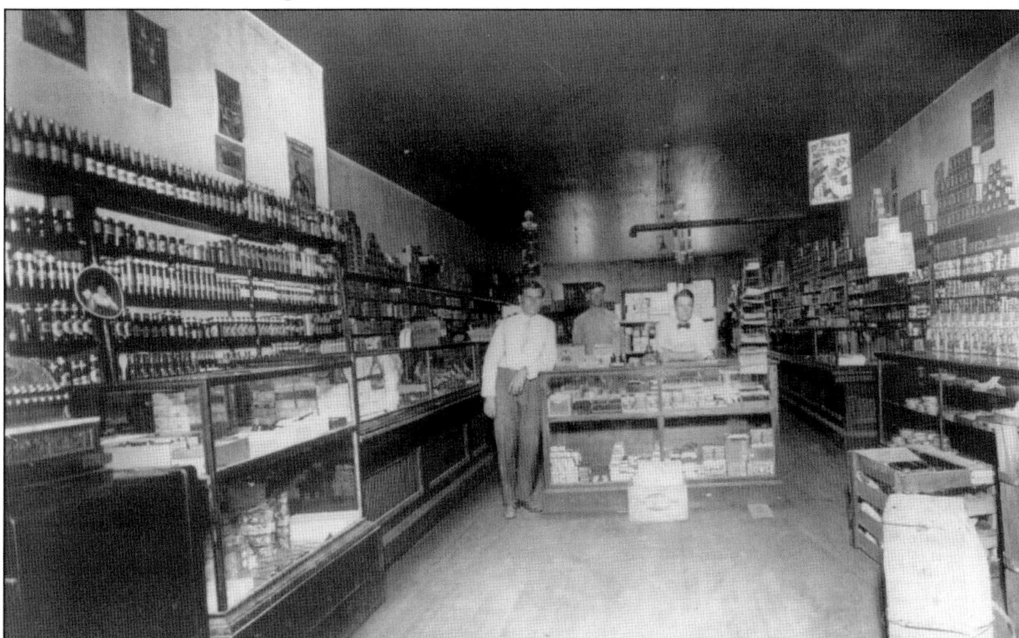

General Store. Establishments like this one were common in small towns and rural areas. They carried a broad selection of routine merchandise, such as canned and bottled goods, as well as various household items, such as hardware. Due to the close connection with their customers, general retailers would adjust their merchandise to the preferences of their community. They also obtained special orders, which would be placed with a manufacturer or supplier.

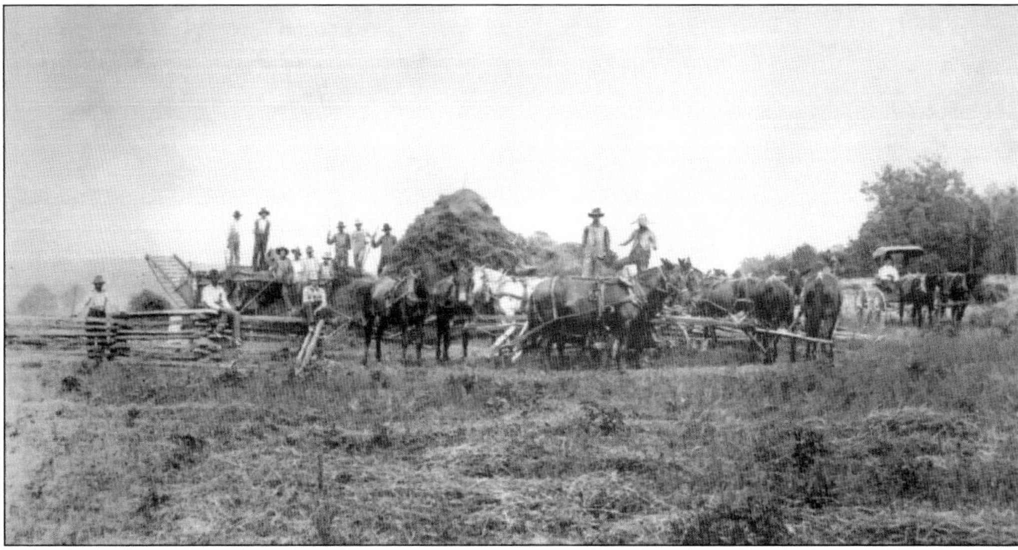

Threshing with Horses, 1905. Threshers were used to grind wheat, oats, rye, barley, corn, and other grains into flour, as well as to bale straw. Horses were used in pairs to power the thresher. The thresher had its beginnings in Europe as the industrial revolution spread to agriculture. This photograph was taken near Crooked Creek.

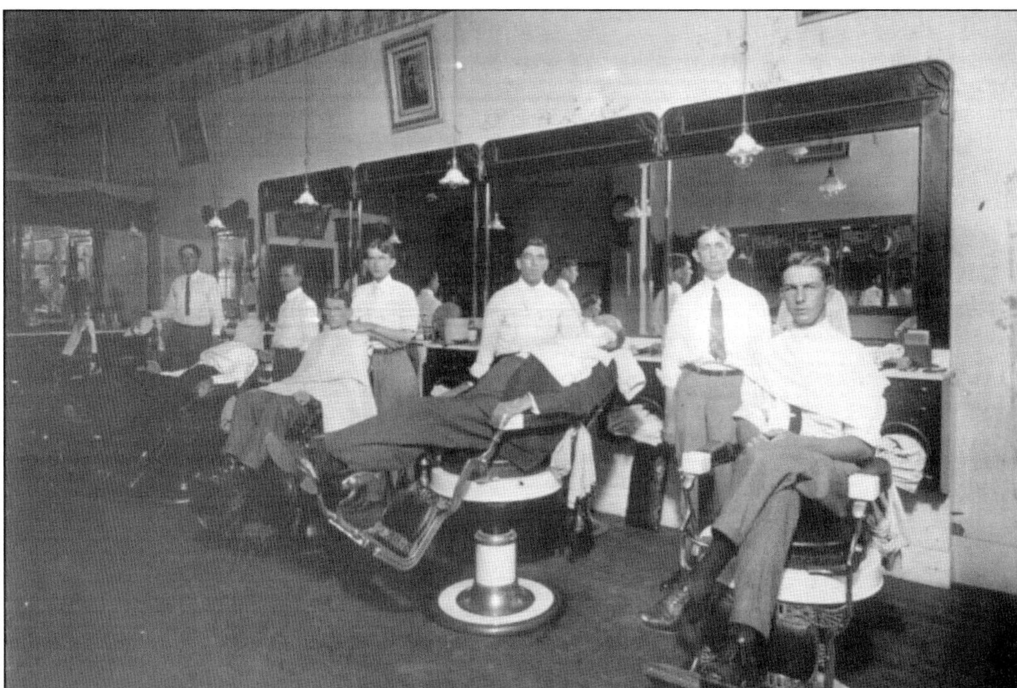

Barbershop, 1906. Beginning at the turn of the century, barbershops became a place for men to socialize, hear daily news, and talk about events in and around the community. Most barbershops like this one were owned by tradesmen who set up their shops in storefronts of small towns. Barbers not only cut hair, but shaved and manicured facial hair among other things, as seen here.

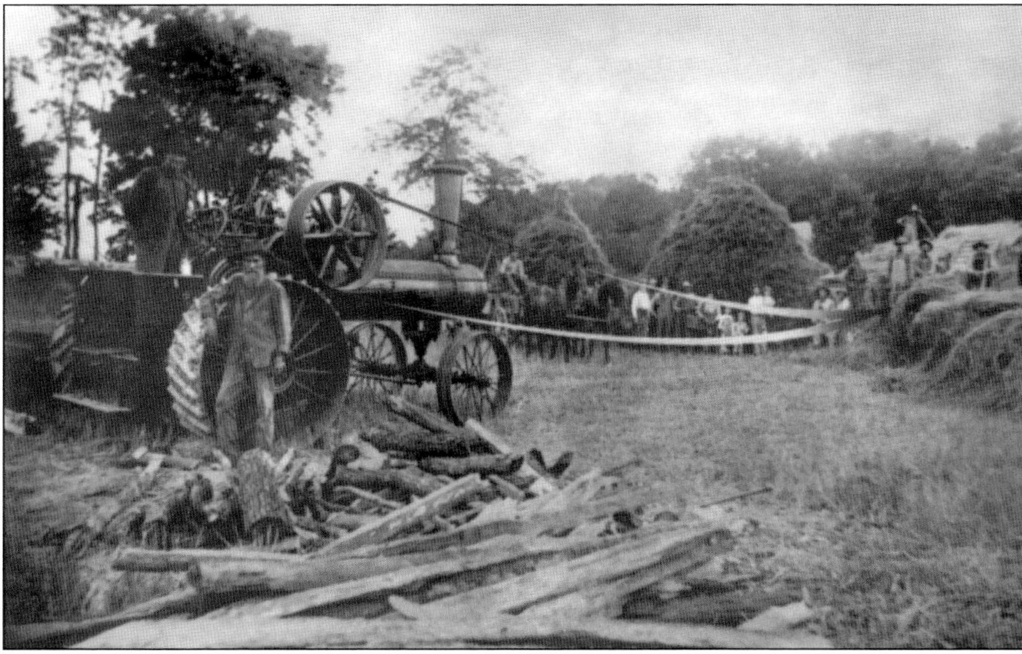

Threshing on Denton Farm, 1911. Threshing with steam-powered tractors was an innovation that saved manual-labor hours. Steam-powered machines used belts connected to a traction engine. It was common for both engine and thresher to belong to a contractor who toured the farms of a district. Steam power remained a viable commercial option until after World War II.

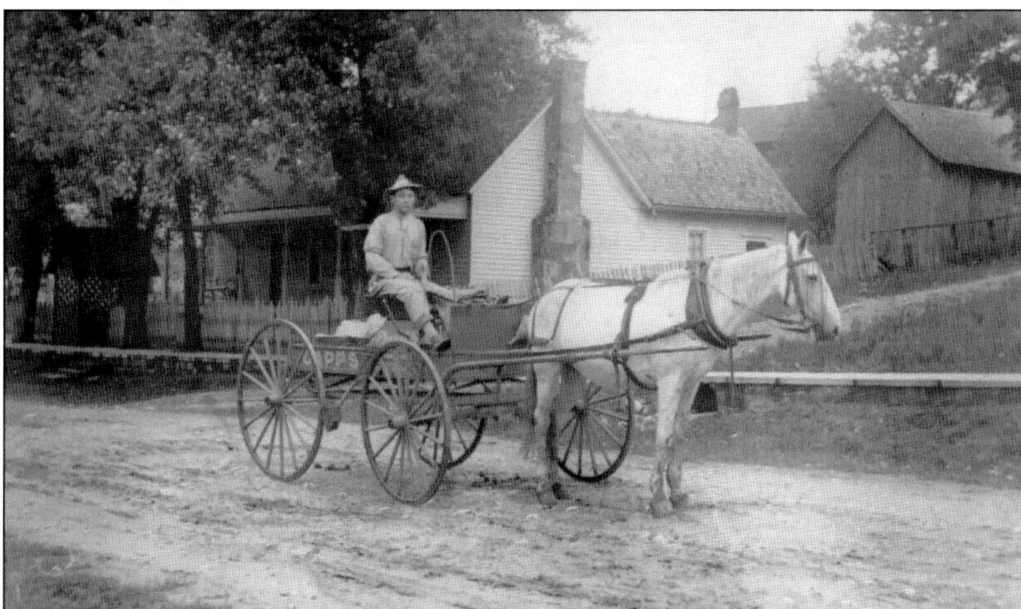

Grocery Wagon, 1914. Glen Coker delivers groceries in a horse-pulled wagon. Home delivery of grocery orders was common in the years before automobiles became common. It would be quite some time before cars were common in this area of the Ozarks. This had much to do with the lack of good roads. Travel by horse remained the default here for much longer than in other areas of Arkansas.

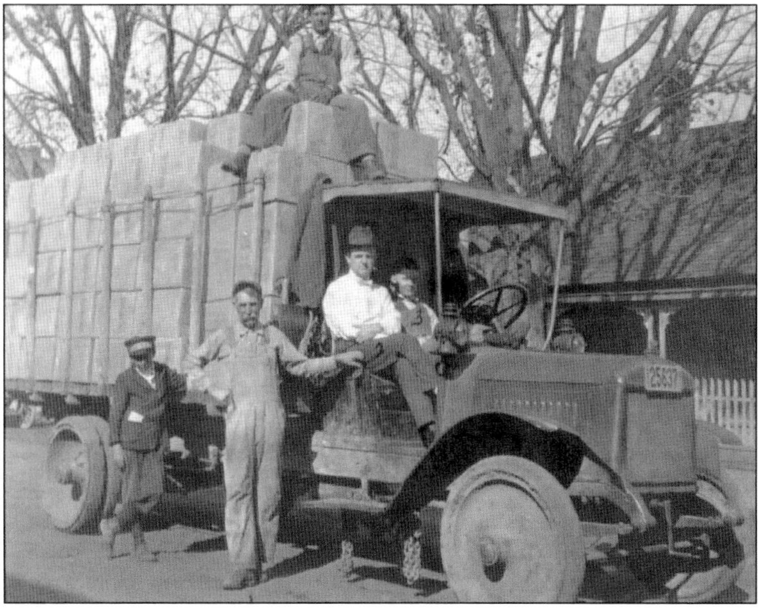

Ulysses Grant Coker's Truck, 1914. Coker owned the first large truck in Harrison. He used it to haul freight between Harrison and Bergman. He was very generous with the use of his truck, which quickly became a sort of community vehicle. Shown here are, from left to right, an unidentified boy, Ulysses Grant Coker, Sam Cecil, and Glen Coker; the man on top of the truck is unidentified.

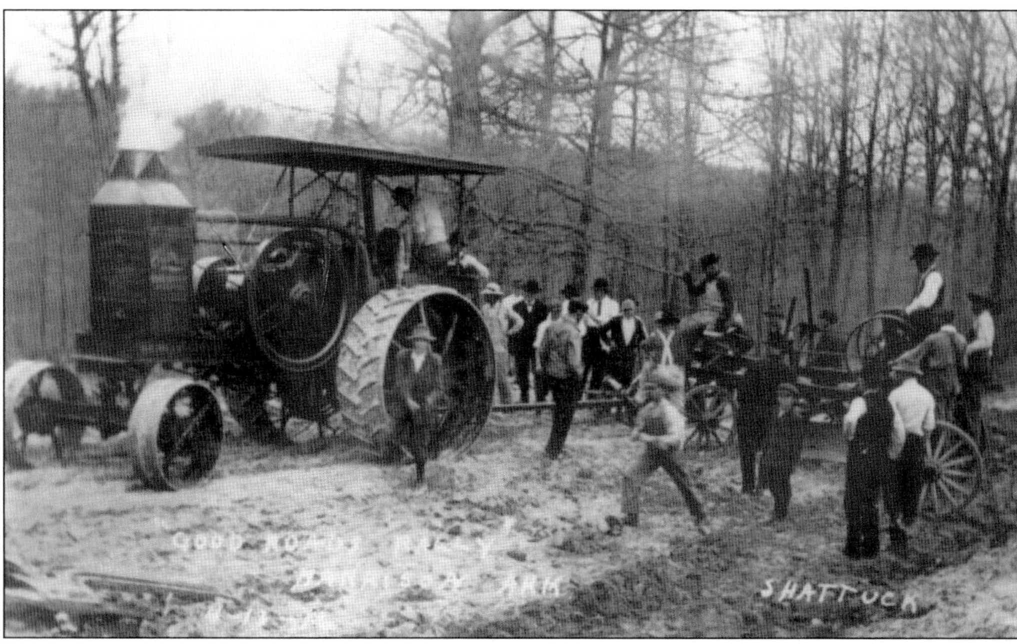

Road-Building Scene, 1916. Roads were difficult to build in this region of Arkansas, thus not many were created until the 1920s. Before then, people navigated the land using Indian trails and what were called "white man's bridle traces" until wagon roads were navigable. Wagon roads were marked by "blazes" on tree trunks. A "three notch road" was known as a "big road" or highway.

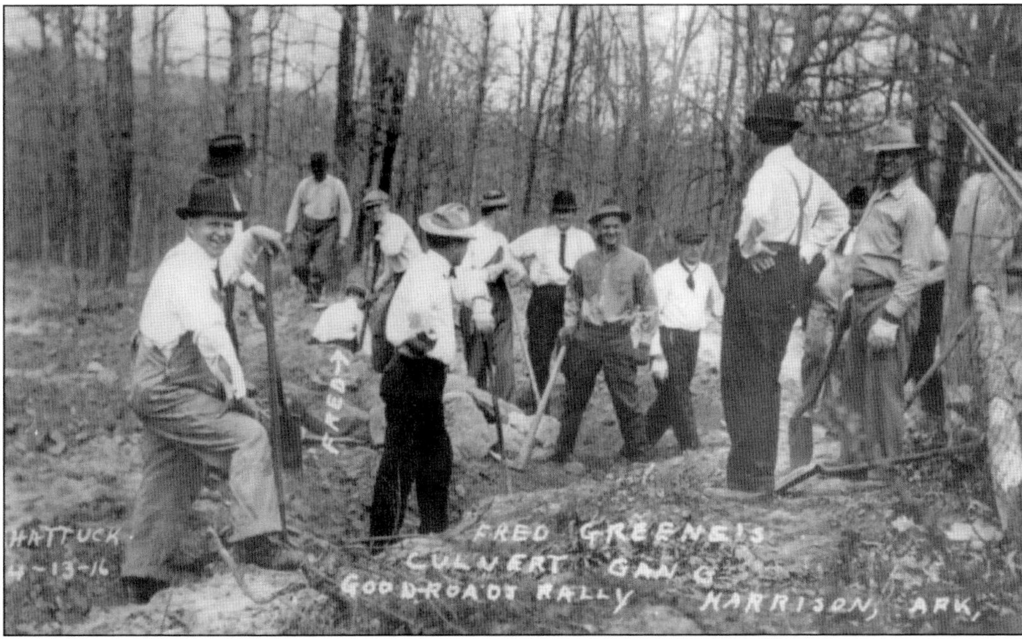

Building a Culvert, April 13, 1916. These men are building what was known as Good Roads Rally. They are referred to as "Fred Greene's Culvert Gang." The only member identified in this photograph is Greene, the man in the background with his back to the camera with an arrow pointing to him reading "Fred."

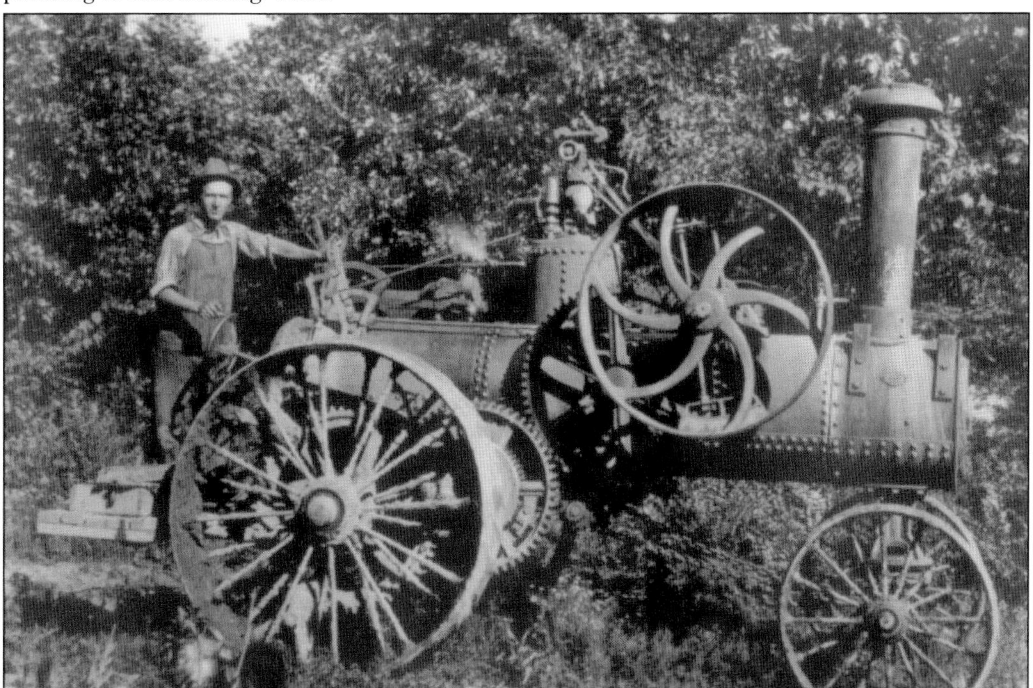

Steam Tractor, 1918. Dewey Erwin poses with an 1890 model. He was delivering the tractor to a mill to which it had been sold. A mill could use the drive belt to transfer power from the engine to the mill itself instead of relying on waterwheels or horses and other livestock for power.

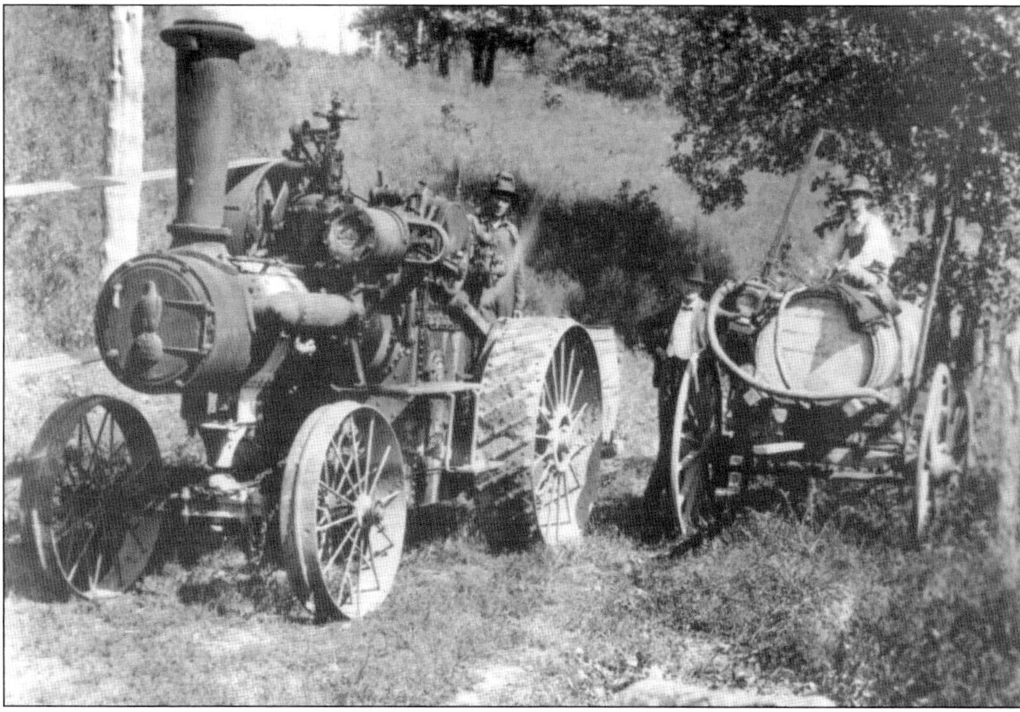

Threshing with Steam Tractors, 1918. Pictured here are, from left to right, Dewey Erwin, Bill Taylor, and David Fearnside. They are threshing for Willis Jones near Capps Road. On a threshing day, neighbors would gather at that day's farmstead to complete a massive job by cooperating and sharing resources.

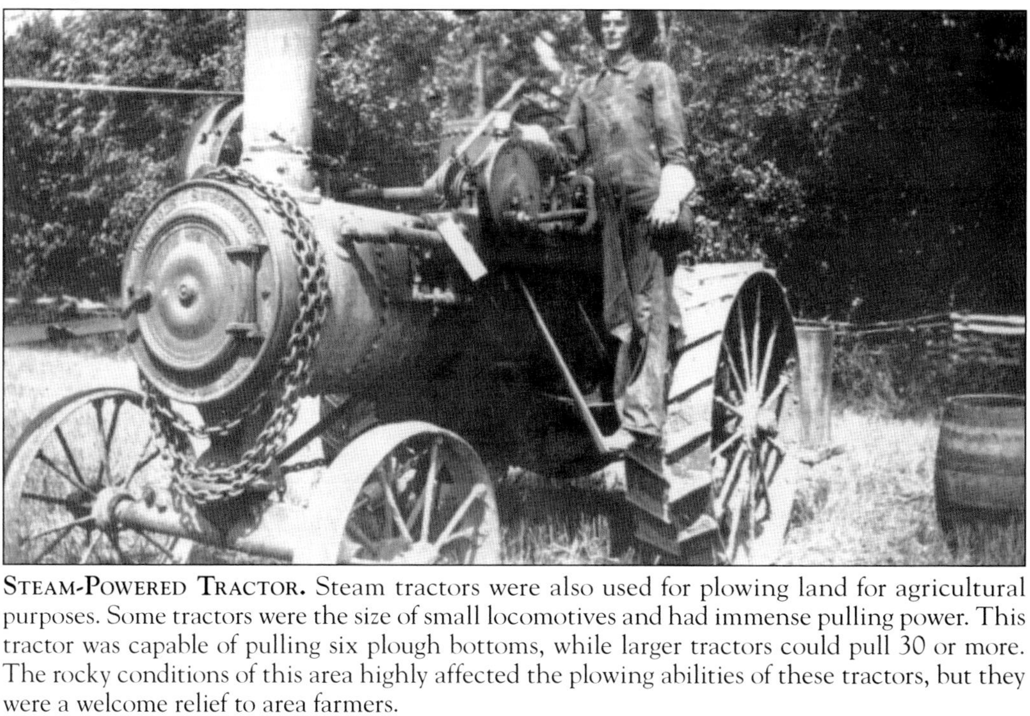

Steam-Powered Tractor. Steam tractors were also used for plowing land for agricultural purposes. Some tractors were the size of small locomotives and had immense pulling power. This tractor was capable of pulling six plough bottoms, while larger tractors could pull 30 or more. The rocky conditions of this area highly affected the plowing abilities of these tractors, but they were a welcome relief to area farmers.

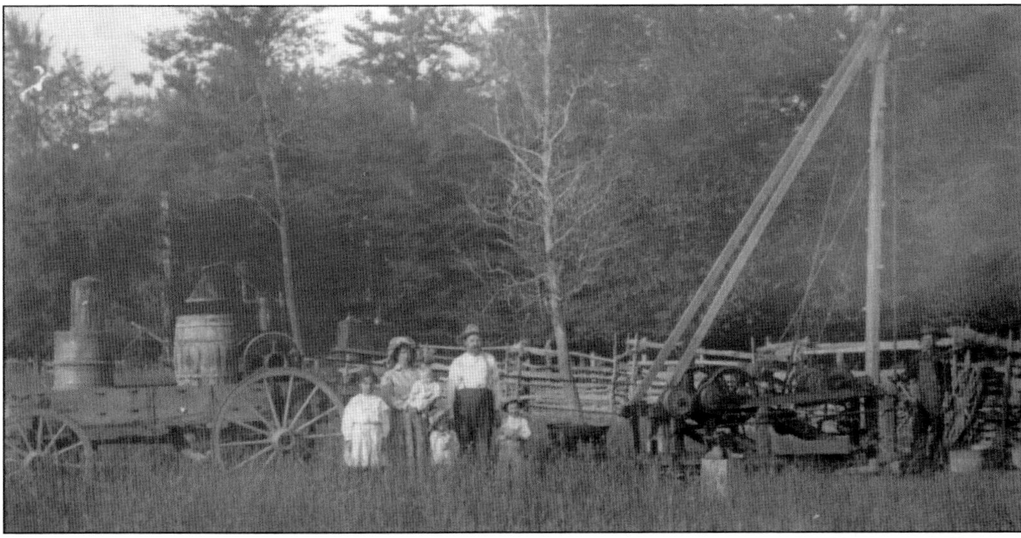

Steam-Powered, Well-Drilling Rig. Before steam power was invented, all water wells were either dug manually or by drilling rigs powered by horses walking around a circular track. By the 1890s, steam power was used in many well-drilling platforms and remained the primary source of power for the next 50 years until the internal-combustion engine was invented.

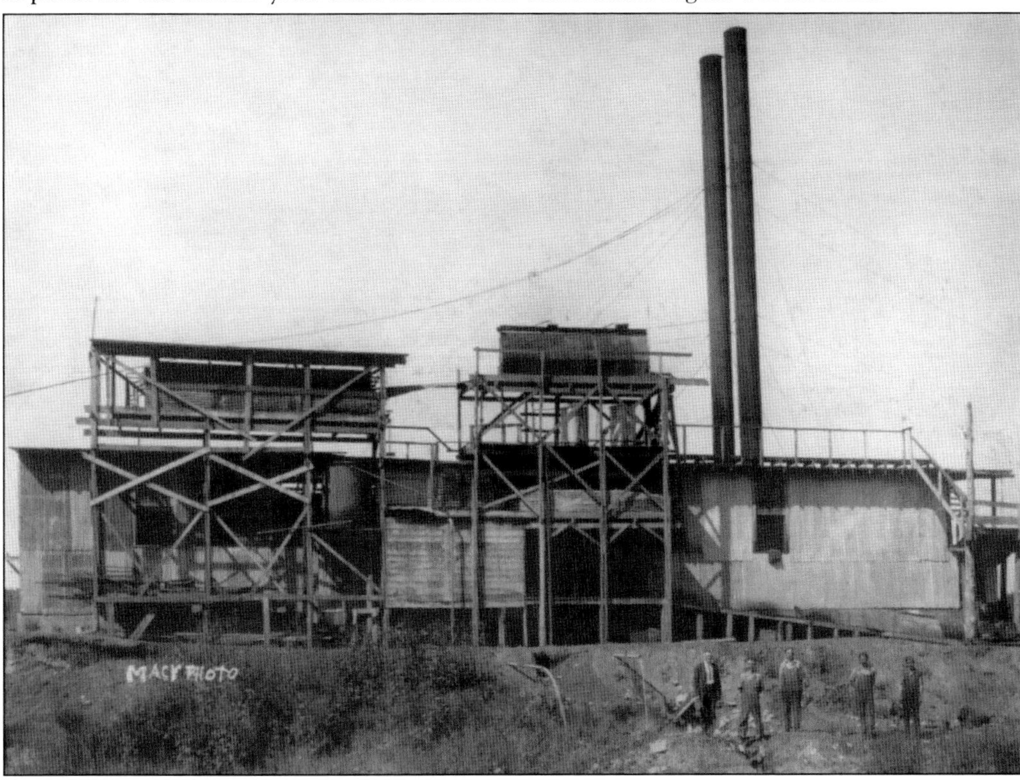

Harrison Light & Ice Company, 1919. In an effort to conserve fuel, the power plant sometimes operated only during certain hours of the day. The plant was in operation until about 1925, when it was acquired by the Southwest Power Company. Arkansas Power & Light purchased the plant in 1929.

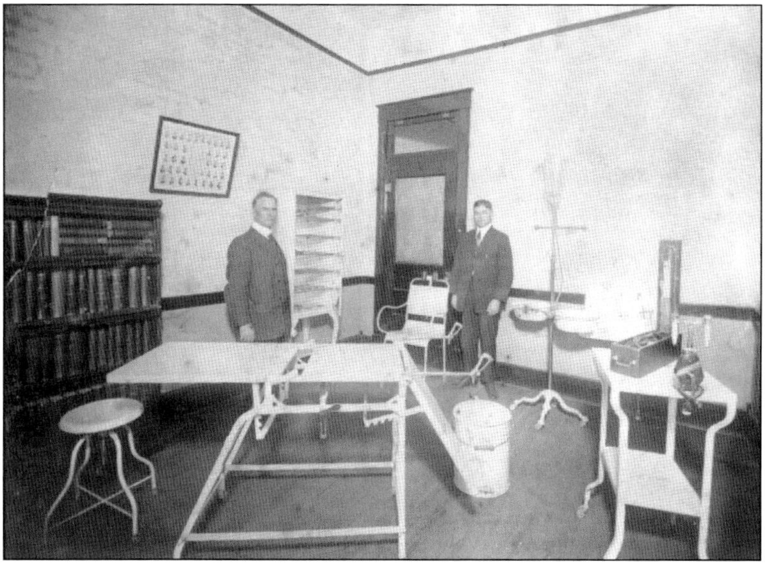

Surgeon's Office, 1920s. Early in the 20th century, surgery was considered almost barbaric. The medical profession did not have the benefits of anesthetics, hygiene requirements, and all forms of scientific advancements. Here, Dr. Jim Fowler (left) and Dr. Buchner pose in Fowler's office.

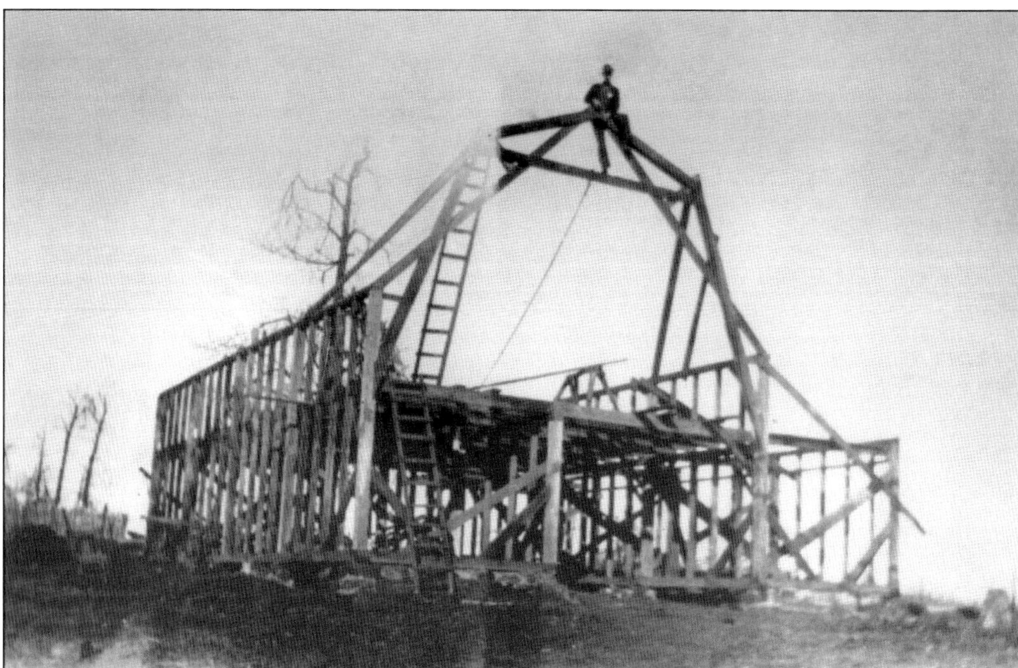

Barn Raising, 1927. Billie Erwin is pictured on top of the barn. In early rural life, barn raising was a community activity. Barns are large and costly structures, the construction of which required more labor than a single family could provide. Members of the community were recruited to help, and they would happily do so because the volunteer cooperation would be returned to everyone involved.

Power Company Truck. This is the first power company truck in Harrison, most likely owned by the Arkansas Power & Light Company, the primary electrical utility company for the majority of the state from 1913 to 1989. It was the predecessor of Entergy Arkansas Incorporated, the electrical company serving much of Arkansas in the 21st century.

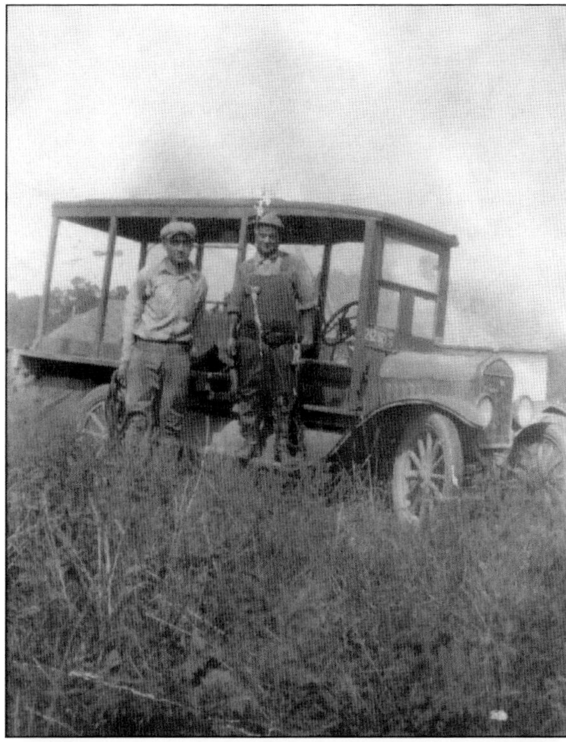

Tire Shop. By the 1930s, the automobile was a common feature in Harrison. Ford and General Motors were the major car manufacturers of the day, and they were fiercely competitive. This kept car prices within reach for many middle-class families. The industry also created a need for service stations like this one. The only identified person in this photograph is Tom Bill Rogers (right).

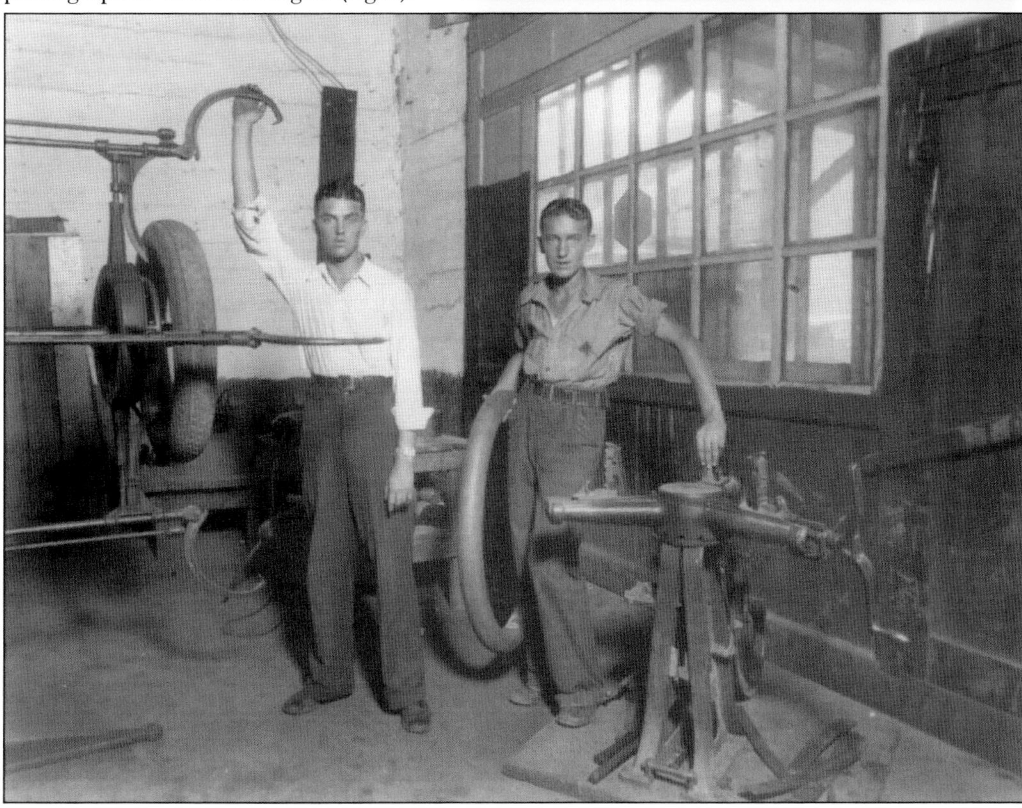

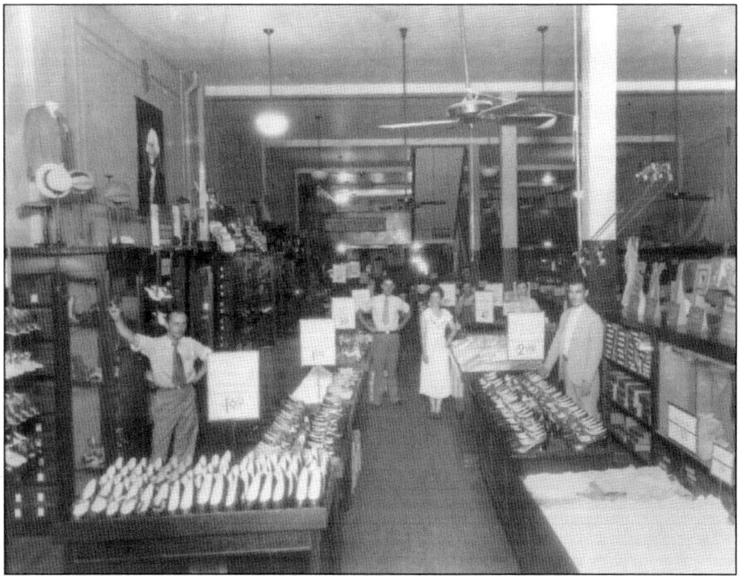

Montgomery Ward. Located at 120 North Willow Street, on the west side of the town square, the Montgomery Ward building was constructed in 1929 and was occupied by that firm for 50 years. Montgomery Ward was a popular retailer, thought to be frequented by James Crawford Angel, a Boone County resident and discoverer of Angel Falls in Venezuela, the highest waterfall in the world, in 1935.

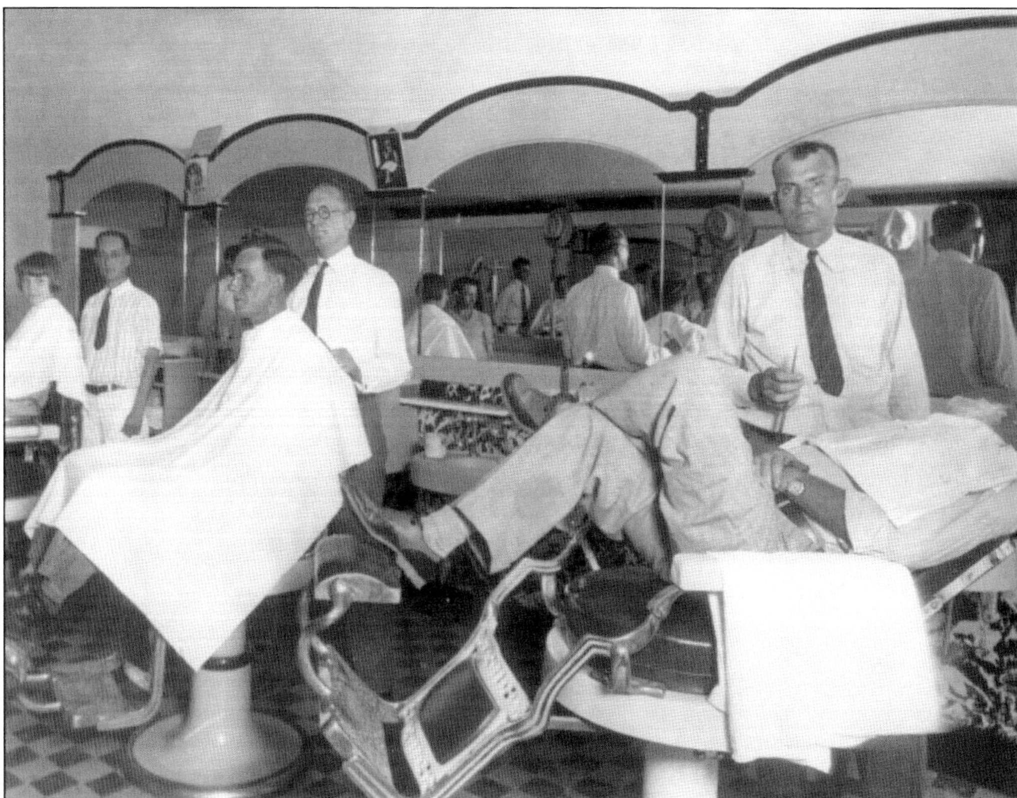

Barbershop, 1930s. During this era, it was common for men in town to visit the barber every week to get manicured. It became a cultural standard to look neat and presentable at all times. To this day, barbershops continue to be gathering places where men can get news of local events, discuss politics, and socialize.

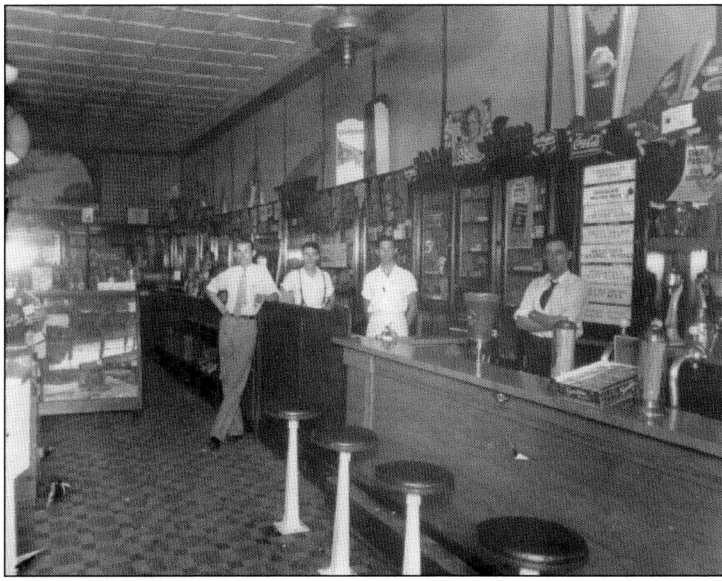

Bennett's Drugstore, 1931. More than a drugstore, this establishment was also a soda fountain, selling sodas, ice cream, milk shakes, popsicles, malted milk, and other treats. The store opened in November 1929. Posing here are, from left to right, Vol Bennett, Ralph Wallace, John Ed Watkins, and Paul Bennett.

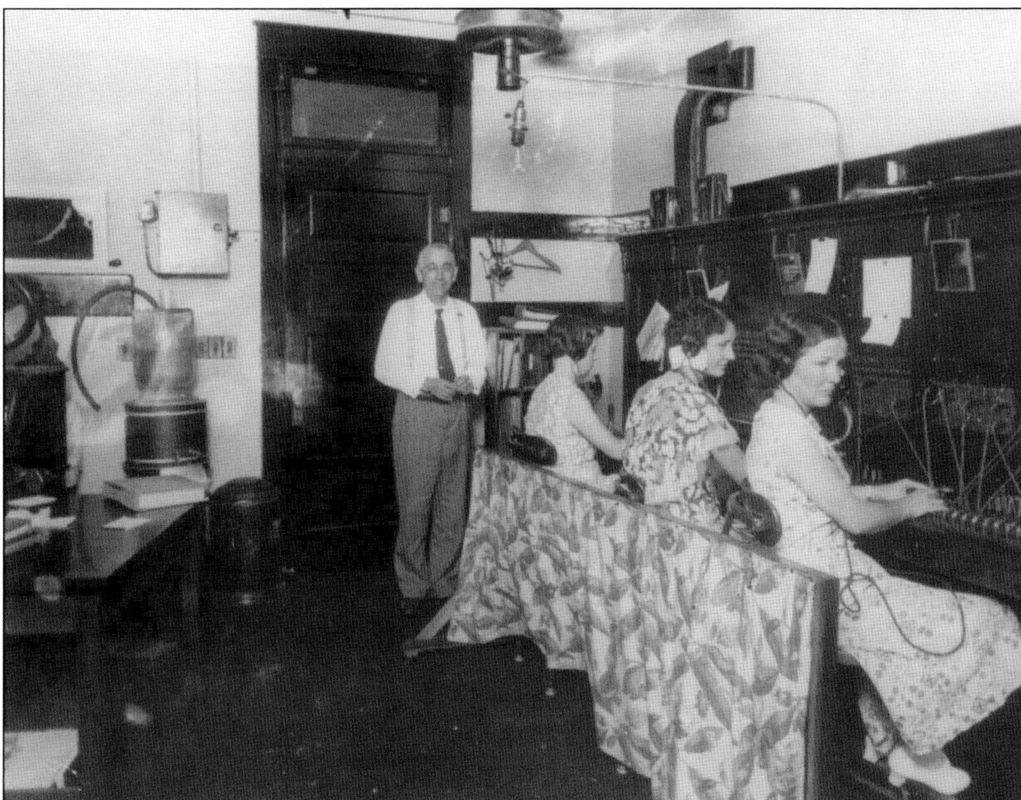

William J. Moore and Telephone Operators, 1932. Harrison received its first telephone line in 1897. It was brought to Harrison from Springfield, Missouri, by Charles Morris, who operated the business from his home. Here, Morris stands near the switchboard of the Boone County Telephone Company with three operators. They are, from left to right, Electra Moore, Anna Lee Porter, and Hersey Wasson.

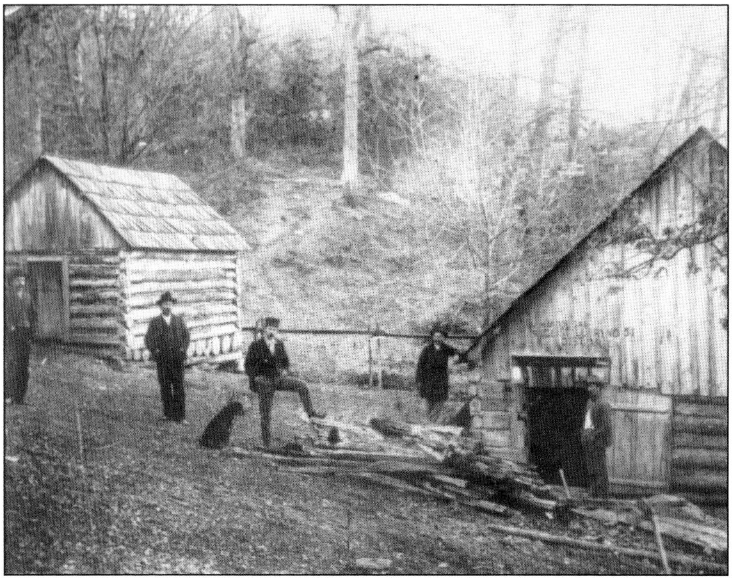

LEGAL DISTILLERY NO. 51. Prohibition was a nationwide constitutional ban on the sale, production, importation, and transportation of alcoholic beverages. It was mandated as the 18th Amendment to the US Constitution in 1920. It was repealed by the 21st Amendment on December 5, 1933. It also ended a long period of bootlegging and crime. This distillery was located near Hurricane Cave.

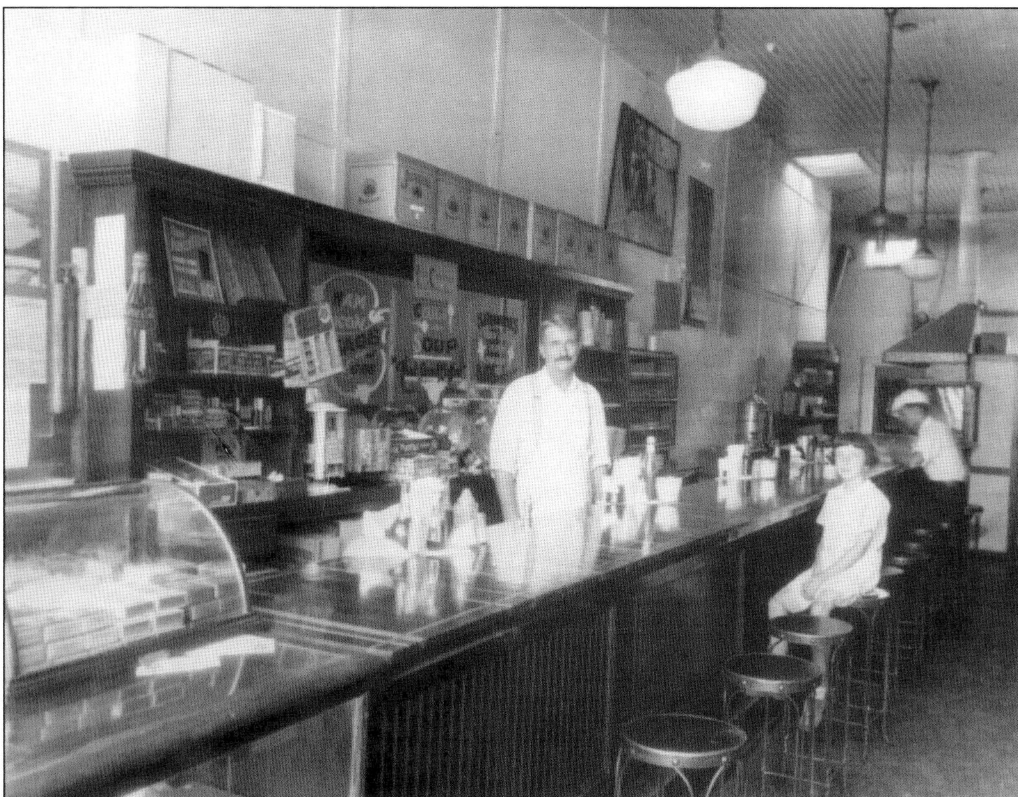

TIM'S CHILI KITCHEN. Diners were a common feature in American culture by the 1930s. The traditional diner setup, as seen here, included a service counter that dominated the interior, with stools bolted to the floor for seating customers in front. A preparation area was located against the back wall. Tim served more than chili; like most diners, his establishment offered other quickly prepared items, like sandwiches and bacon and eggs.

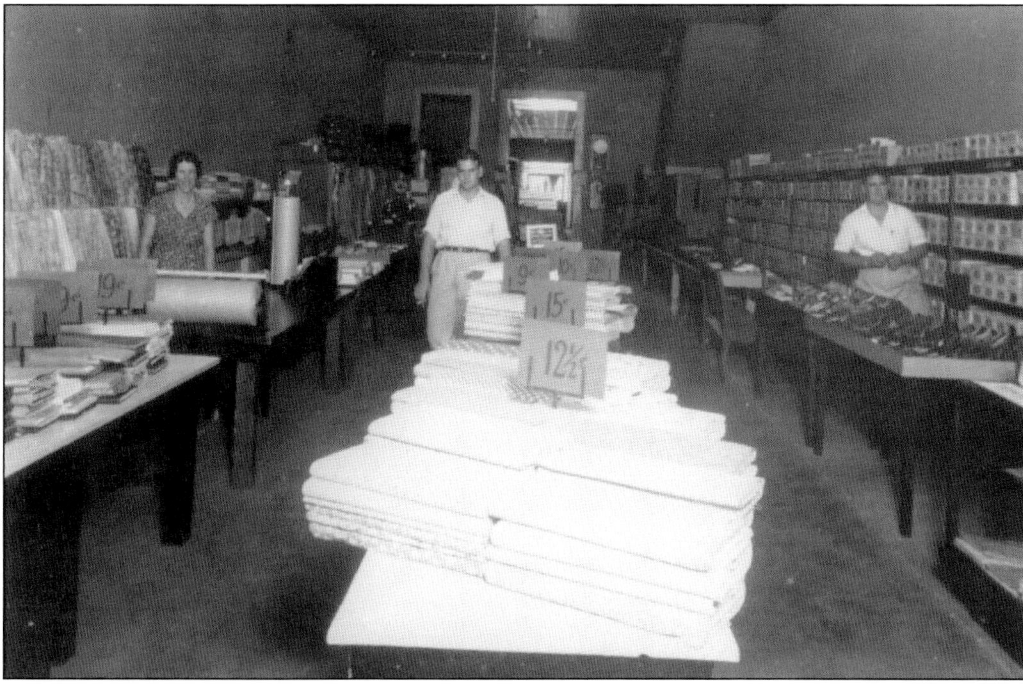

Store Interior, 1934. Here, three unidentified employees pose in a retail store selling sewing materials and shoes. Cloth is priced from 9¢ to 19¢ a yard. It was common for people to make and tailor their own clothes at a time when buying premade clothes was expensive.

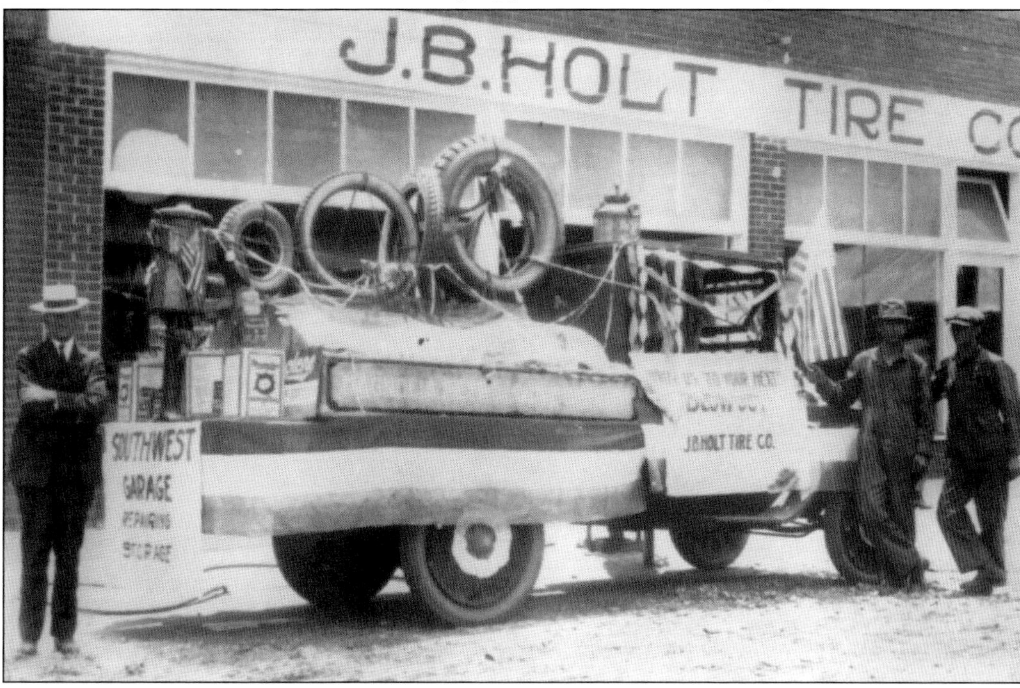

J.B. Holt Tire Company. William Jennings Bryan Holt operated businesses in Harrison for over 40 years. He was also a deputy sheriff and served on the Harrison City Council. He is seen here at the far left wearing a suit and a white straw boater hat.

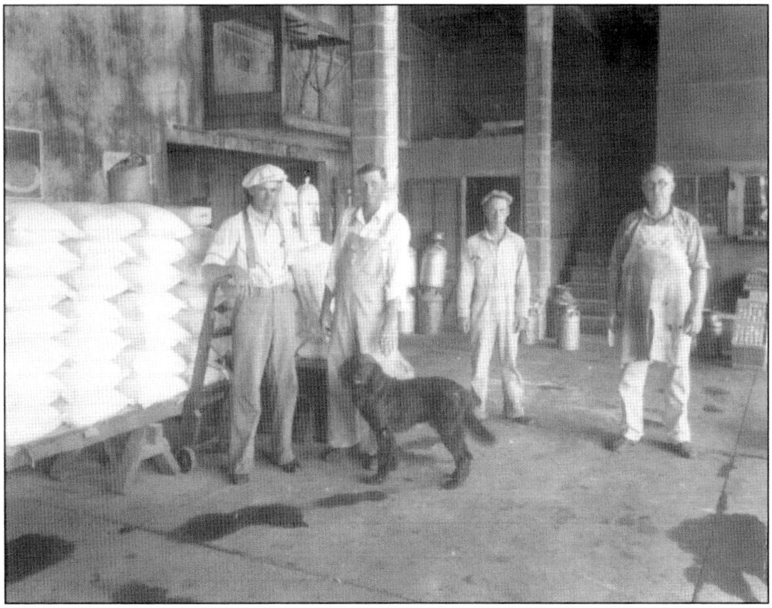

Feed Store. For a rural area, feed stores like this one were a mainstay. To this day, the area continues to be rural, and several feed stores remain in Harrison. Many Boone County residents raise livestock, such as cattle, pigs, sheep, and chickens. Feed is especially important during the winter months, when livestock do not go outside to forage as much.

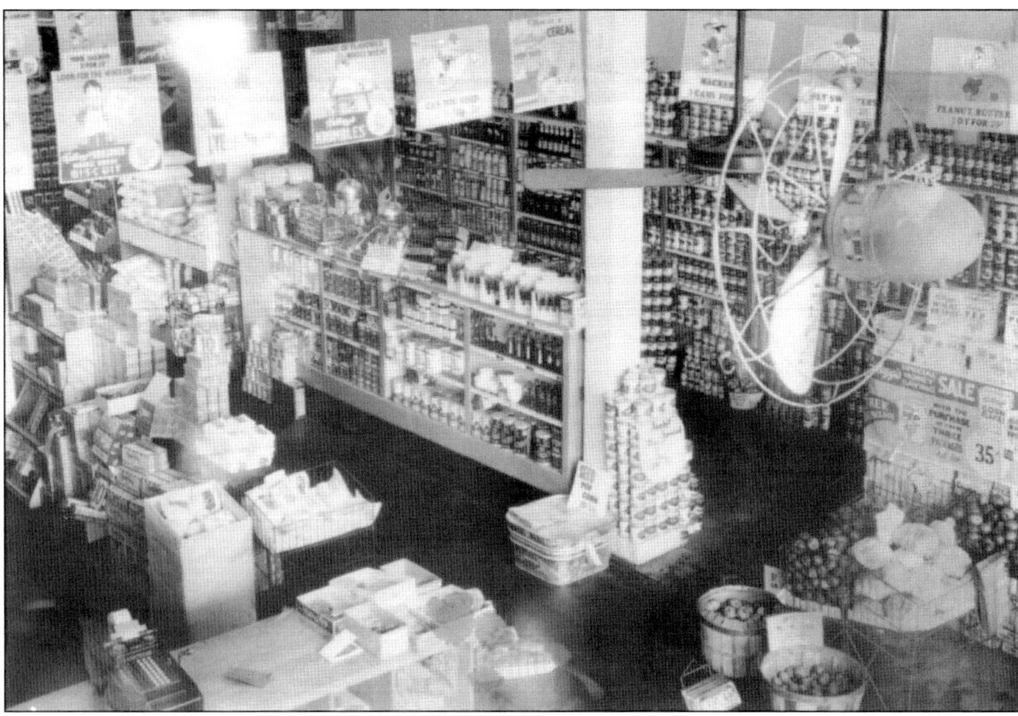

Grocery Store Scene. Kellogg's whole wheat Krumbles is on sale, two for 25¢, and canned dog food is on sale, three cans for 25¢. Popcorn is being sold in bulk for 15¢ a pound, and apples are on sale for 5¢ a pound. Note the old Victor Adding Machine Model 110, introduced in 1919, on the counter at the bottom left.

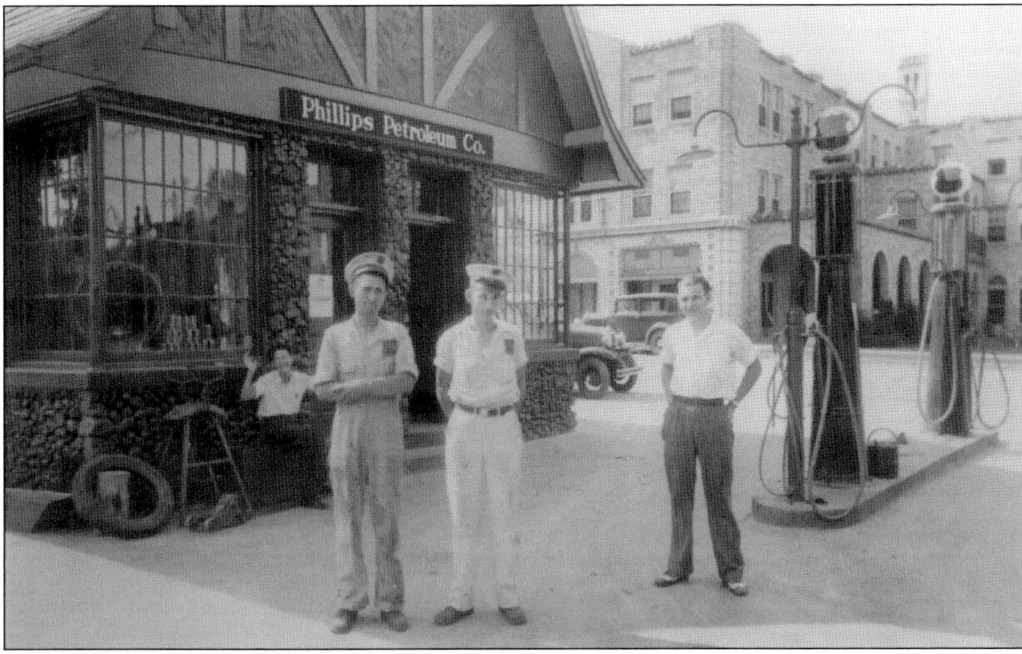

PHILLIPS SERVICE STATION, 1930S. This is one of the first filling stations in Harrison. The building was constructed around 1915 by W.H. Lewis, who originally sold kerosene and oil products in town. The gas pumps seen here had to be operated by hand. In the background is the historic Hotel Seville, which used to be Harrison's finest social and civic meeting place.

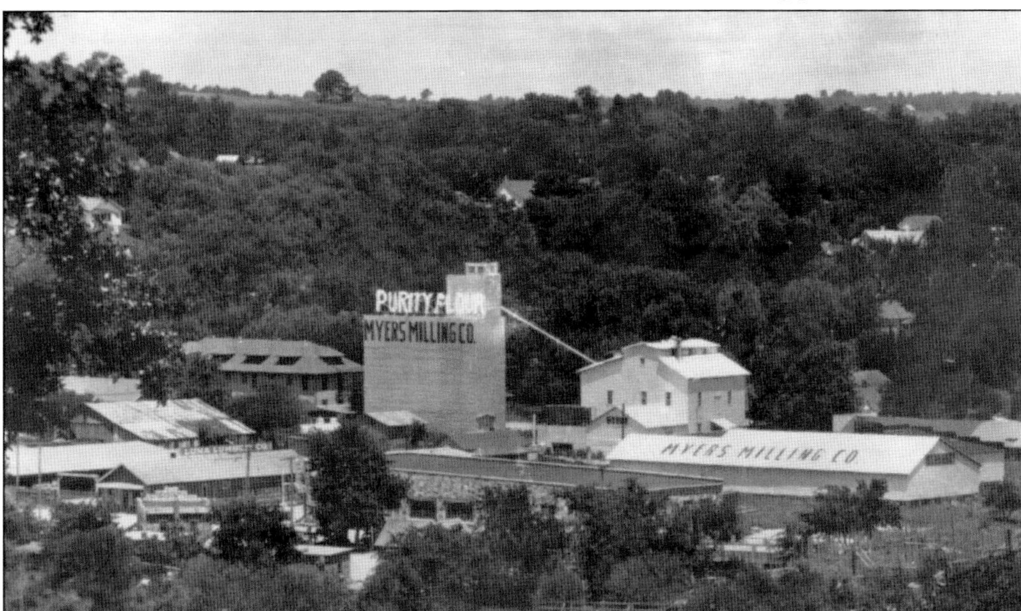

MYERS MILLING COMPANY, 1939. Charles Myers and William Myers were business partners in this venture. Their company manufactured flour, as well as poultry and dairy feeds. Their business was greatly damaged by the abandonment of the railroad by the Arkansas Ozarks Railway Corporation. They registered a complaint against the corporation, and an injunction was issued by Chief Judge John E. Miller on June 30, 1960.

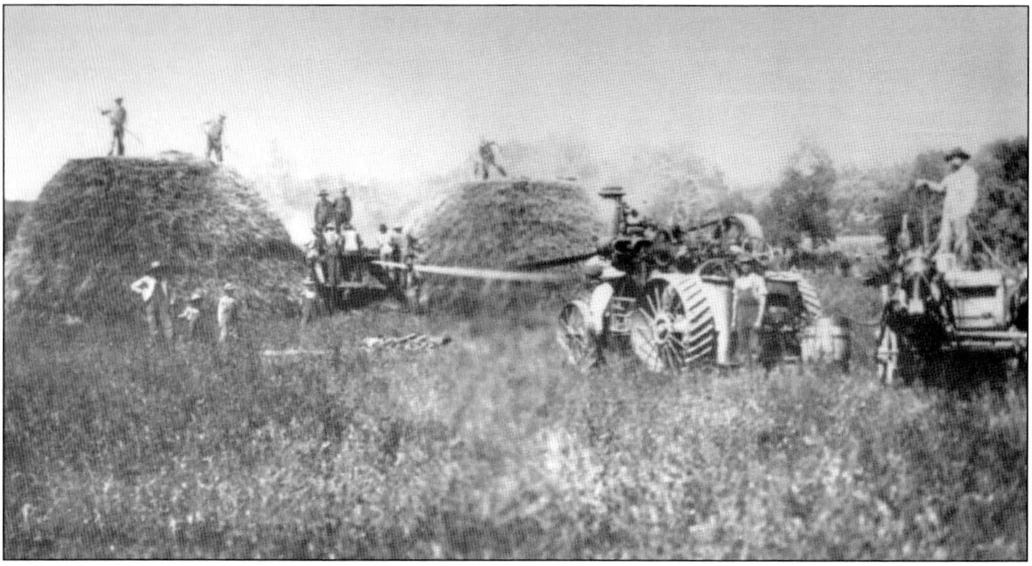

Dewey Erwin's Thresher. Several men are seen threshing on Vol Denton's farm near Alpena. Dewey Erwin assisted farmers in the area with their threshing. He was born on September 15, 1899, and married Sylvia Alene Fearnside in 1929. They had no children. Sylvia died in 1975, and Dewey died on February 14, 1982, at 82 years of age.

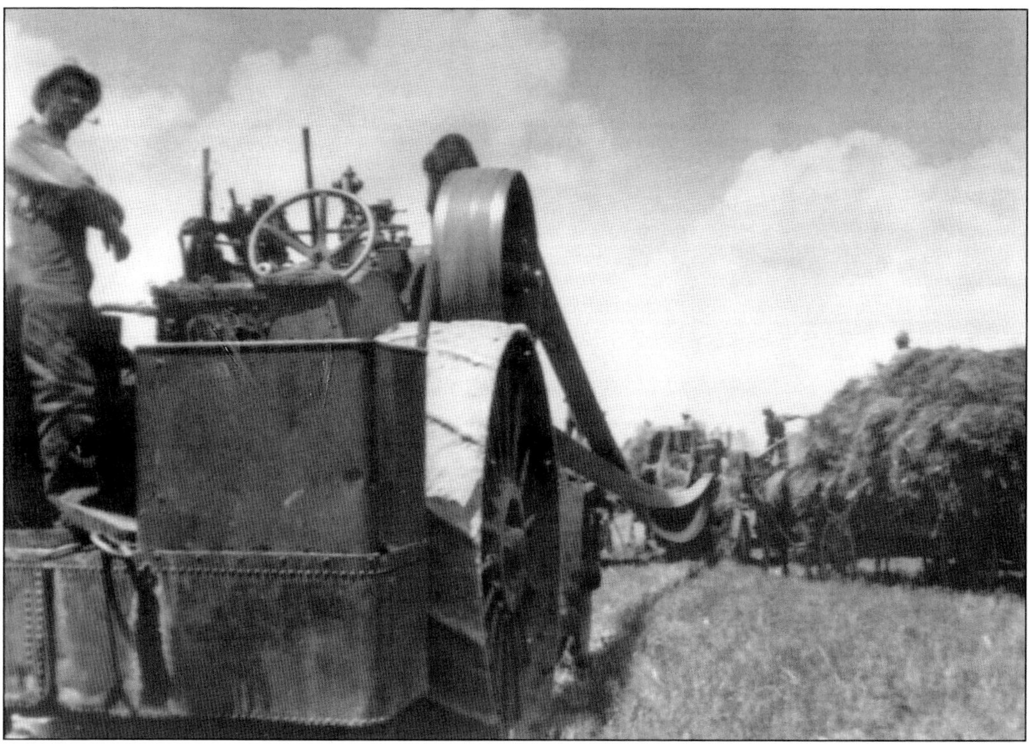

Threshing on Farm, 1940. Jim Majors's farm was located in west Harrison near Dry Jordan Creek. The thresher in this photograph belonged to Dewey Erwin. Dwight Sims is on the steam tractor, looking at the camera. The belt from the steam-powered tractor is clearly seen stretching to the threshing machine in the background.

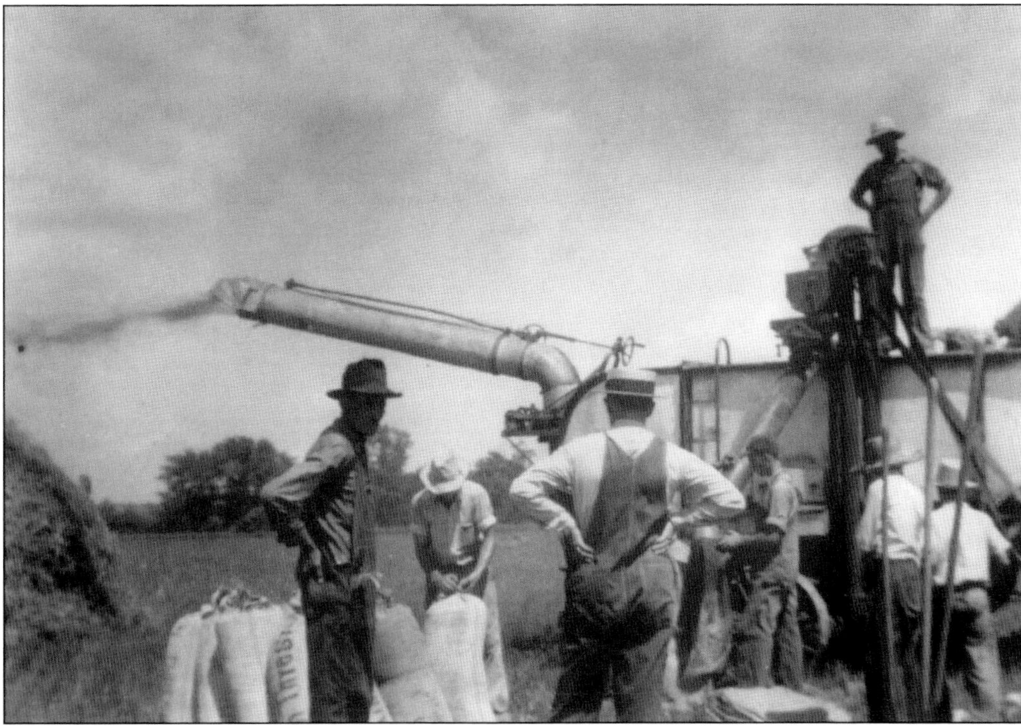

Jim Majors's Farm, 1940. Seen here with Dewey Erwin's thresher are, from left to right, Jim Majors, Arch Rose (tying a sack), Ben Beene, an unidentified young man monitoring the spout, Ben Majors (back to camera, wearing straw hat), and Clay Majors; Dewey Erwin stands on top of the separator.

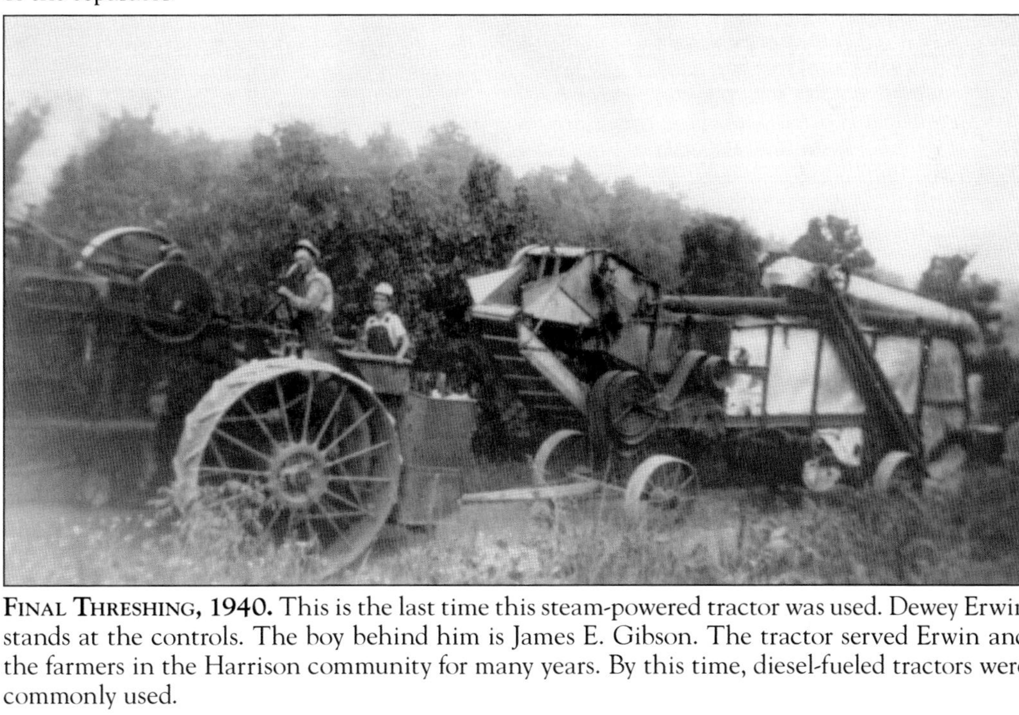

Final Threshing, 1940. This is the last time this steam-powered tractor was used. Dewey Erwin stands at the controls. The boy behind him is James E. Gibson. The tractor served Erwin and the farmers in the Harrison community for many years. By this time, diesel-fueled tractors were commonly used.

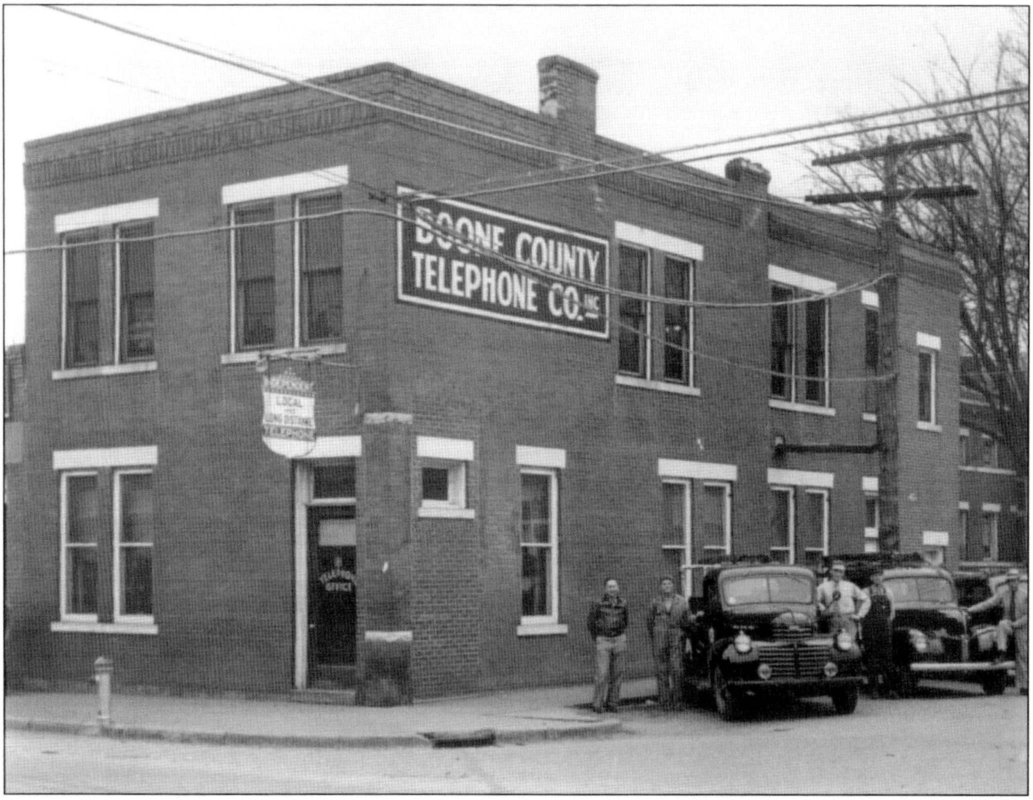

Boone County Telephone Company, Inc. This is the telephone company's headquarters. Telephone lines in Harrison were first constructed in 1900, connecting the town to communities as far away as Eureka Springs and Marshall. By 1905, one hundred seventy-five miles of lines and 435 telephones had been installed. The five men seen here stand beside the company's service trucks.

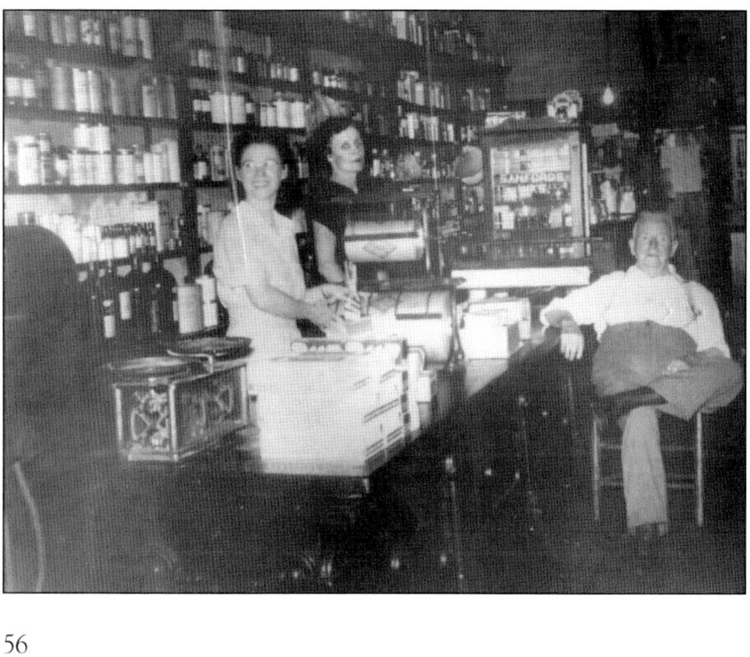

Store Scene, 1940s. The wood-framed glass case on the counter holds Sanford's Inks for sale. Such inks were used for dip pens, commonly used until the ballpoint pen dominated the market. Though patented in 1888, the ballpoint pen would not be a commercial success until after World War II.

Three

THE RAILROAD

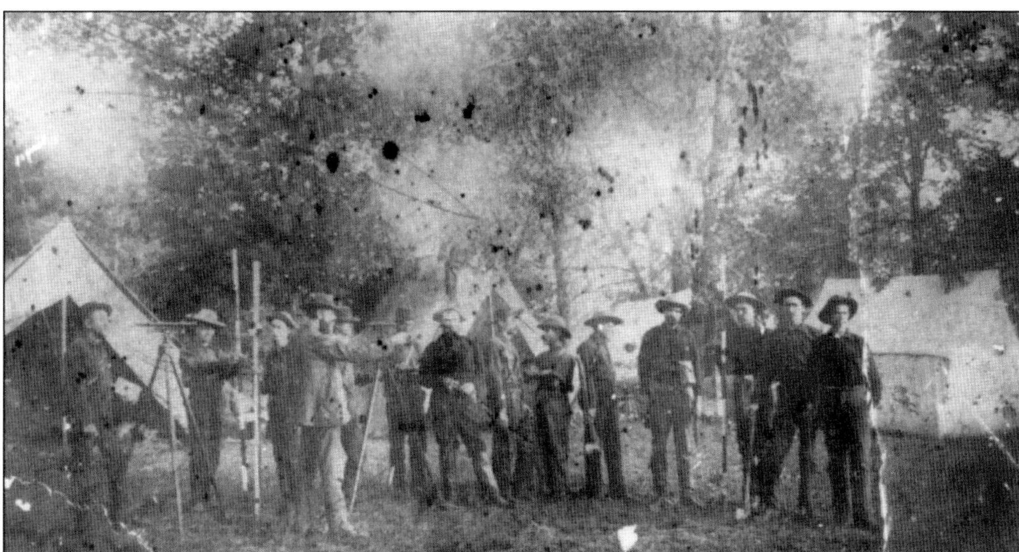

RAILROAD SURVEY CREW. Marcus LaRue Harrison was part of a survey crew like the one shown here when he was recruited to survey land for the town that was eventually named in his honor. The development of railroads in America is one of the most important aspects of the industrial revolution. With their formation, construction, and operation, railroads brought profound social, political, and economic change to Harrison.

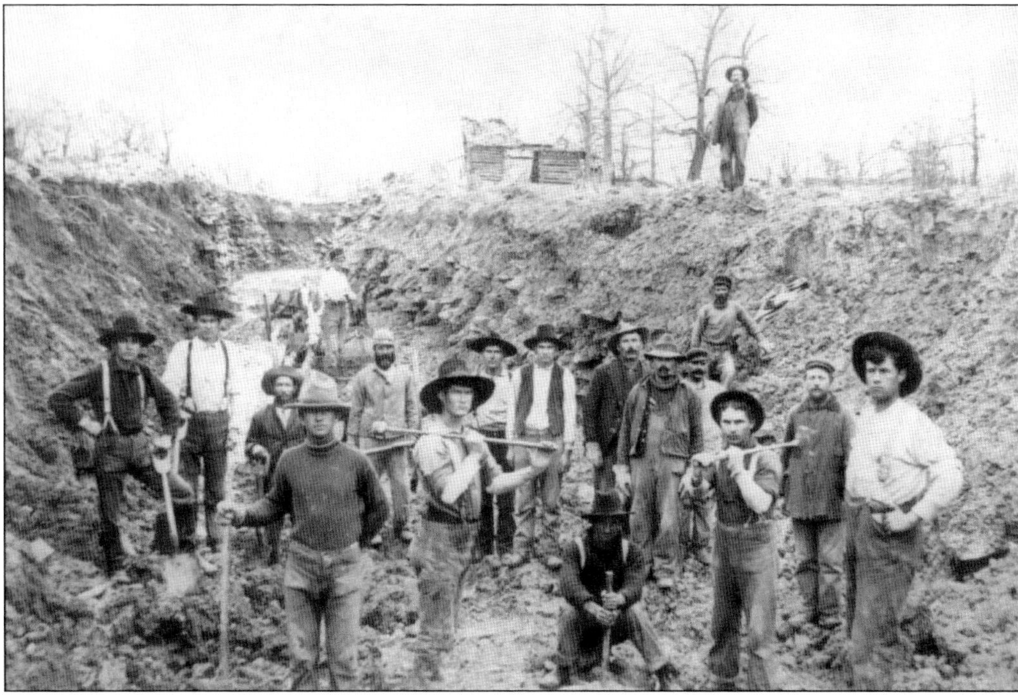

Missouri Pacific Railroad Crew. A crew is working on a Missouri Pacific Railroad bed before the turn of the century. This section of track was cut out of the Riddlesperger farm. Moving great amounts of dirt before the days of modern machinery was a strenuous task.

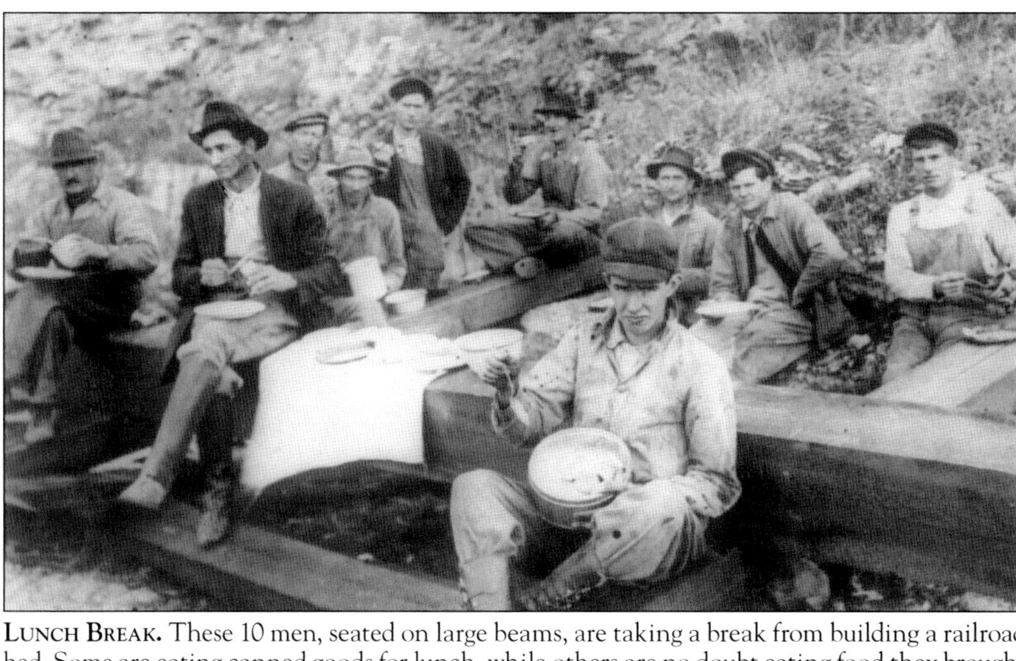

Lunch Break. These 10 men, seated on large beams, are taking a break from building a railroad bed. Some are eating canned goods for lunch, while others are no doubt eating food they brought from home. The only person identified is J.E. Fitzgerald (far right).

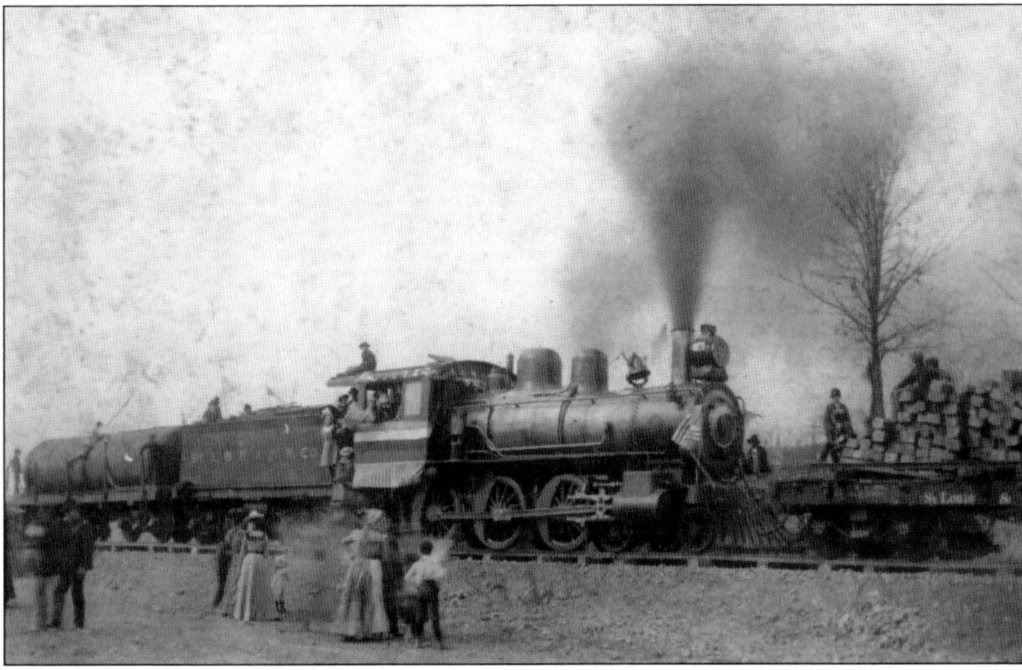

First Train in Harrison, 1901. The first locomotive arrived in Harrison via the St. Louis & North Arkansas Railroad on March 22, 1901, at 9:15 a.m. The line was planned to link to the capital city of Little Rock in Pulaski County along what became US Route 65. Ralph Rea, in *Boone County and Its People*, wrote that the businessmen of Harrison paid $40,000 toward the project.

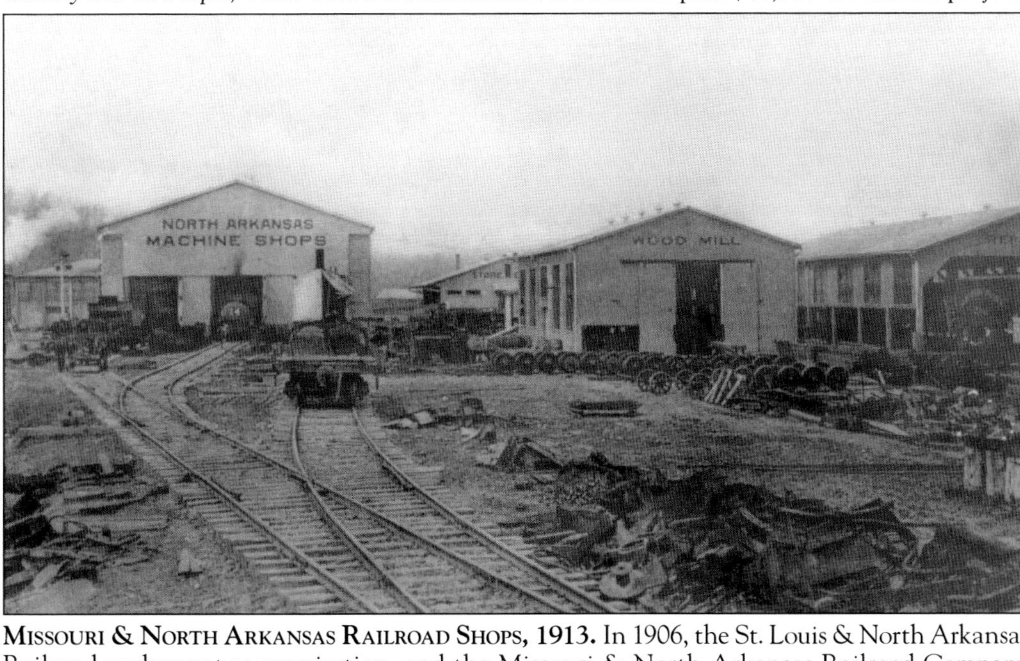

Missouri & North Arkansas Railroad Shops, 1913. In 1906, the St. Louis & North Arkansas Railroad underwent reorganization, and the Missouri & North Arkansas Railroad Company was formed. The regional carrier stretched from Joplin, Missouri, to Helena, Arkansas. In 1913, the company moved its headquarters and shops to Harrison. The city raised $25,000 for the construction of railroad offices on the town square.

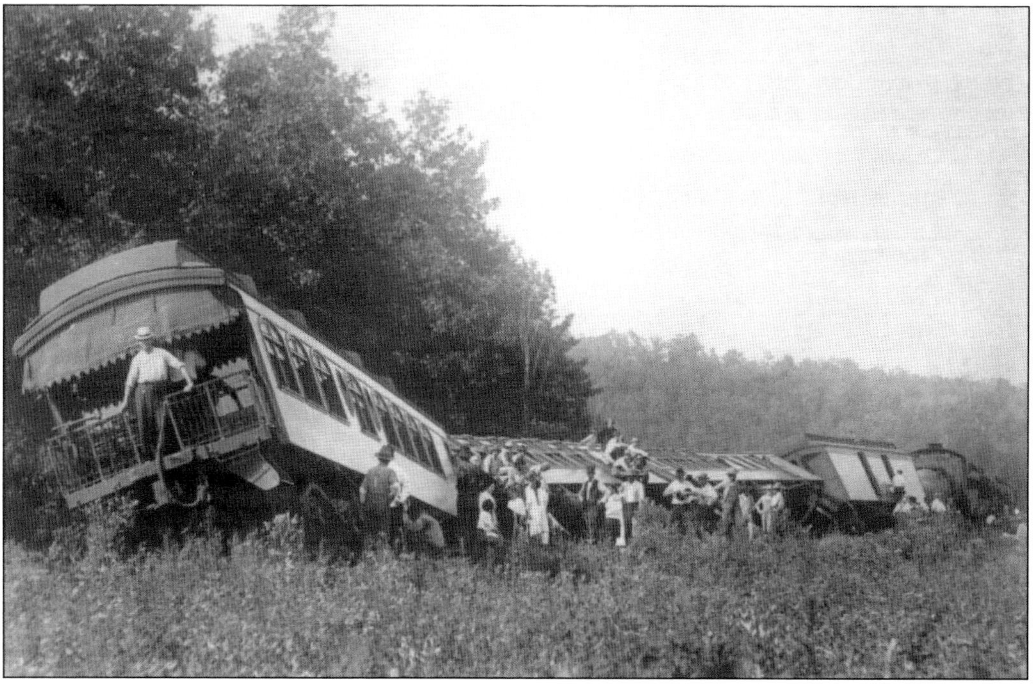

Missouri & North Arkansas Wreck, 1914. The line to Helena, Arkansas, was completed at a cost of $6 million. Service began over the entire Missouri & North Arkansas line on March 1, 1909. Through a policy of "spending money to make money," the railroad was put in first-class condition. Pullman sleeper service was initially offered on the route from Kansas City, Missouri, to Helena; however, affluence for the company would be short-lived.

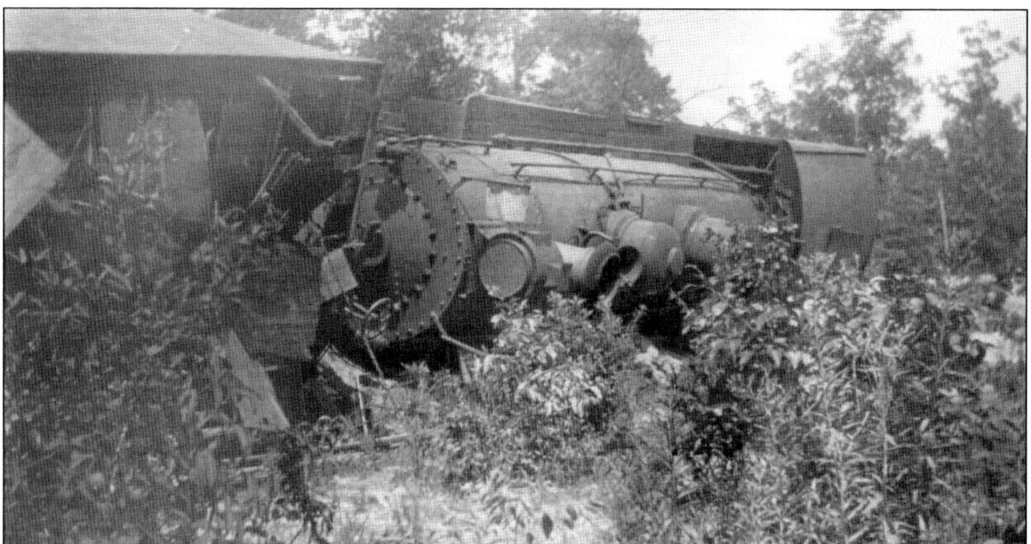

Wrecked Engine, 1914. Due to irregular dependability in its early years, the Missouri & North Arkansas (MNA) acronym came to stand for "May Never Arrive." In this case, it never did. After several years of running deficits, the railroad company ultimately entered into receivership.

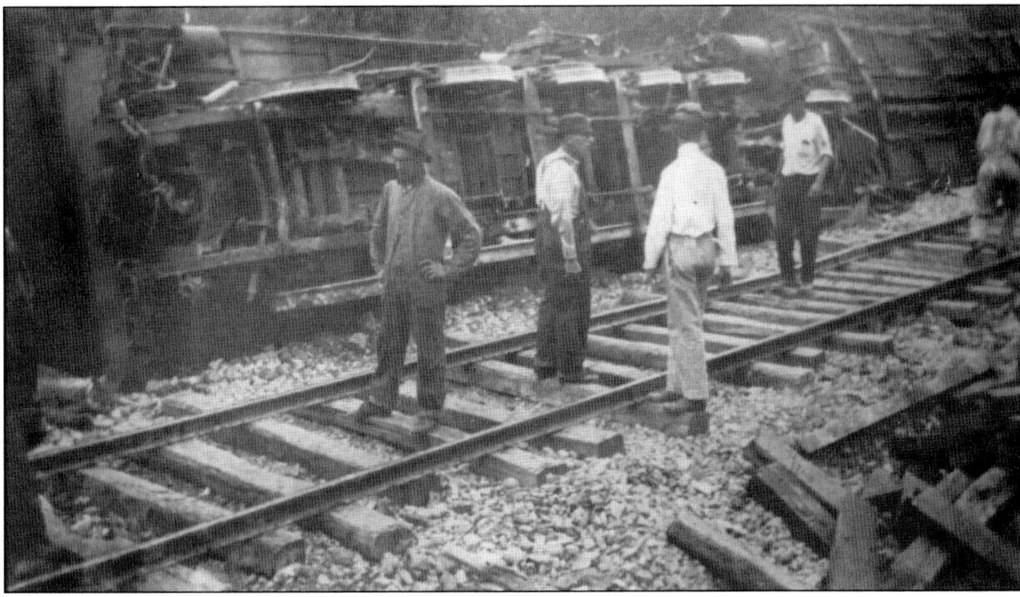

Train Collision, 1914. A miscommunication in train orders led to this horrifying head-on collision on the Missouri & North Arkansas line near Tipton Ford, Missouri, in August 1914. It was one of many tragedies the Missouri & North Arkansas Railroad Company would experience, which ultimately led to its demise.

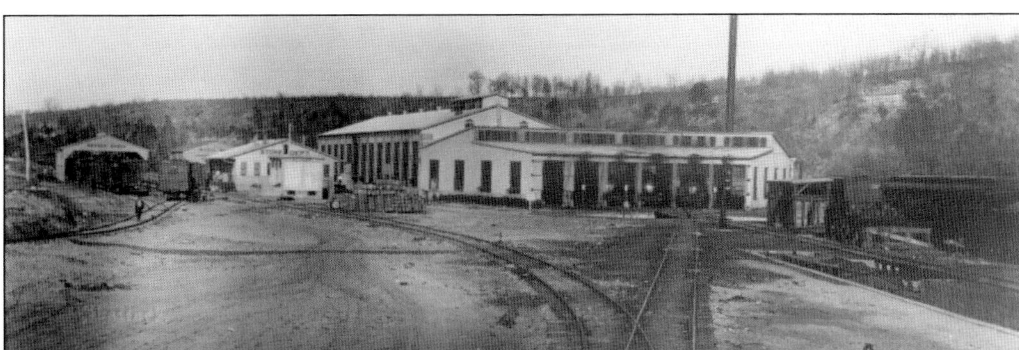

MNA Railroad Shops, 1915. With the railroad shops fully established in Harrison, the local economy experienced a boost. By 1916, the railroad was experiencing profits; however, the government's takeover of the railroads in 1917 to support World War I would prove detrimental. Due to a policy guaranteeing income based on a railroad's 1914–1917 average, the Missouri & North Arkansas Railroad Company suffered a period of loss.

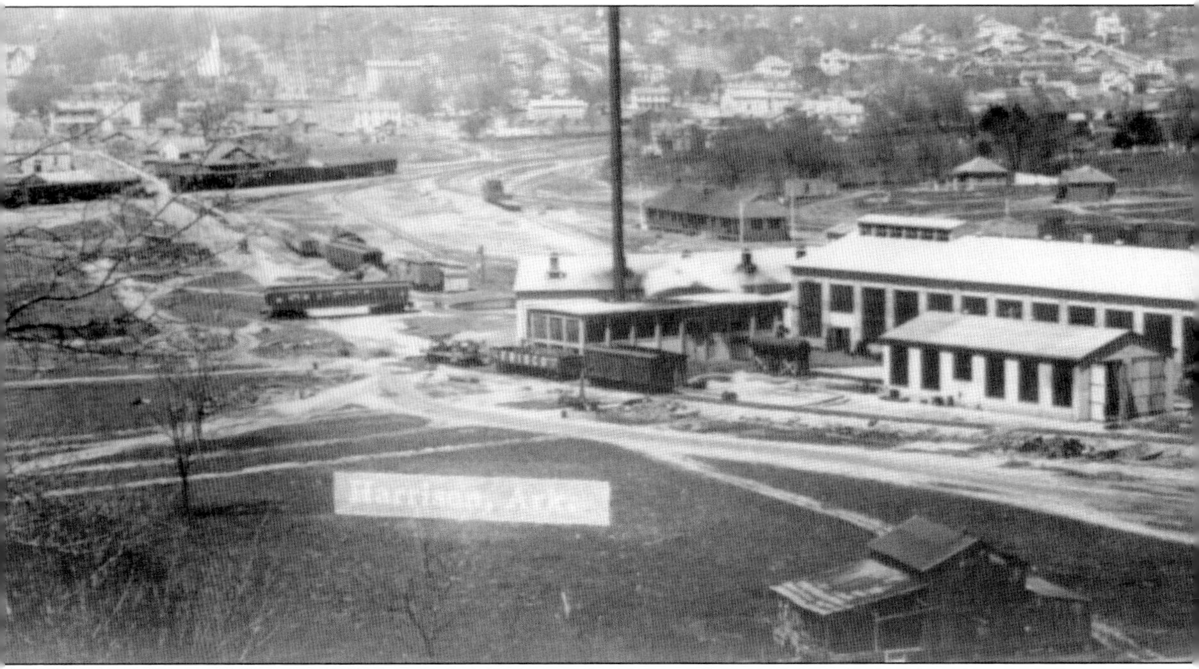

MNA Railroad Complex, 1915. Though hopes were high that the railroad would be an economic boon to Harrison and Boone County, unfortunately it was a failure for many reasons. The railroad was plagued with weather-induced disasters, labor dissent, questionable decisions by absentee managers and owners, unforgiving topography, economic difficulties, fires, and just

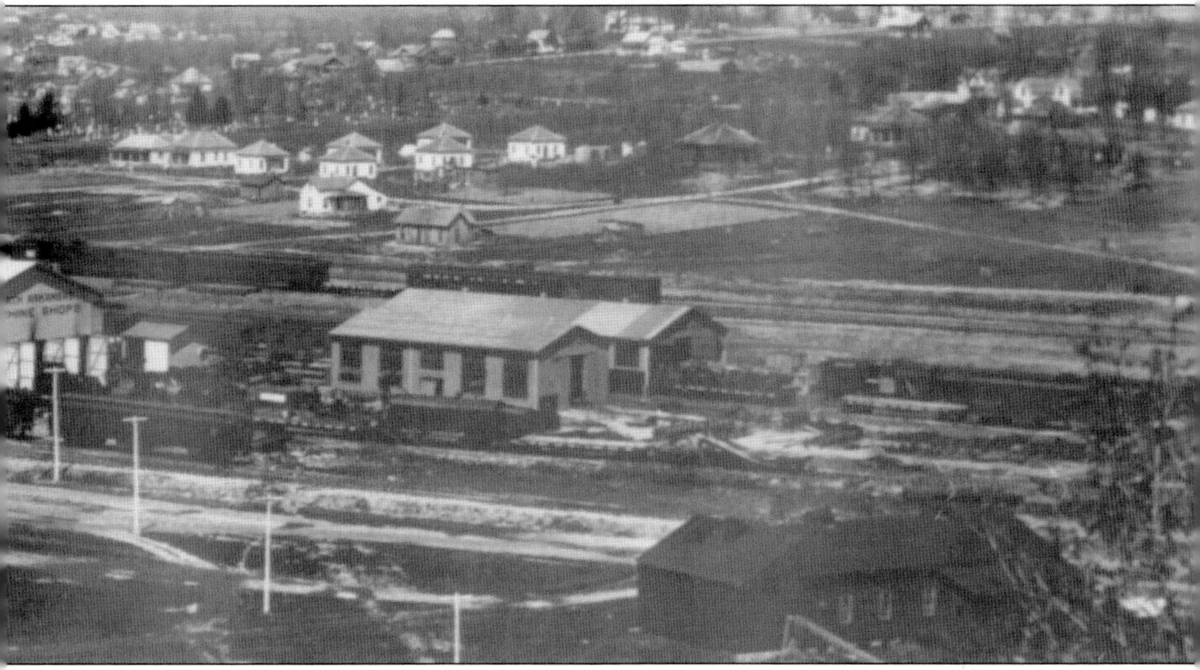

plain bad luck. The railroad also brought in outsiders, who became a source of contention for an exclusive community and culture. The race riots of 1905 and 1909, in which white residents of Harrison drove out nearly all of its black residents, can be partly blamed on the railroad. The line was completed in 1906, but the railroad was abandoned just four decades later.

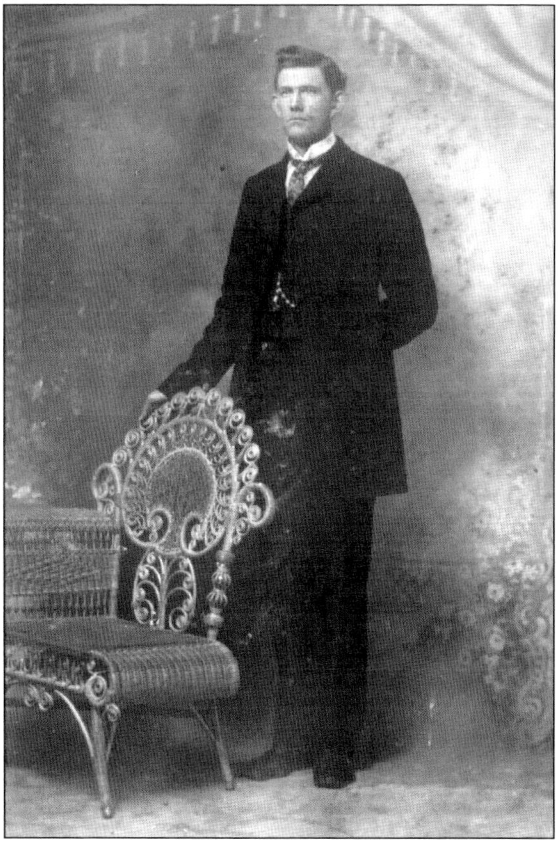

J. Sam Rowland. Rowland began serving as attorney for the Missouri & North Arkansas Railroad Company in 1921. During the early part of his active career, he served as Boone County representative in the Arkansas Legislature. This photograph was taken while he was serving in the legislature. Later in life, Rowland became active in Harrison as a volunteer and philanthropist.

Arkansas & Ozarks Railway Engine. In 1949, two sections of the former Missouri & North Arkansas Railroad Company returned to service under new ownership. The largest segment in place stretched from Seligman, Missouri, to Harrison and was operated by the diesel-powered Arkansas & Ozarks Railroad. Due to declining revenues, the owners of the Arkansas & Ozarks Railroad filed for complete abandonment in 1960. By 1962, all rails were removed.

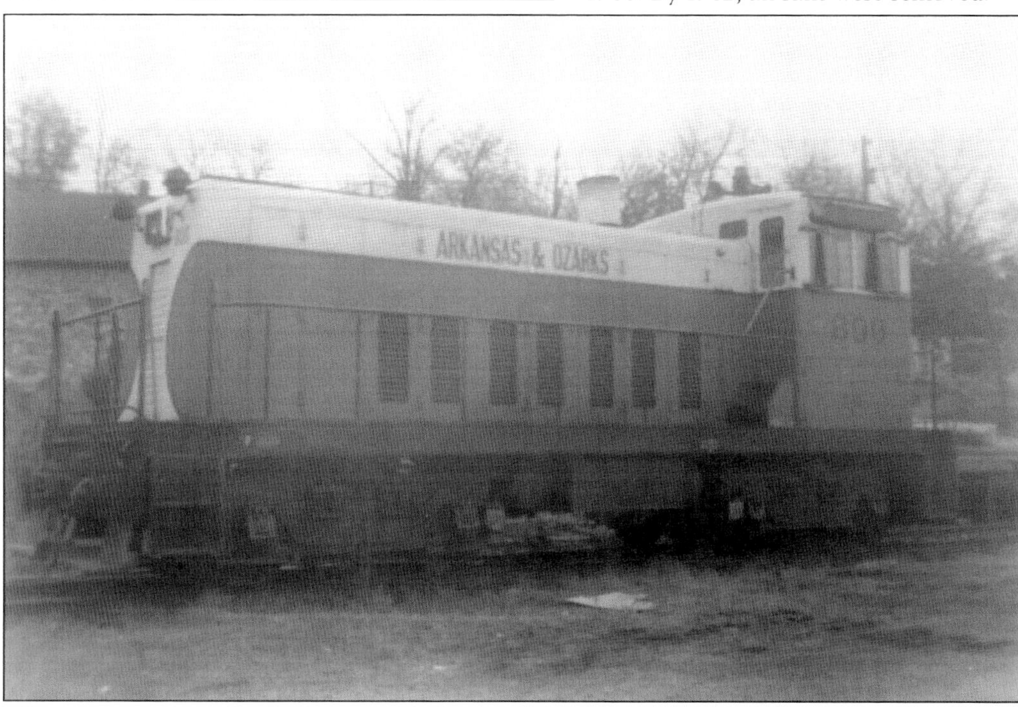

Four

EDUCATION AND RELIGIOUS LIFE

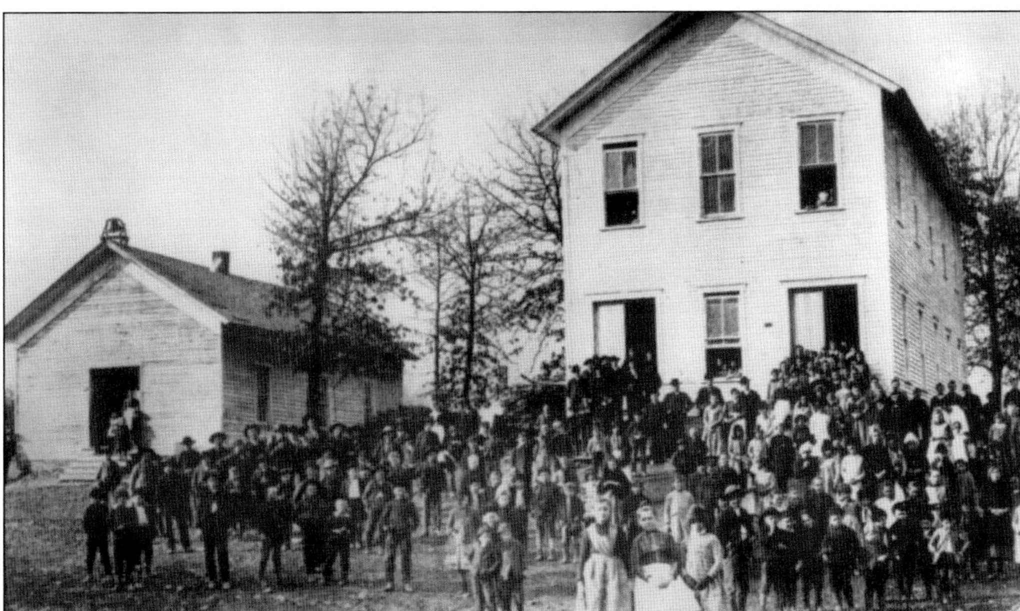

SCHOOL GROUP, 1885. Most schools at this time were conducted in one-room schoolhouses, where children of all ages and levels were given various lessons at different times. This two-schoolhouse complex was known as the Harrison Academy. The older schoolhouse on the left was undoubtedly used for younger children. The two-story schoolhouse on the right, built in the 1870s, was used to teach students up to the 10th grade.

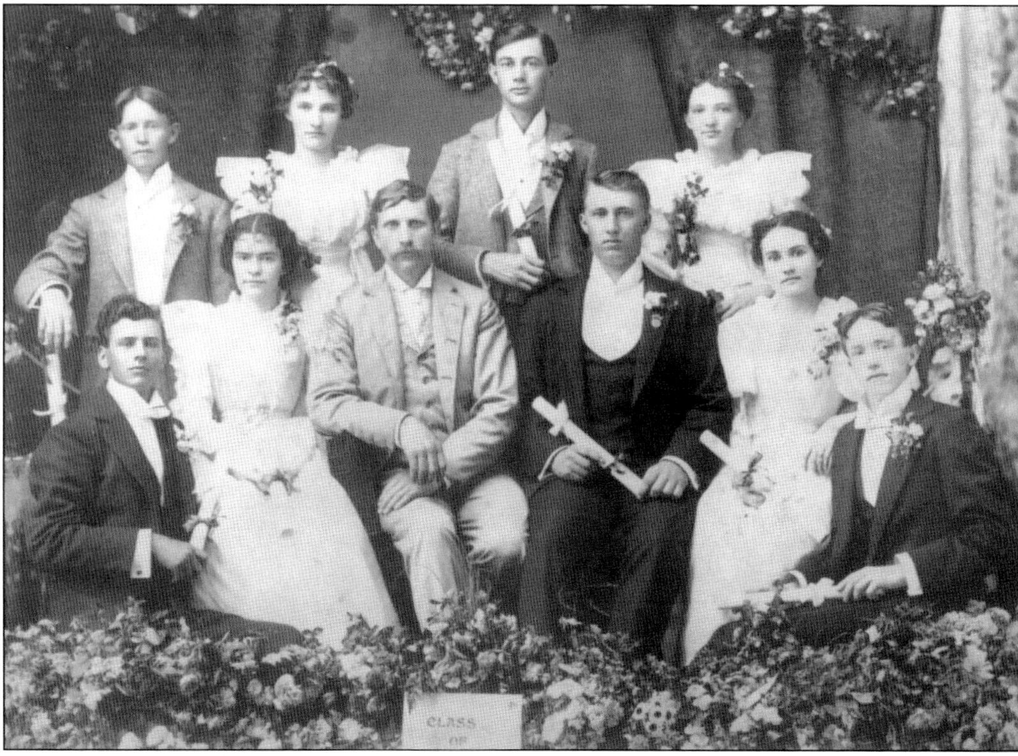

CLASS OF 1898. Pictured here is a graduating class with its teacher. Graduation was quite an accomplishment in these times. Students and teachers worked with the most basic of supplies. Typically, only one textbook was used by each student for the year. Most students worked with a slate and soapstone pencil, which cost the equivalent of two weeks wages for a grown man.

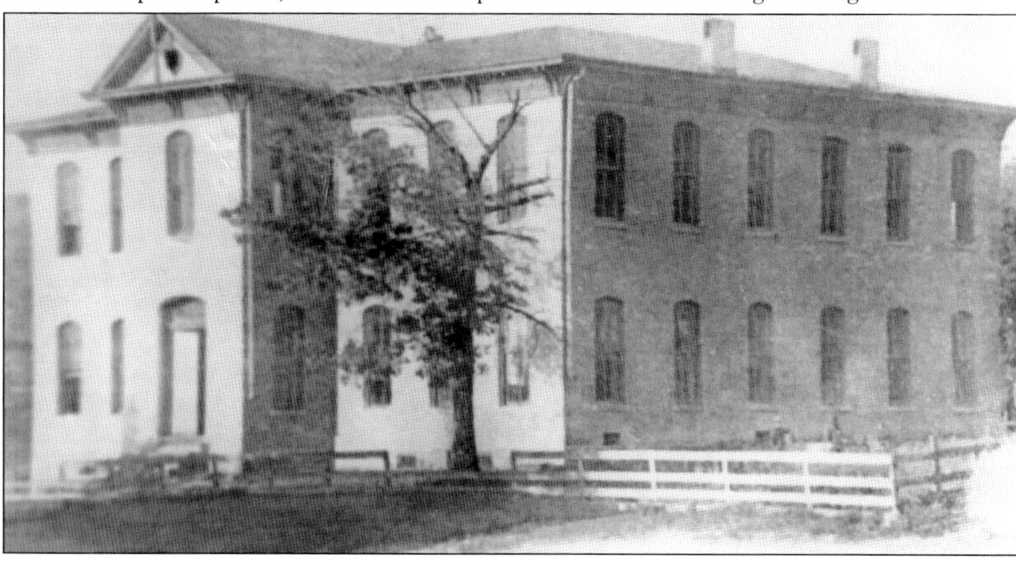

HARRISON GRAMMAR SCHOOL. Located next to the high school, the grammar school was built in 1895. When erected, it was used as a high school. Later, after the construction of the Harrison High School building, this structure was used as a grade school and was referred to as Central Grade School. It was torn down in 1939.

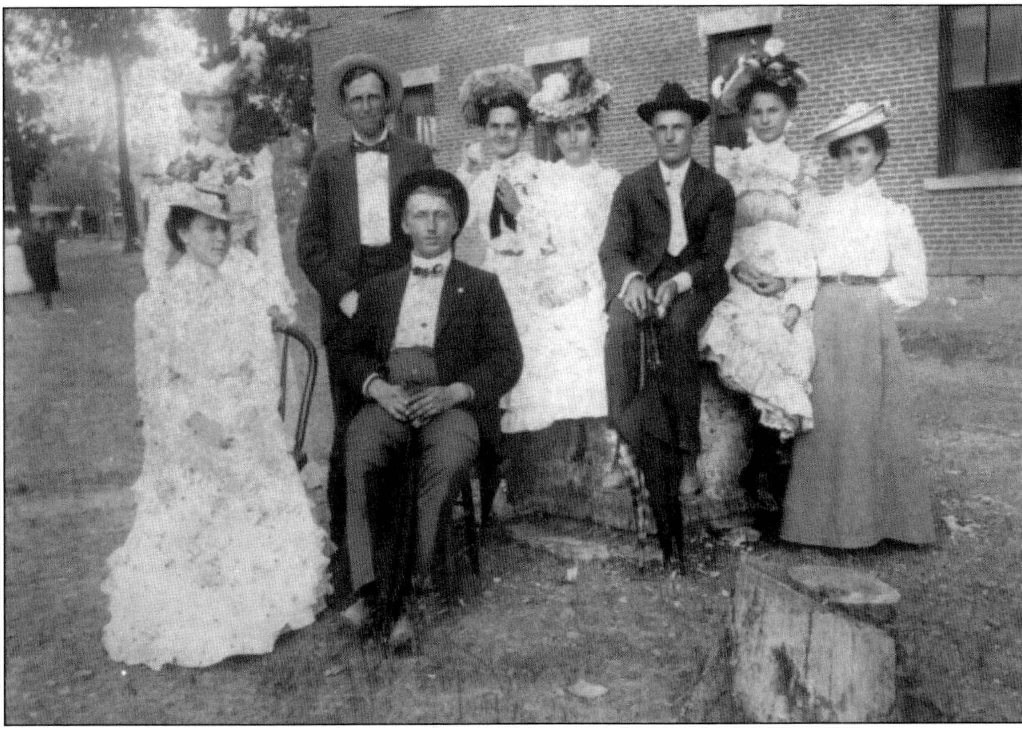

CLASS ON COURTHOUSE SQUARE, EARLY 1900S. Members of the Harrison High School class stand outside the old courthouse with their teacher. The only identified person is Dr. Frank Beverly Kirby (third from right). The young women wear dresses and hats, fashion reminiscent of the Victorian era.

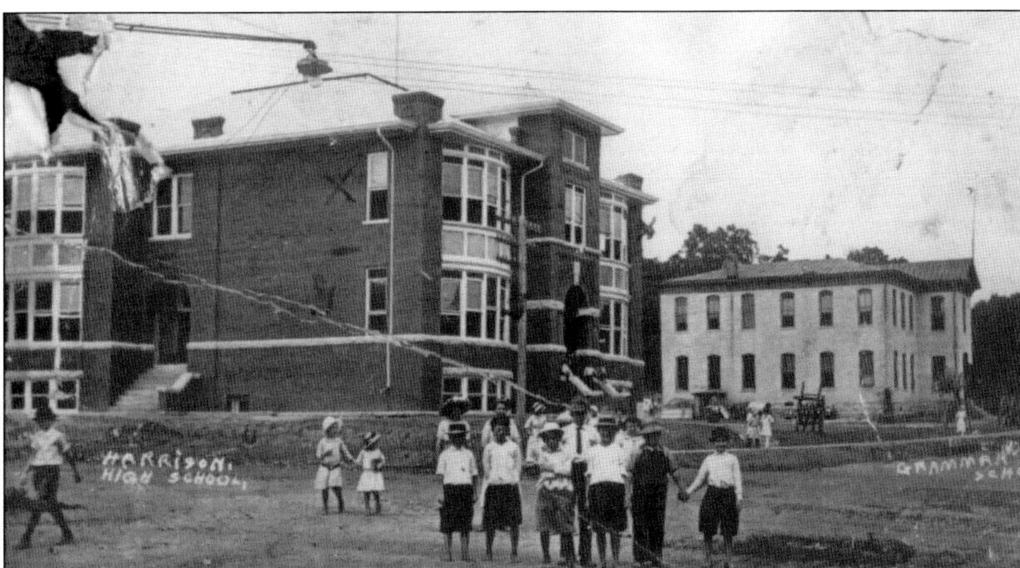

HARRISON HIGH SCHOOL, SEPTEMBER 9, 1915. The school, built in 1912, is located at the corner of West Central Avenue and North Cherry Street. It remained a high school until it was remodeled in 1952 and became the junior high. During renovation, the bay windows and most of the wood were removed, and fire escapes were added. This is now the Boone County Heritage Museum.

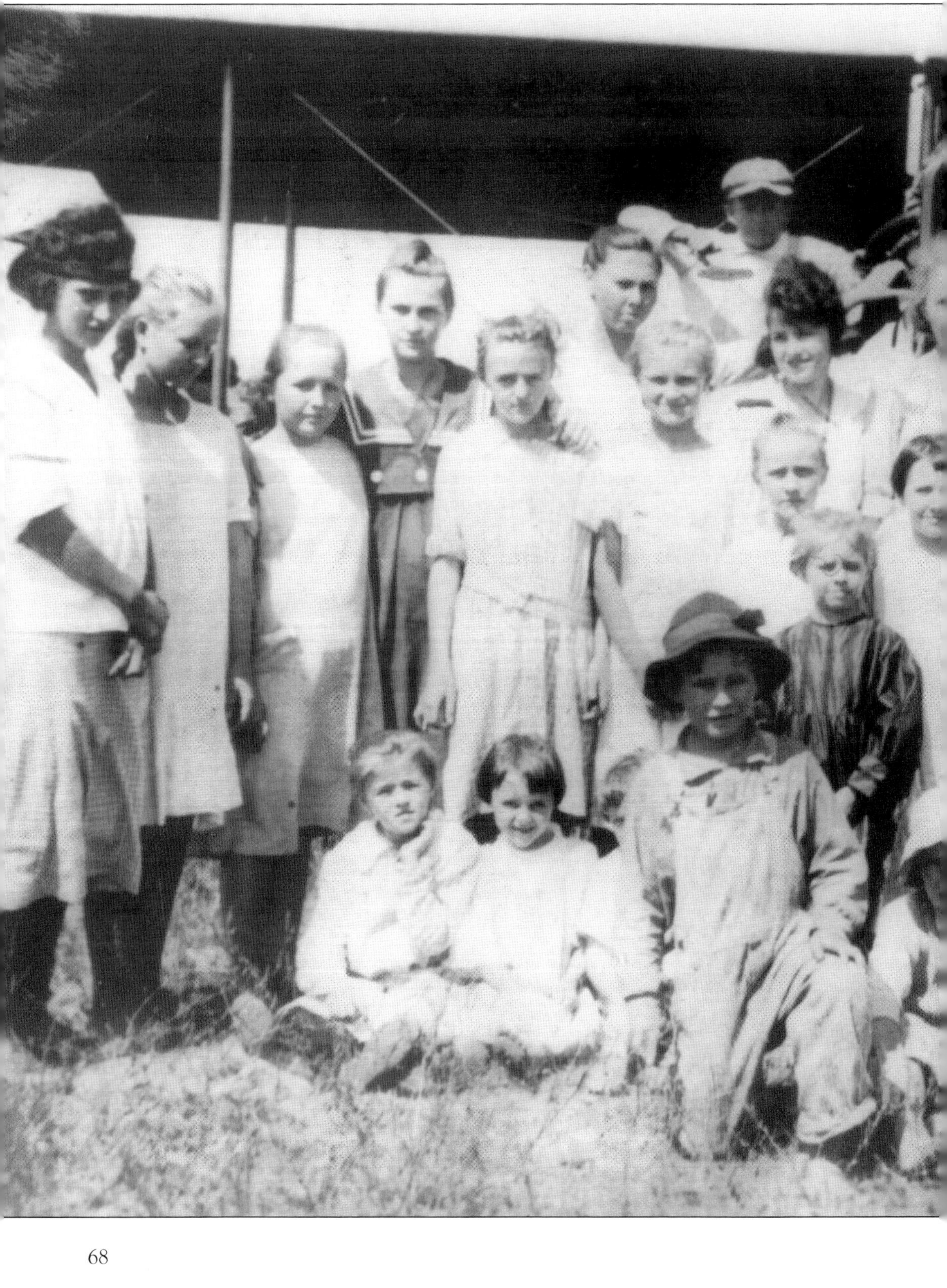

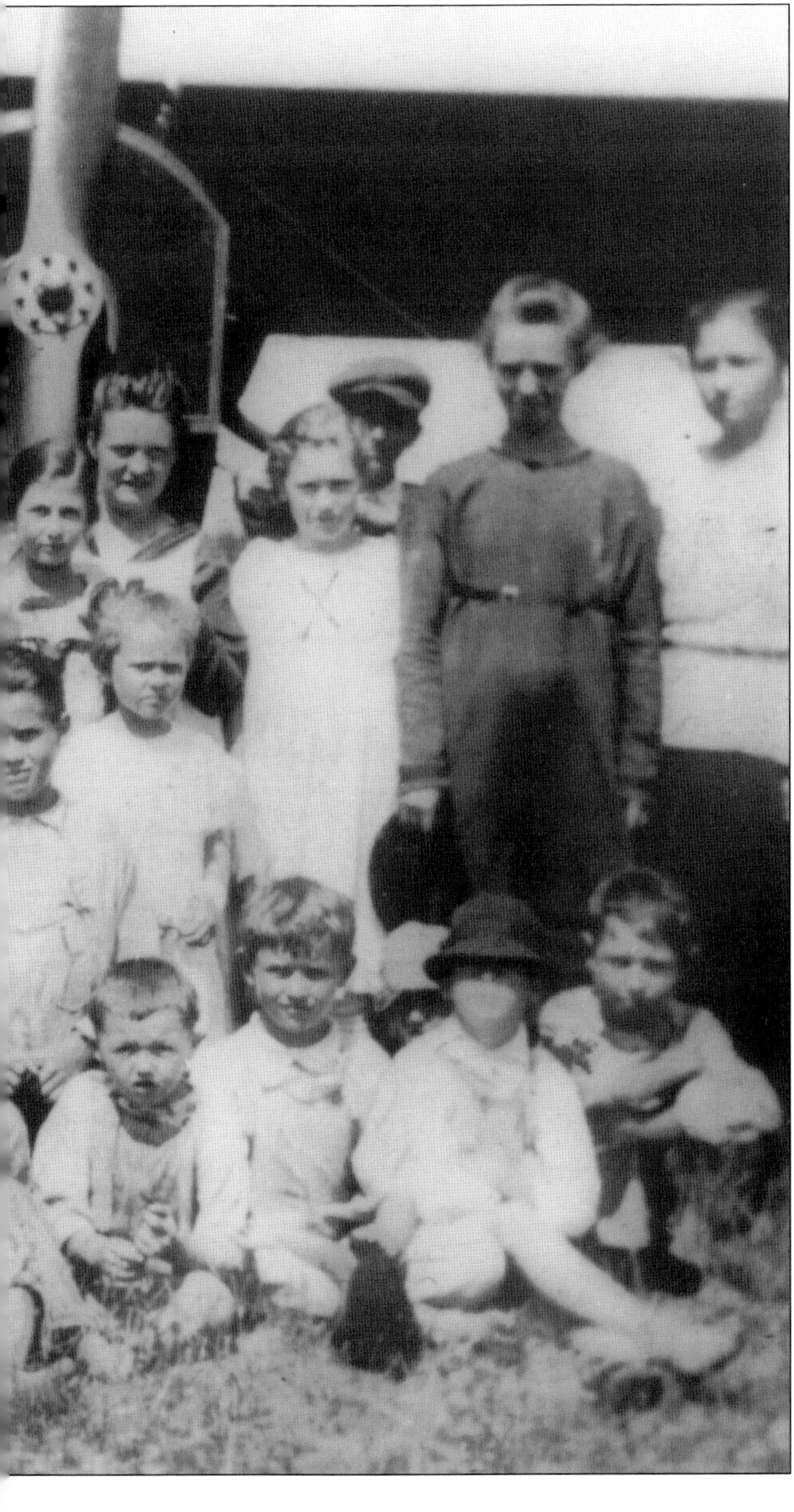

FIRST AIRPLANE TO LAND IN HARRISON, 1920. The biplane shown here made an emergency landing on Bob Jackson's farm near Oregon Flat. When it landed, the children's excitement precluded conducting class, so they went out to see what was going on. They posed for a photograph in front of the flying machine, which they had heard of but had never seen with their own eyes. Standing at the far right is the teacher, Pearl Small. Shown here in no particular order are Edith Smith, Audrey Price, Dorothy Price, Winnie Maxey, Mildred Jackson, Edith Lankford, Norton Archer, Steely Swafford, Thelma Sands, Janice Price, Myrtle Guynn, Dorothy Willis, Margie ? , Lora Miller, Lota Swafford, Bonnie Taylor, Kathleen Jackson, Virginia Davis, Jack Davis, Ruth Davis, Neal Taylor, Gail Price, Paul Sands, Robert Jackson, Carson Taylor, Theodore Guynn, Marvin Swafford, and Henry Price.

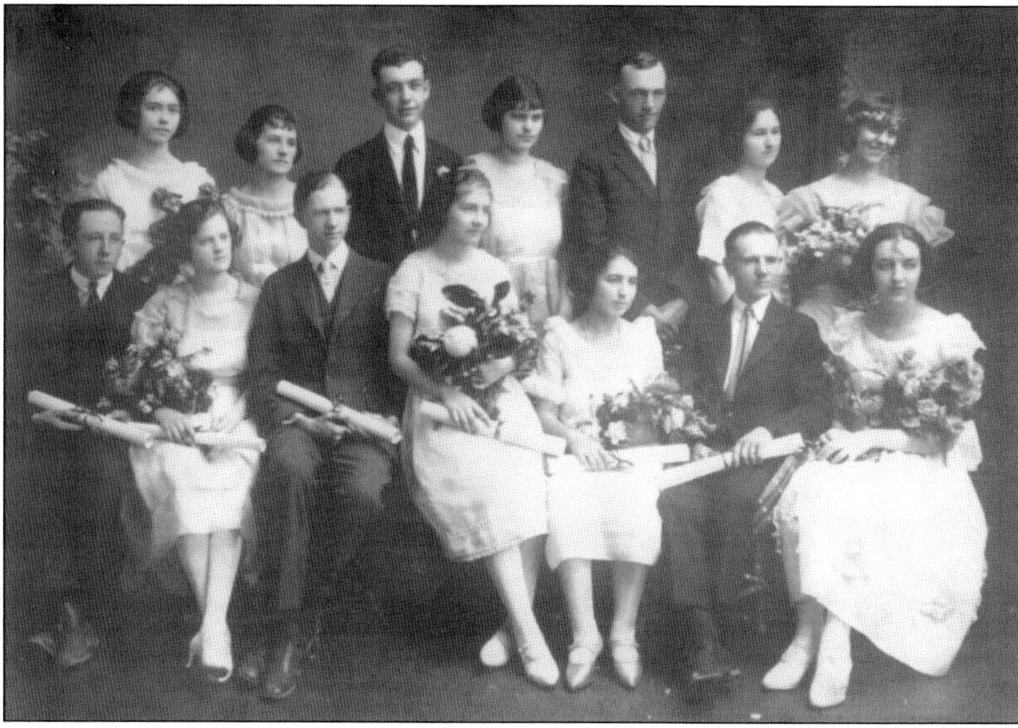

Harrison High School Graduating Class, 1922. Shown here are, from left to right, (first row) Delbert James, Agnes McFerrin, Ernest Nicholson, Gladys Parks, Florence Evans, Ben Beene, and Mildred Slover; (second row) Hattie Holland, Helen Graham, Rex Slover, Nina Holder, Slyvia Morris, Lena Allbright, and Jane Frank Trimble. Some names may be misspelled, as the original caption was written in poor script.

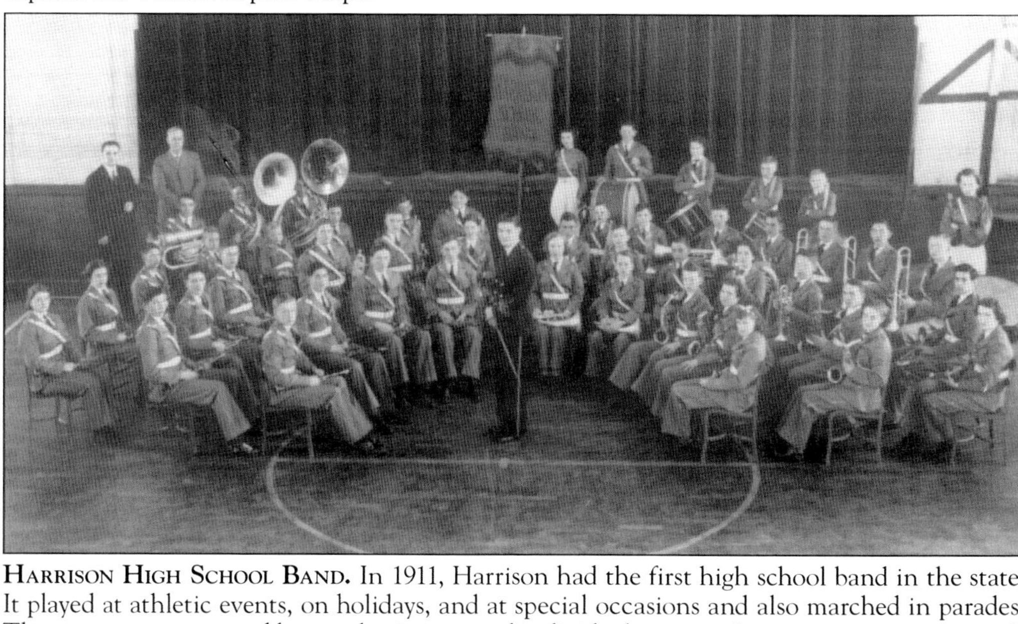

Harrison High School Band. In 1911, Harrison had the first high school band in the state. It played at athletic events, on holidays, and at special occasions and also marched in parades. The group was sponsored by area businesses and individual citizens. It continues to receive such support today and competes in many events across the state.

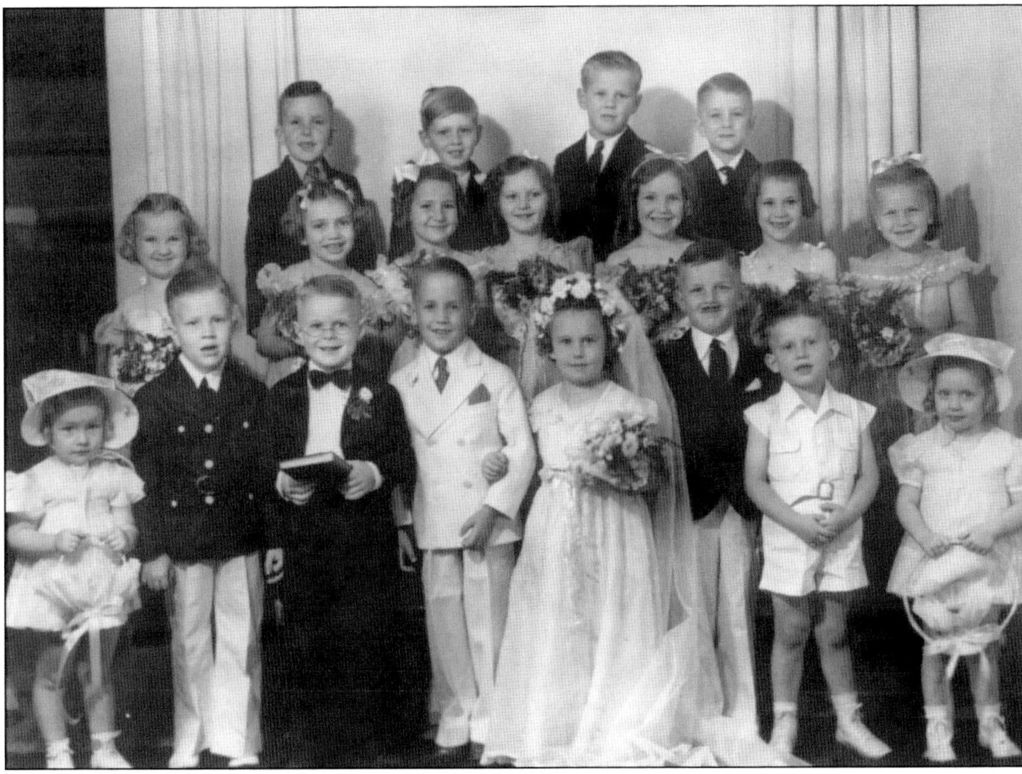

Tom Thumb Wedding, 1939. Pictured here is Virginia Ernest's kindergarten class. The children are, from left to right, (first row) Ruthie Wasson, John Rush, Joe Bill Wilson, David Carr, Kay McCoy, Roger Collier, Mike McCoy, and Jackie Boyd; (second row) Bonnie Barker, Shirley Hinley, Joyce Gibson, Joan Sugg, Lucianna Cassidity, Mary Rogers, and Linnie Creed; (third row) Joe Fast, David Moore, John Ragland, and Alfred Alsup.

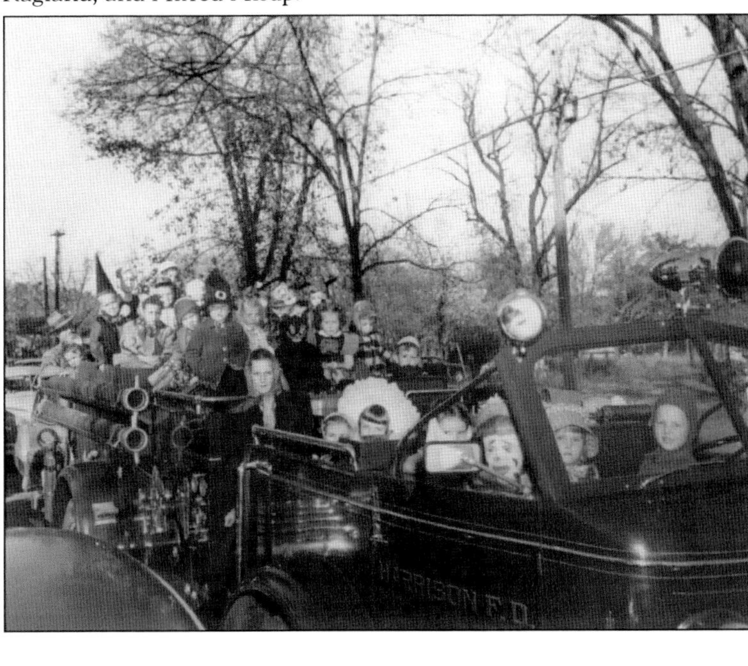

Schoolchildren and Fire Truck, 1946. Several students and their teacher take a ride in a Harrison Fire Department truck on Halloween. Fire trucks were a common feature on the streets of Harrison during holidays and parades, and they remain so today. Fire Station No. 1 is located at 120 South Spring Street, next to City Hall.

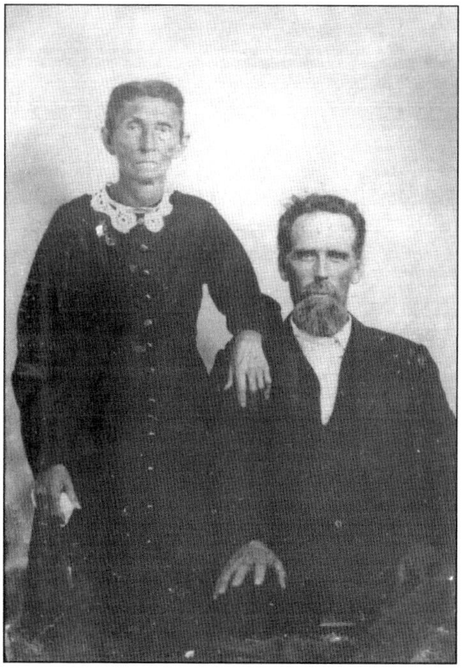

Rev. William Andrew Dees and Margaret Miram Choate. Born on May 19, 1835, in Greenville, Missouri, Dees served in the Missouri Cavalry for the Confederate army. Choate was born on November 24, 1835, in Tennessee. They were married on June 18, 1854. Dees, a Methodist preacher, started churches in Bellefonte and Cedar Ridge. He died on July 10, 1923, at age 88.

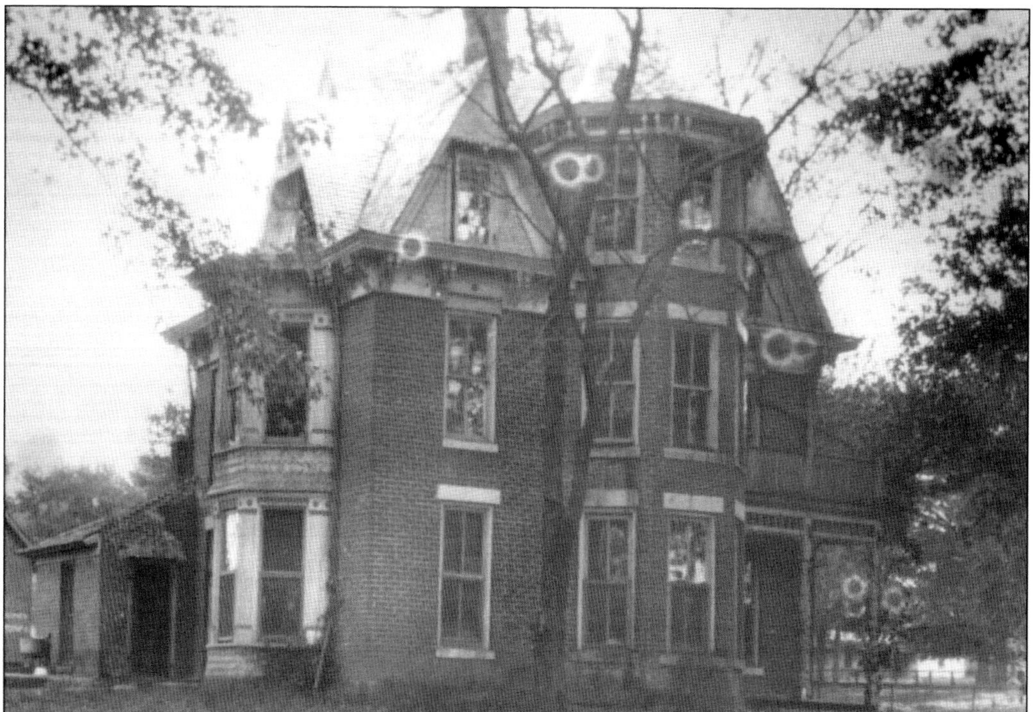

Home of James Townsend "Town" Hopper. On May 18, 1876, at this home, 21 Disciples of Christ met to organize their church. This was just two months after Harrison was incorporated. James Hopper's house was considered one of the finest in the county. He would later donate a significant portion of his property to First Christian Church and sold much of it for development in Harrison.

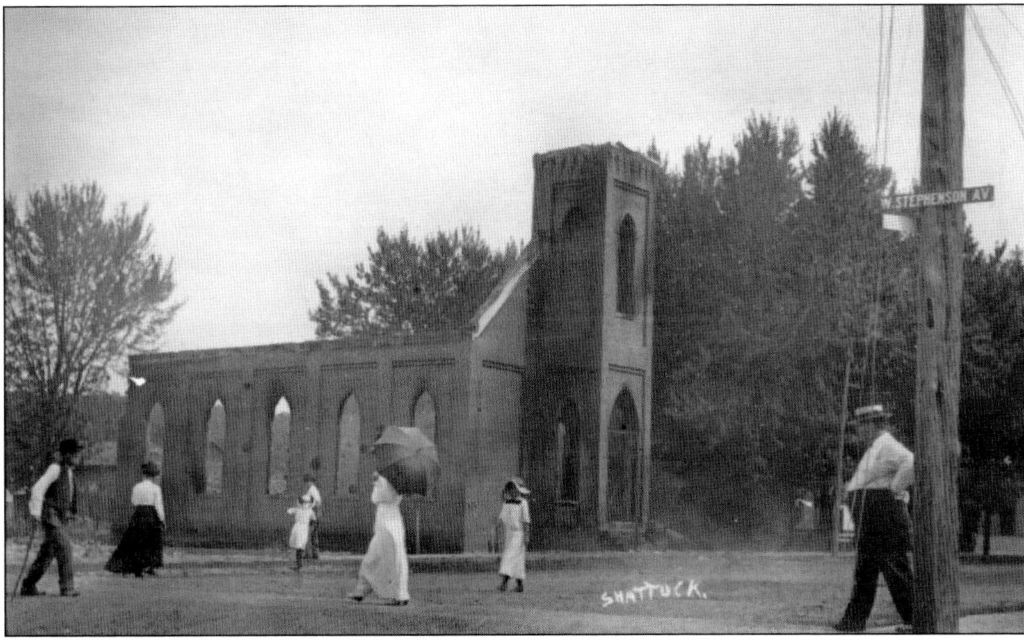

FIRST PRESBYTERIAN CHURCH REMAINS, 1913. Harrison Presbyterians had been congregating since 1870. Members of the Presbyterian Church began holding services at this building, located at the corner of North Spring Street and West Stephenson Avenue, in 1906. The church burned down on July 8. Nothing was saved except the exterior brick shell of the building. All records between 1870 and 1913 were lost.

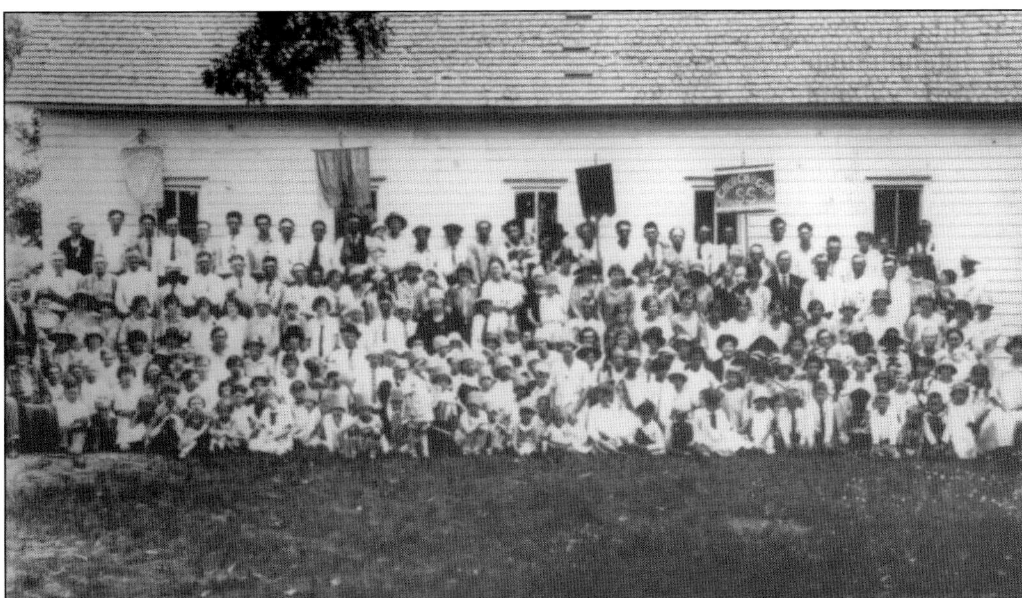

CHURCH OF GOD CONGREGATION. The Church of God has its roots in Pentecostalism, which has always been a popular movement in the Ozarks. Though the particular church seen here remains unidentified, it is most likely linked to one of the three Churches of God located in Harrison today.

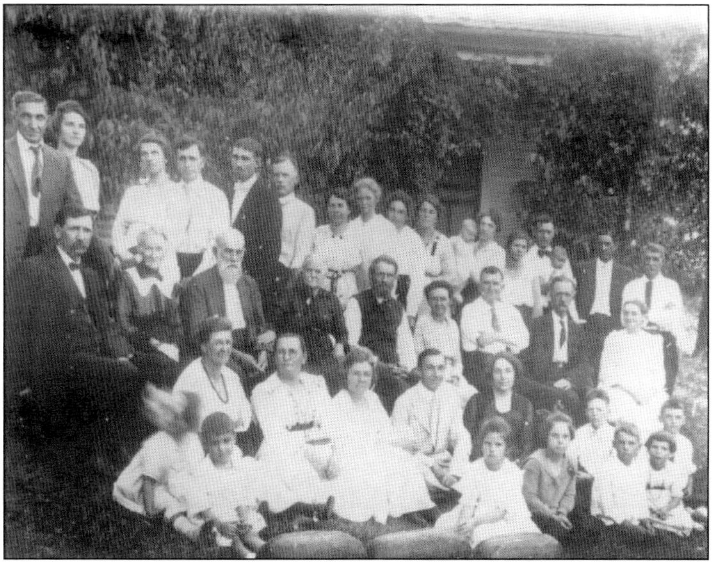

First Christian Church Picnic. The Christian Church (Disciples of Christ) celebrates itself as being a uniquely American denomination in the Protestant tradition. It was formed on January 1, 1832, in Lexington, Kentucky. Though a large and influential denomination, each local church is governed on the congregation level. This group from the congregation enjoys a picnic on Independence Day.

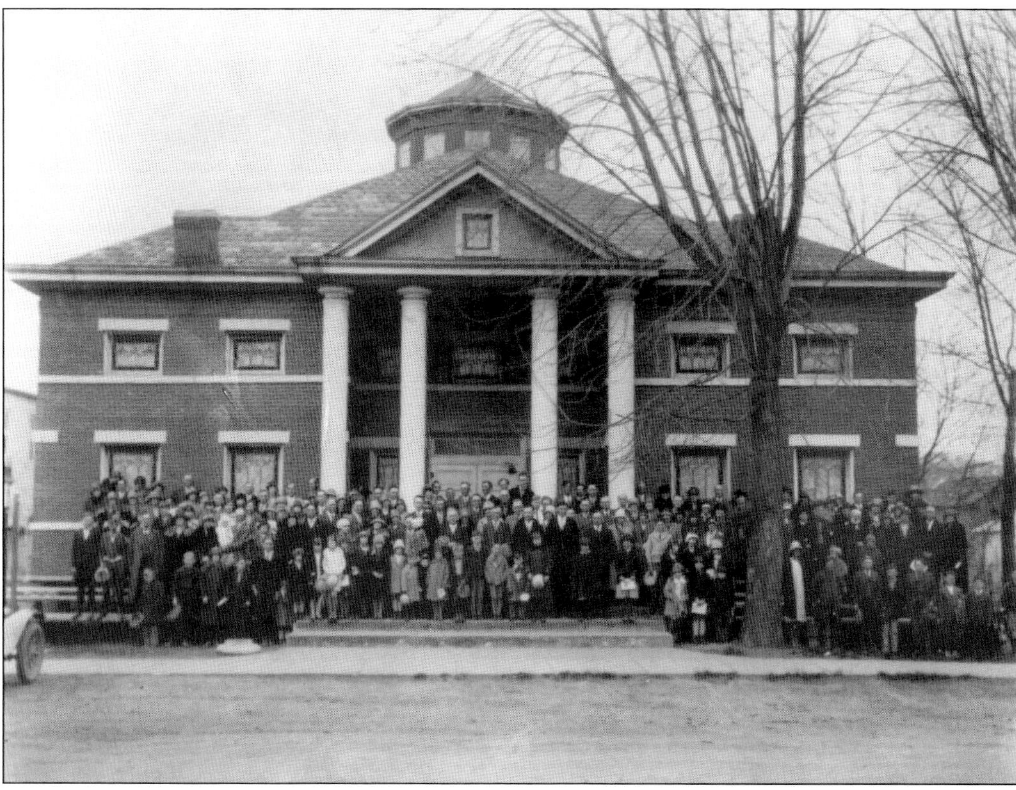

Congregation of First Presbyterian Church, 1926. After the first church burned down in 1913, construction of this new building began. It was erected over the next two years on the same block, just a bit south of the original location. The building still stands, located across from city hall, and it looks much the same.

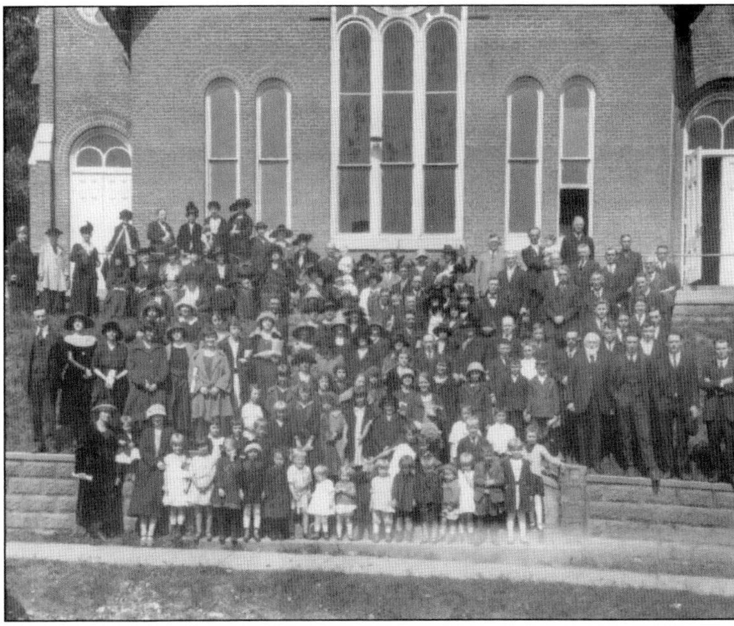

Congregation of First Christian Church, 1920s. Construction on this building was completed in November 1876, just six months after it was organized. The church immediately started holding services there. Despite the speed with which it was built, the church was very well constructed, for it still stands today and looks much the same. The building is located on West Stephenson Avenue between North Pine and North Cherry Streets.

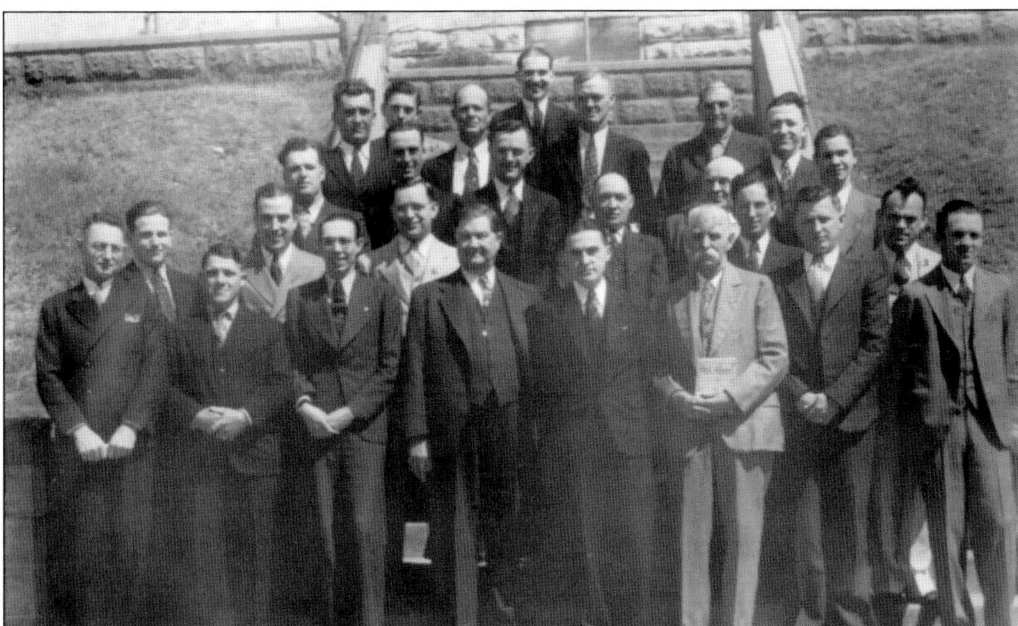

Men's Bible Class, 1940. Membership at First Christian Church was quite large at this time, and it was soon decided that the congregation needed a new building. A construction meeting was held on September 28, 1955. Ground-breaking ceremonies were held on May 6, 1956, and work began on June 1. The first service was held on June 23, 1957. The church, located at 915 South Maple Street, is still in use.

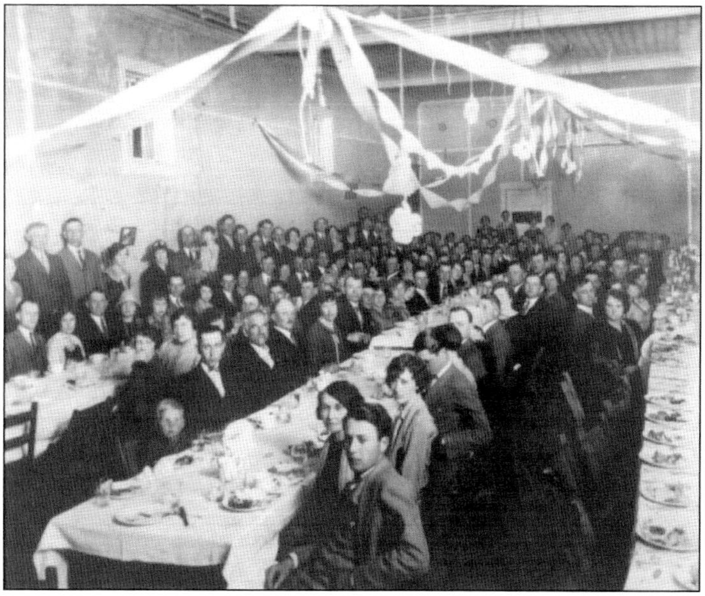

BANQUET SCENE. Shown here is the Sunday school class of First Baptist Church, taught by Reverend Conroy. It was held on the first floor of the Masonic Lodge, located on North Vine Street. Space was a commodity in Harrison's early days. Many civic groups and churches used buildings owned by other organizations in order to accommodate large groups.

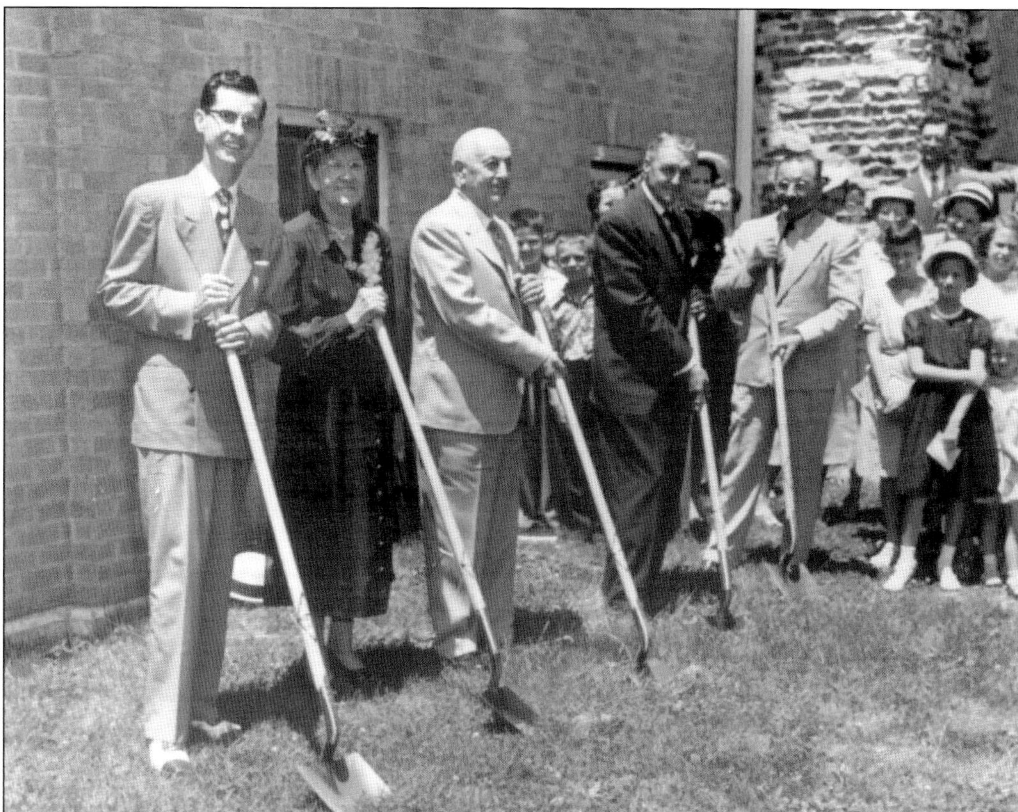

FIRST BAPTIST CHURCH, MAY 24, 1953. This is the ground-breaking ceremony for the new First Baptist Church, located at 1400 South Pine Street. The individuals with the shovels are, from left to right, Rev. Lehman H. Webb, Mrs. Hastings, William J. Moore, Ralph Hudson, and circuit judge Woody Murray. Hastings was the oldest member of the congregation at the time.

Five

Civic and Professional Clubs

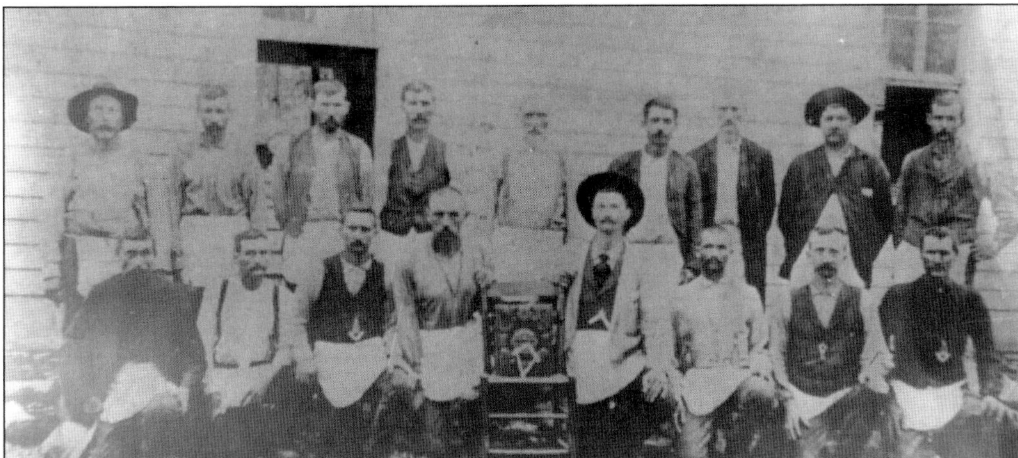

Freemasons Meeting, 1895. Freemasonry is closely linked to the history of Arkansas. Many founders of the state were Masonic leaders. Several of the state's early judges, representatives, senators, and governors were members of the fraternity. Freemasonry has been described as a system of morality, veiled in allegory and illustrated by symbols, with a goal to take good men and make them better.

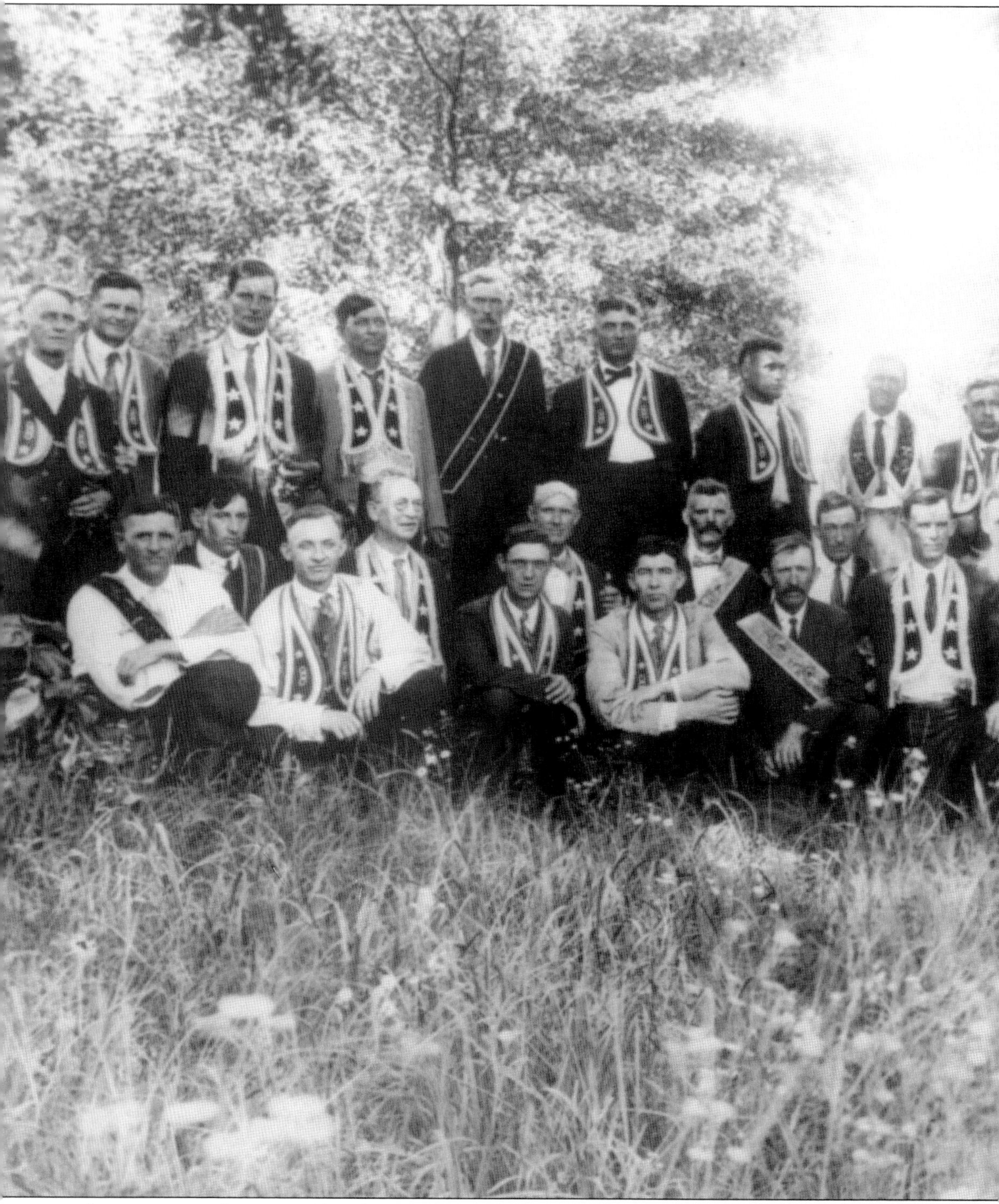

Independent Order of Odd Fellows, June 6, 1920. The Order of Odd Fellows, founded in 18th-century England, is an altruistic and fraternal organization with chapters around the world. The American Independent Order of Odd Fellows was founded in Baltimore, Maryland, on April 26, 1819, by Thomas Wildey and four members of the order from England. In the 18th century, it

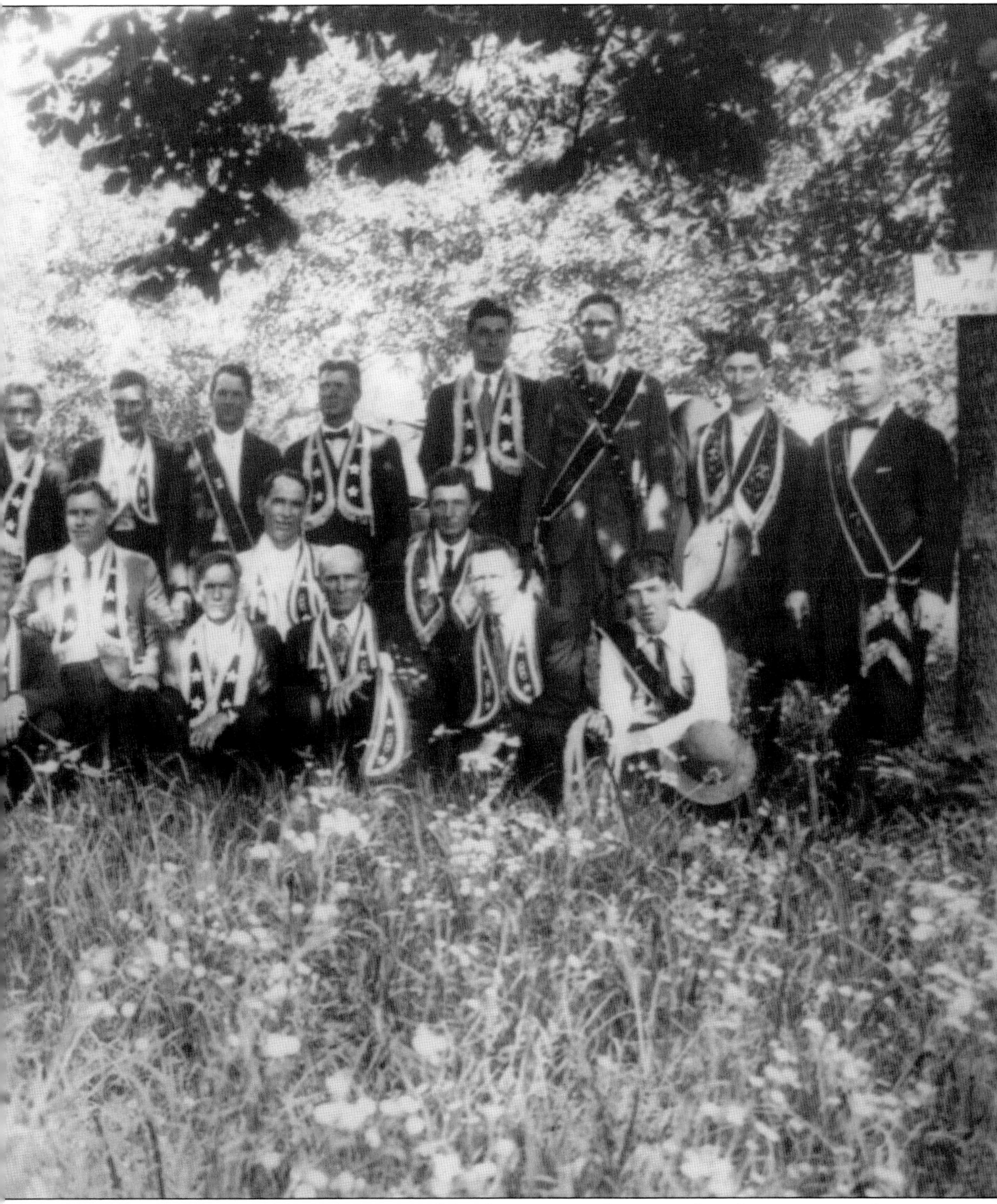

was odd to find a group of people organized for the purpose of giving aid and assistance to those in need and pursuing projects that would benefit all mankind. These groups of people began to be known as odd fellows. The order is known as the "Three Link Fraternity," which refers to its "Triple Links" logo containing the letters F, L, and T (friendship, love, and truth).

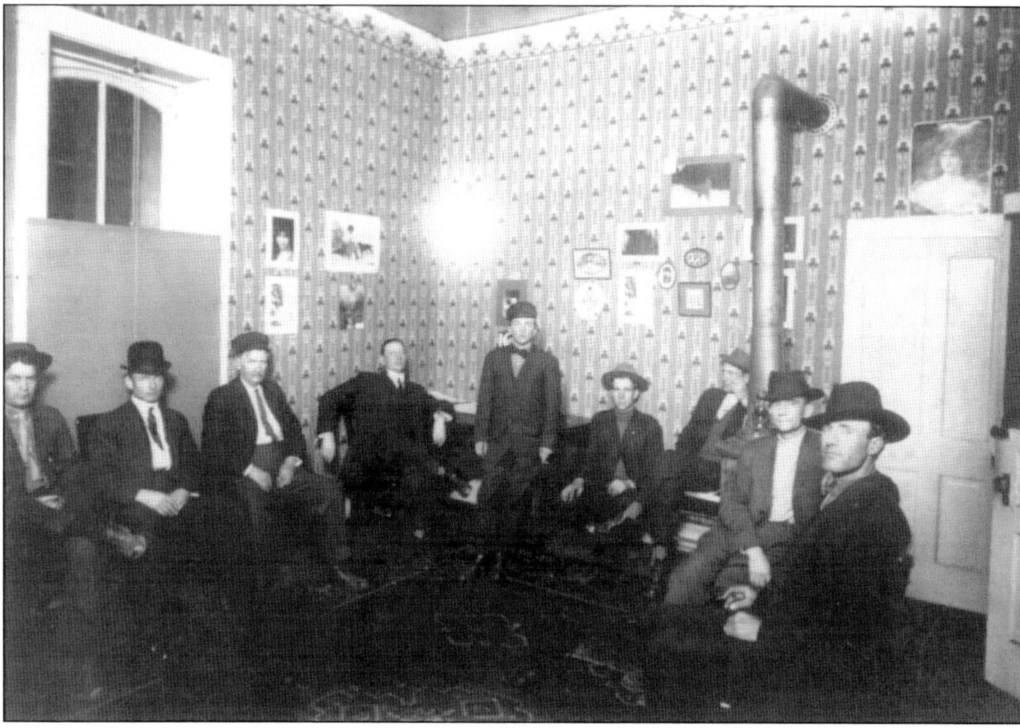

ELKS LODGE. The Benevolent and Protective Order of Elks, often known as the Elks Lodge or simply the Elks, is an American fraternal order and social club founded in 1868. Claiming nearly one million members, it is one of the leading fraternal orders in the United States. The lodge in Harrison is known as Harrison Lodge No. 2311.

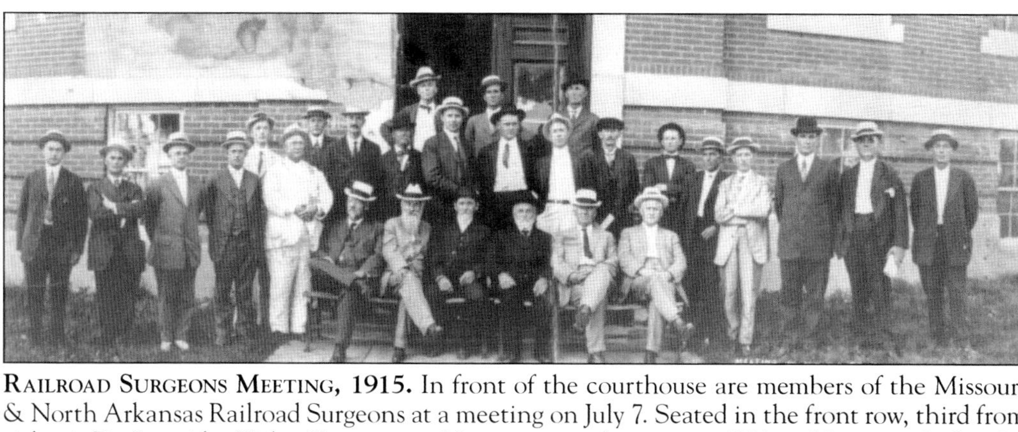

RAILROAD SURGEONS MEETING, 1915. In front of the courthouse are members of the Missouri & North Arkansas Railroad Surgeons at a meeting on July 7. Seated in the front row, third from right, is Dr. Leonidas Kirby. He came to Harrison as a druggist in 1871 and later studied at St. Louis Medical College. He earned a reputation as one of the outstanding doctors in the state.

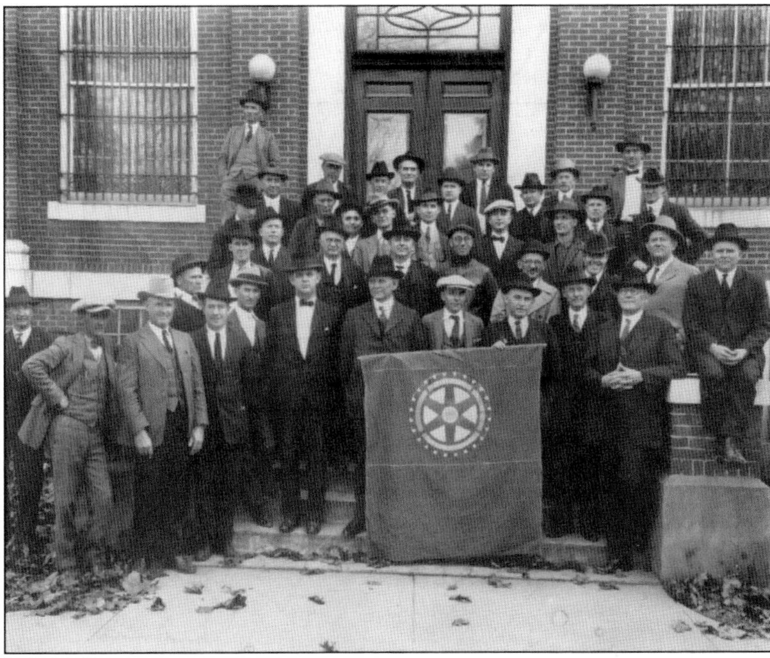

Rotary Club, 1919. The Rotary Club of Harrison, Arkansas, was founded on March 1, 1919. In a city with a population of approximately 5,000, it was the smallest club to be granted a charter by Rotary International. J. Sam Rowland was elected the club's first president. He is seated in the second row on the far right wearing a gray suit and hat.

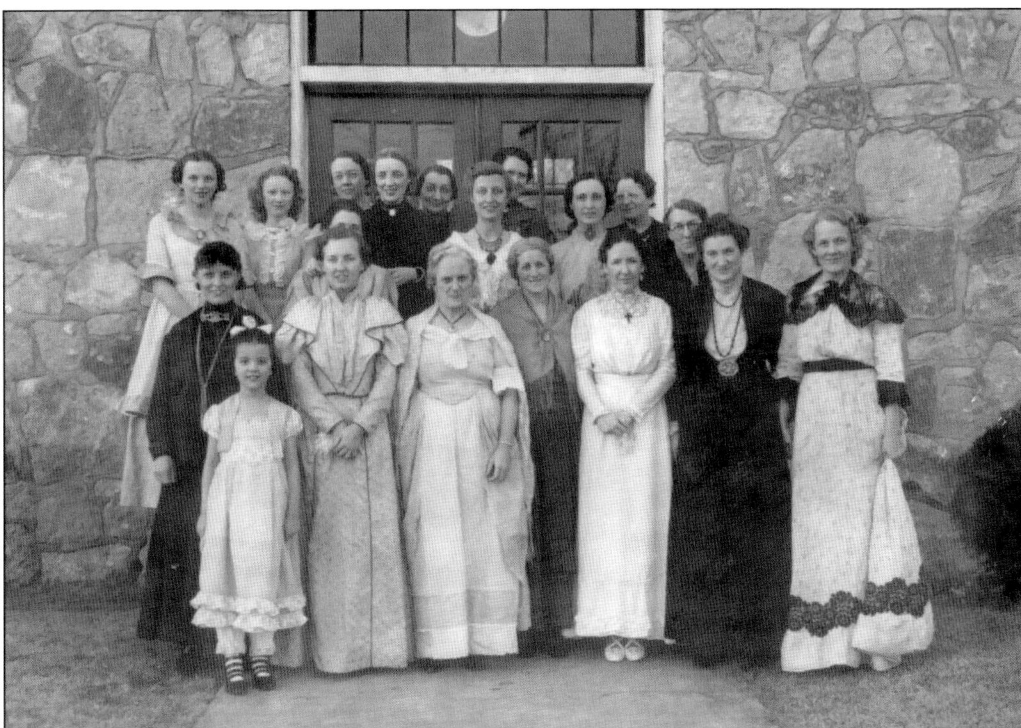

PEO Sisterhood. The Philanthropic Educational Organization was founded on January 21, 1869, by seven students at Iowa Wesleyan College in Mount Pleasant, Iowa. PEO exists to be a source of encouragement and support for women to realize their potential in whatever worthwhile endeavor they choose, though education continues to be the group's primary philanthropy.

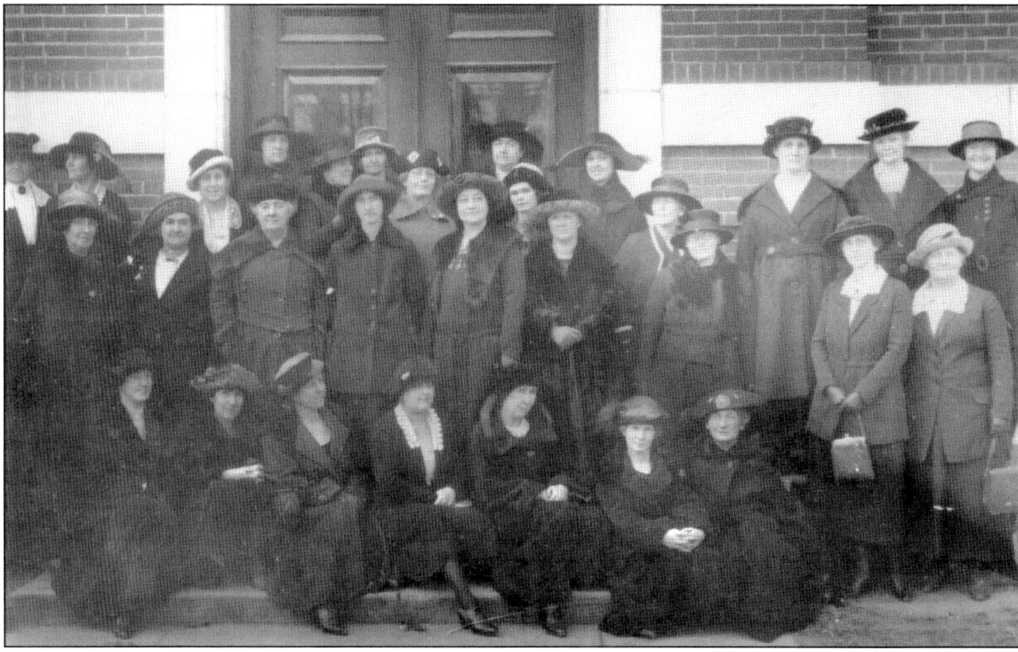

MOTHER'S CLUB OF HARRISON. The Mother's Club was organized about 1920 as a volunteer group to help purchase school supplies and keep the Harrison High School open. It paid the tuition of students who could not afford it and teachers' salaries and funded repairs to the building and property. The Mother's Club also helped with all charity work in Harrison.

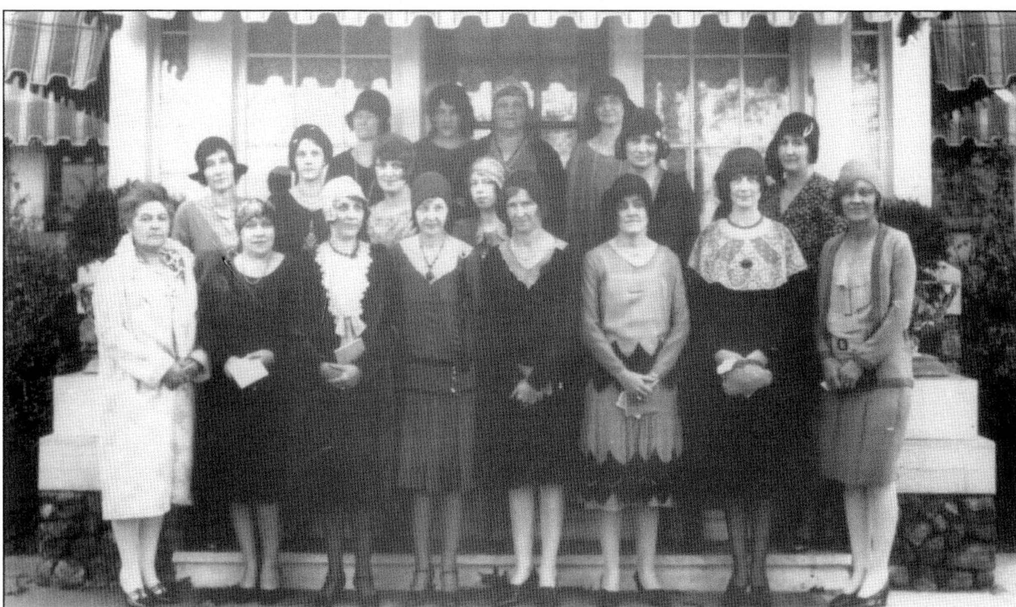

APOLLO CLUB, NOVEMBER 12, 1929. The members of the club are, from left to right (first row), Mrs. J.M. Shinn, Mrs. Will Glass, Effie Chilton, Mrs. Worthington, Bess Ruble, Mrs. Mathis, Mrs. McKinney, and Mrs. Foster; (second row) Mrs. Leo Godwin, Mrs. Wallace Townsend, Ora Lee Cralle, Dorothy Myers, Mrs. Leslie Jackson, and Mrs. Ray Edwards; (third row) Mrs. J.N. Paul and guests Mrs. Prater, Mrs. Harper, and Mrs. McDermitt.

Six

THE PEOPLE

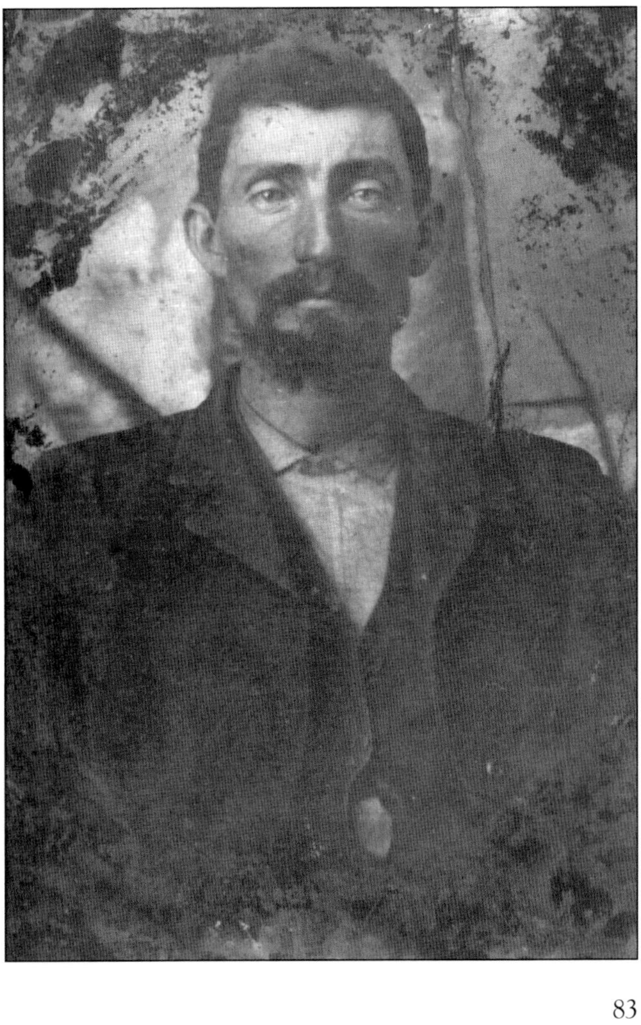

ISAAC BELFIELD MILAM. Born on November 1, 1820, in Hickman County, Tennessee, Milam ran the first water mill in Harrison. It was located on Crooked Creek. He did not fight in the Civil War, but he did witness it. Milam died on January 12, 1899. This photograph is a tintype, dating it most likely to the 1860s or 1870s.

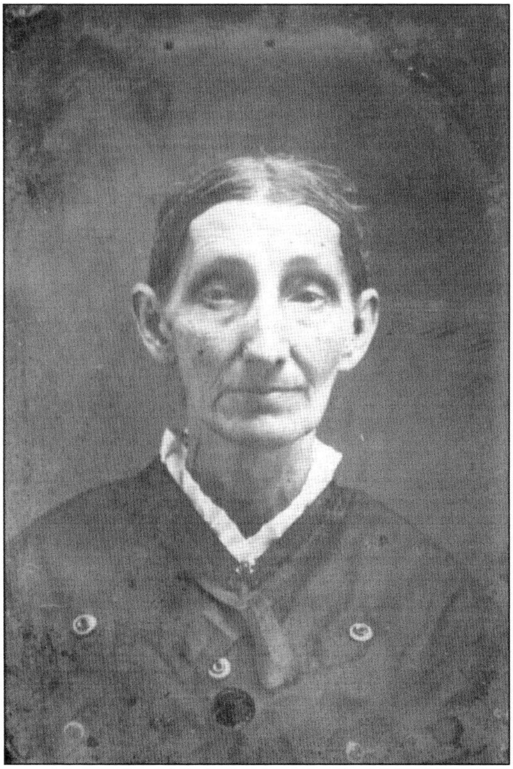

Rebecca Pickard Milam. Milam, born on June 25, 1819, in North Carolina, was the first wife of Isaac Belfield Milam. Together, they ran the first water mill in Harrison. The date of this photograph is unknown, but it is a tintype, dating it most likely to the 1860s or 1870s. She died on January 12, 1891, and is buried with her husband in the old Milam Cemetery near Harrison.

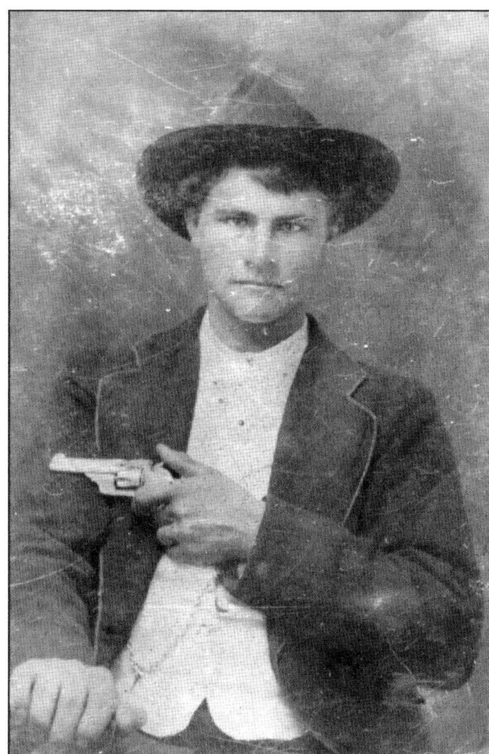

Man with Revolver. The unidentified young man carries a short-barrel revolver. This photograph is also a tintype (or ferrotype). The fact that he is posing with an easily concealed pistol most likely means he did not intend to use it to kill animals. During this era, when men posed for photographs with firearms, they were sending a message.

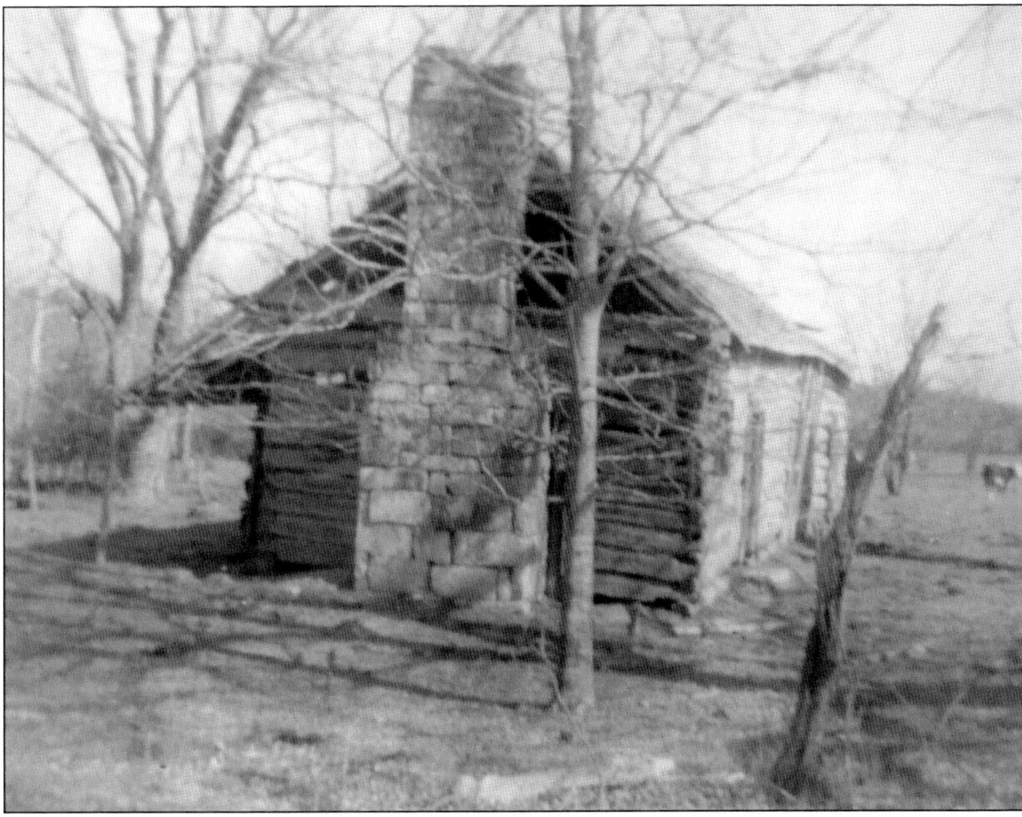

Home of James Douglas Dunlap. Dunlap was born in 1805. His house was built about 1854. His brother Lorenzo Dow Dunlap died at the Mountain Meadows Massacre in southwestern Utah on September 11, 1857. The massacre is shrouded in conspiracy and intrigue. A wagon train of families from Arkansas and Missouri was headed west to California. While they rested at Mountain Meadows, a militia composed of Mormons and Paiutes attacked them. The white men were dressed as Native Americans to make it seem like it was purely an Indian attack. The assault started on September 7 and ended on September 11. There were approximately 120 fatalities and only 17 survivors, all children under the age of seven. James Dunlap helped rescue the survivors and brought them back to Arkansas. His descendants have lived in Boone County for over 150 years.

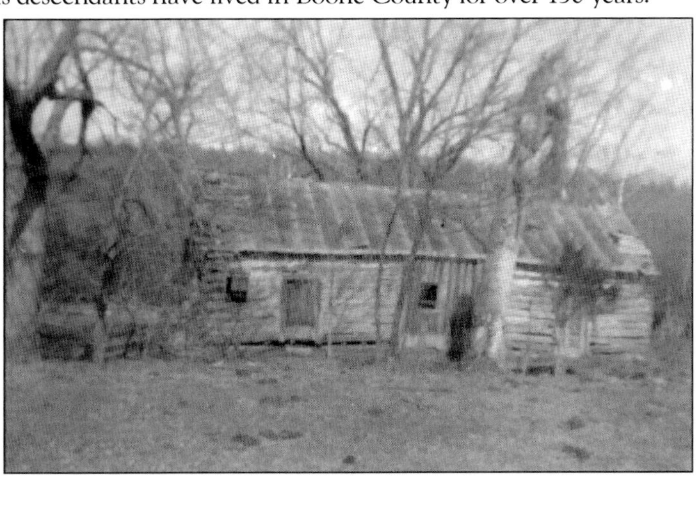

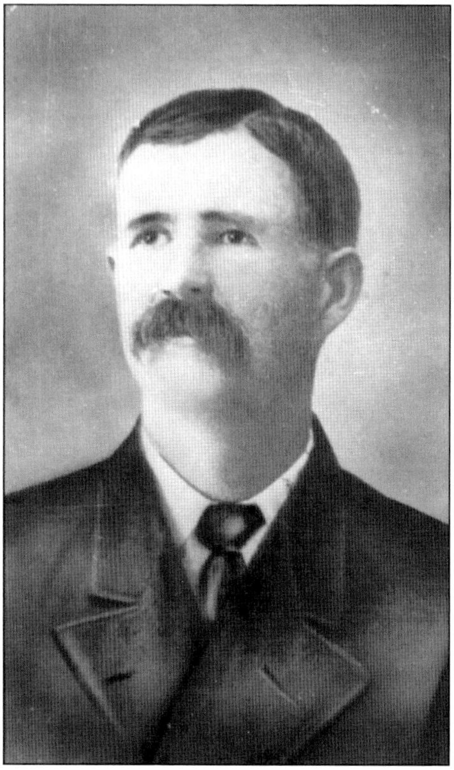

William Twitty Baker. A survivor of the Mountain Meadows Massacre, Baker was nine months old at the time of the attack. Both of his parents and an older sister were killed. Baker was placed with the Ingraham family of Pocketville, Utah. The survivors were returned to Arkansas two years later. Baker lived near Harrison for many years before moving to Marshall. He died in 1937.

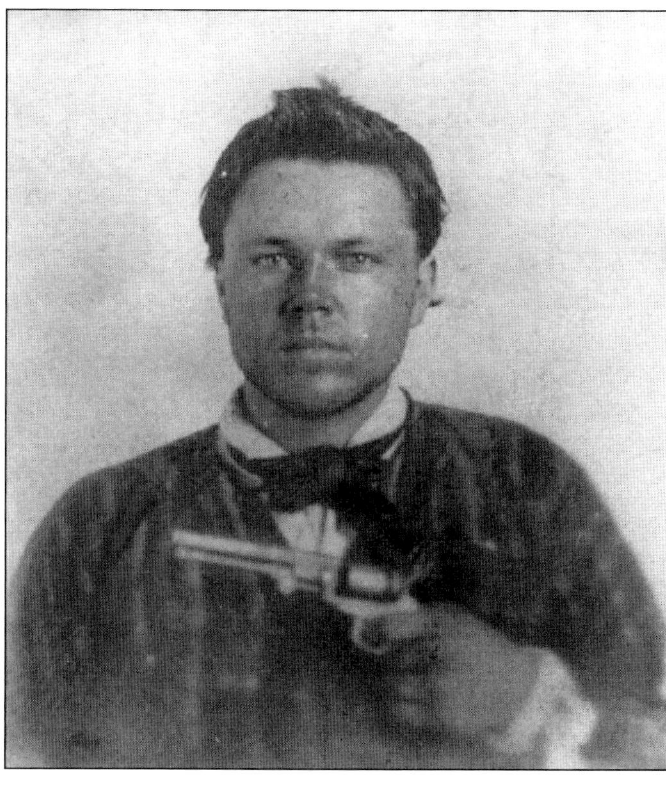

James Richard Buckley, 1862. Pictured here is James Buckley on his way to serve in the Confederate army in May 1862. He fought with the 27th Arkansas Infantry, which led guerilla bands to fight bushwhackers late in the war. Bushwhackers were hated in the Arkansas Ozarks because they did not fight for either side, only for personal gain.

LT. JOHN WOODY, 1878. Woody, a Union officer, served with Andrew Jackson at the Battle of New Orleans in 1814. Woody was influential in founding Fayetteville, Arkansas. The patent for the original town was issued in 1835 by President Jackson. Along with fellow officers Lewis Evans, Larkin Newton, and Samuel Vaughn, Woody chose the name Fayetteville, most likely because two of the men originated from Fayetteville, Tennessee.

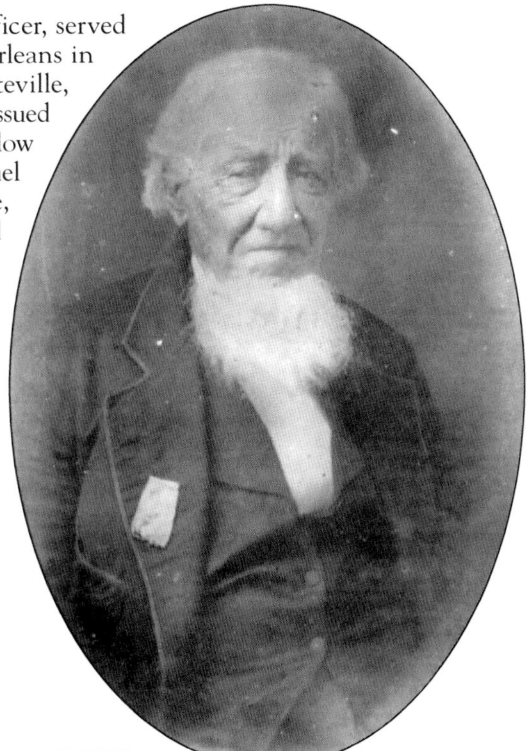

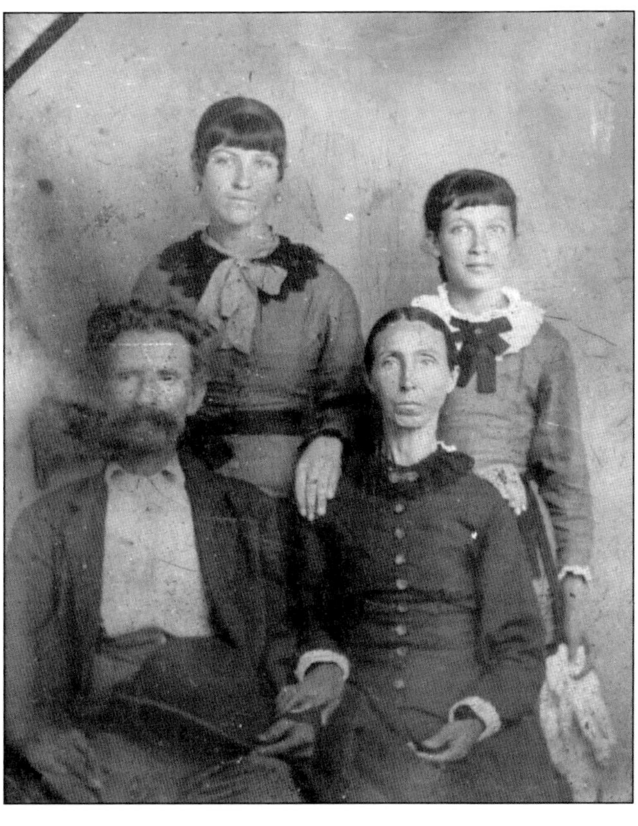

CHANDLER FAMILY. Posing here are, from left to right, (first row) Thomas T. Chandler and wife Cordelia Cox Chandler; (second row) daughters Belle Chandler and Adelia Jane Chandler. Both daughters were born in Boone County. Adelia become the wife of D. Franklin Slagle in 1880. She passed away in 1945.

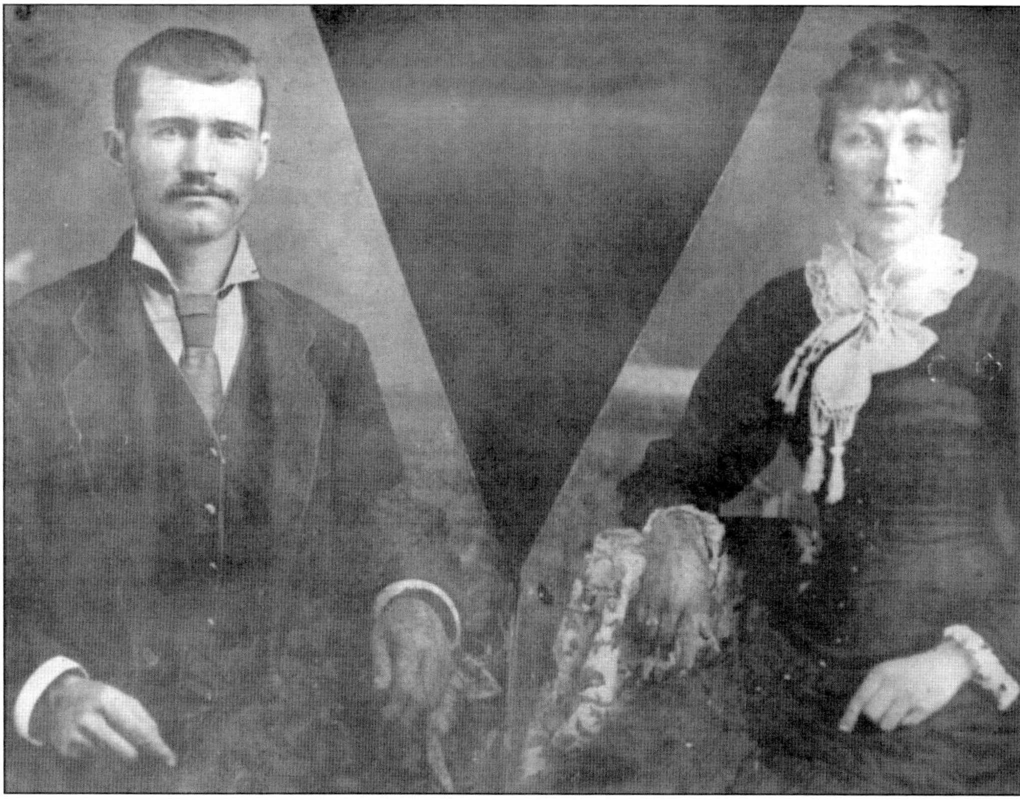

The Slagles, 1885. Pictured here are D. Franklin Slagle and his wife, Adelia Jane Chandler Slagle. Born in 1859, Franklin was orphaned after the Civil War. After growing up in Missouri, he married Adelia in 1880. They built a homestead in Oklahoma, then known as Indian Territory, but returned to Arkansas for health reasons. The Slagles lived in the Harrison area for the rest of their lives.

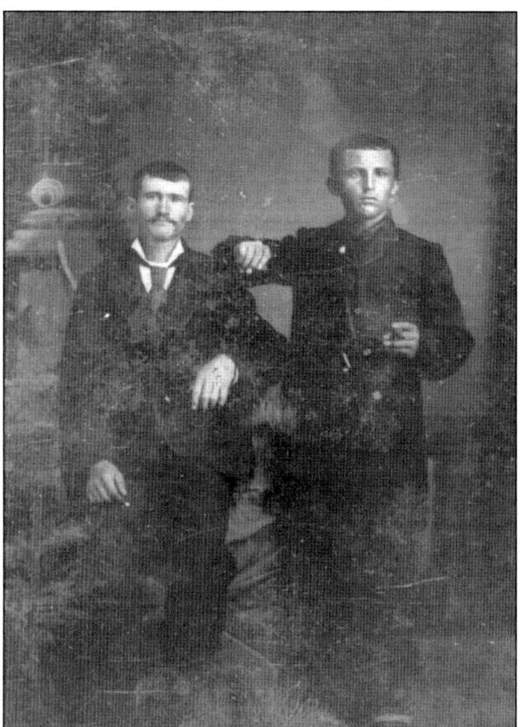

D. Franklin Slagle and Cousin. Slagle (left) was one of thousands of pioneers to participate in the Land Run of 1889, when Pres. Benjamin Harrison proclaimed the two million acres of the Indian Territory of Oklahoma open for settlement. Under the provisions of the Homestead Act of 1862, any settler could claim 160 acres of this unassigned public land, and those who lived on and improved the claim for five years could receive a title.

THE BLANKENSHIPS, AUGUST 6, 1890. Born on October 28, 1858, in Nashville, Tennessee, Joseph Wilson Blankenship was a professor at Rally Hill Academy from 1888 to 1898. Daughter of Gillum Hopper, Nannie Belle Hopper Blankenship was born in Harrison on February 6, 1874. Together, they had four children and one foster child. Professor Blankenship died on October 4, 1952. Nannie Blankenship died on June 20, 1943. They are both buried in Hollister, Missouri.

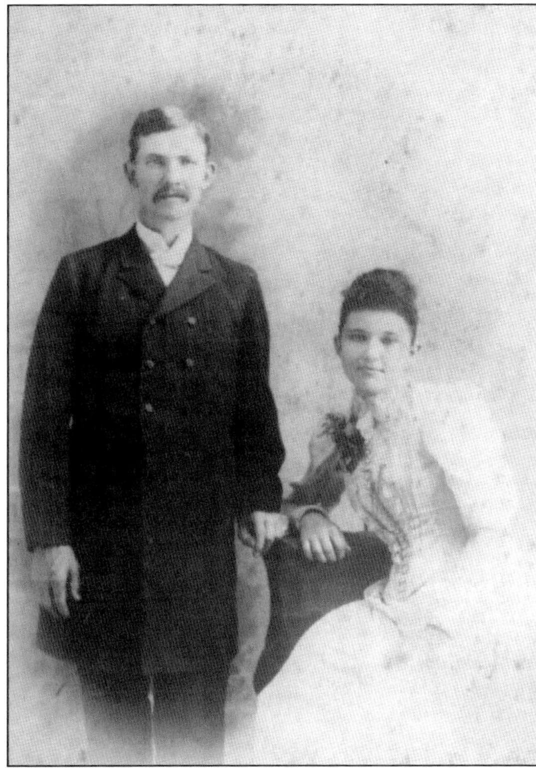

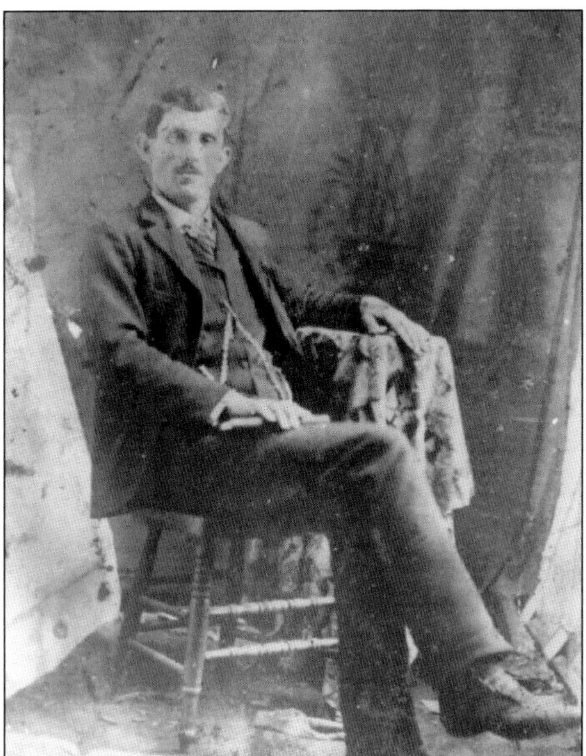

LONNIE LAYTON COFFMAN. Coffman (March 9, 1871–October 8, 1918) married Martha Rose Moore (December 20, 1873–September 5, 1926). He was a local merchant, and they were parents of nine children: Troy, Herbert Roy, John Seaborn, Mae Jean, Hugh White, Garland, Frank Lee, Lonnie Layton Jr., and Jack.

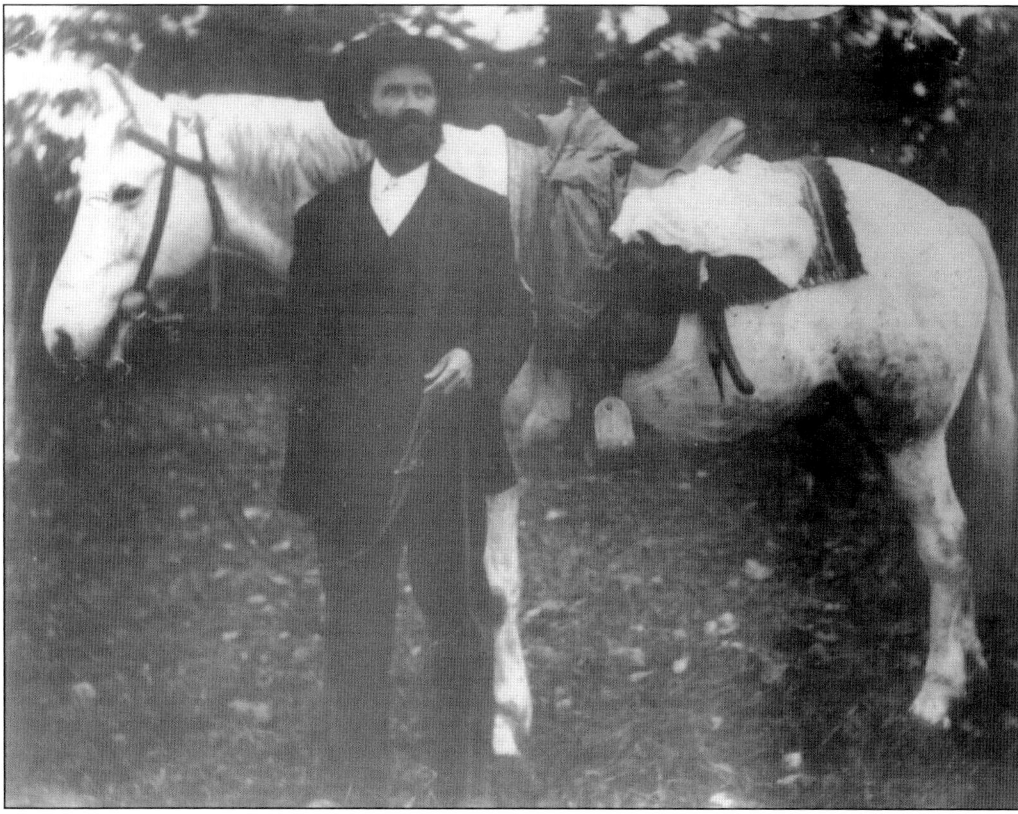

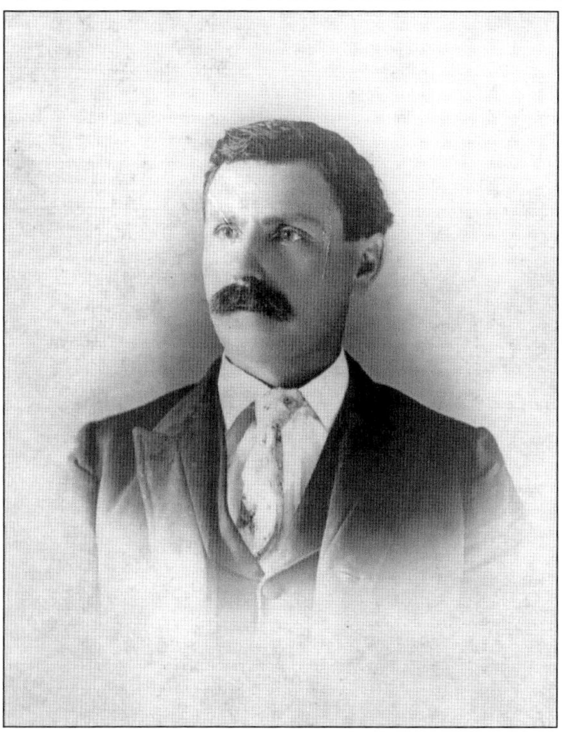

DR. L. FATE ELLISON. Here, Dr. Ellison poses with his horse, Old Bill. Ellison was a traveling dentist. In that era, an infected tooth could be deadly. The most common way of dealing with tooth pain was extraction, a painful operation using methods that would be considered barbaric today.

BOONE COUNTY CLERK, 1892. County clerks wore many hats in these times. Among their responsibilities were keeping and maintaining records, issuing marriage licenses and birth and death certificates, overseeing local elections, compiling documents for court cases, and maintaining county maps. This was the job of John Hicks Roy (pictured).

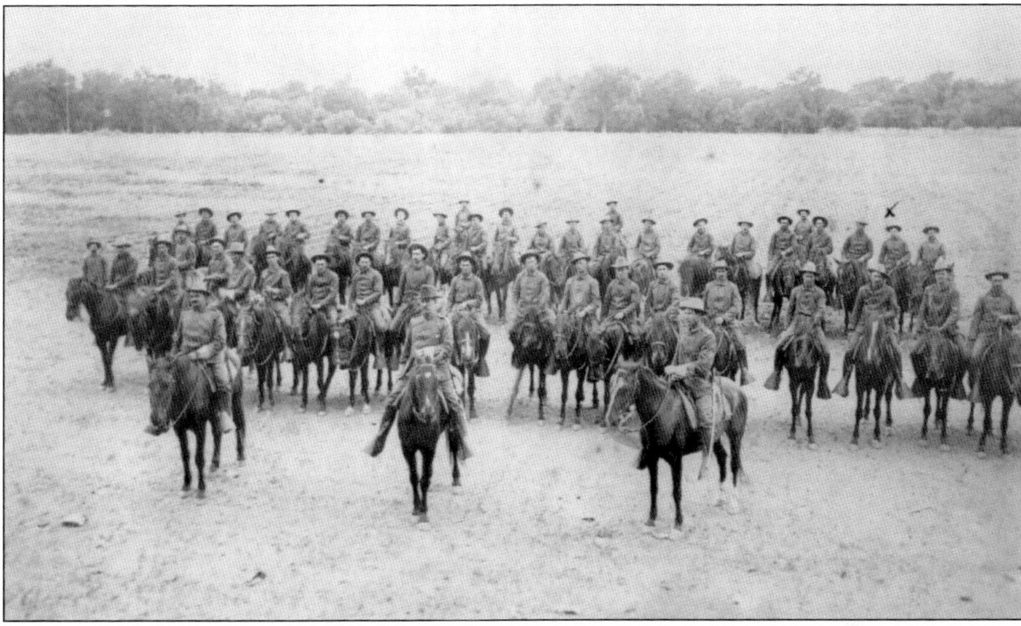

Rough Riders, 1890s. Pictured here is Gen. Greener and Company G of Theodore Roosevelt's Rough Riders. The company's name was bestowed on the 1st United States Volunteer Cavalry, one of three such regiments raised in 1898 for the Spanish-American War. Gen. Greener is shown front and center of the formation. The only other identified person is Garland McKinney (indicated with an "X").

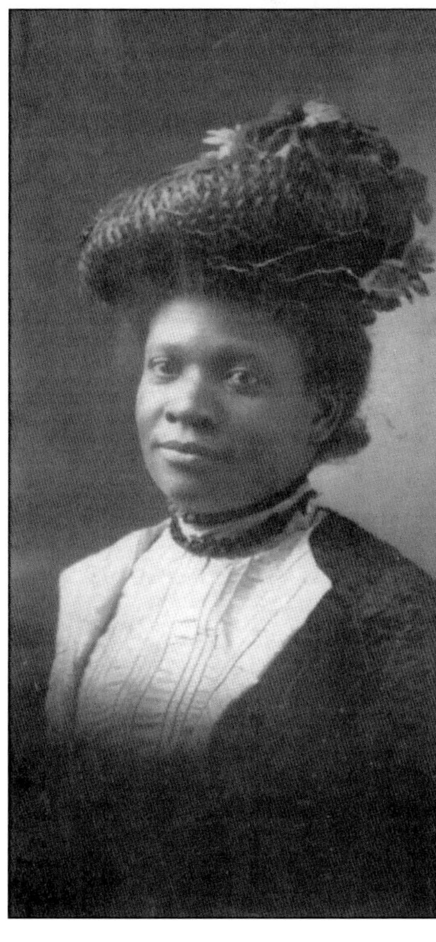

Garvin Family Cook, 1890s. Though her personal identity is not known, this woman has been identified as the cook for the Garvin family, most likely for Ford Morris Garvin. Garvin was a lawyer, banker, and mayor of Harrison around 1884. Garvin was also a charter member of the Rotary Club of Harrison in March 1919.

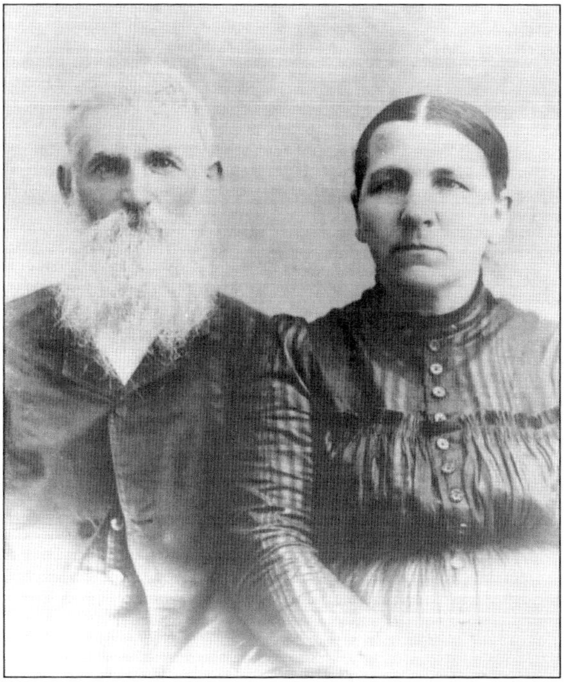

John Wilburn Moore and Mahala Melvina Burchfield. John was born on June 20, 1835, in Sevier, Tennessee. His wife was born on August 15, 1845, in Sevier. They had 14 children, all born in Harrison, most of who lived and died in Harrison. John died on August 16, 1893, in Harrison, at 58 years of age. His wife died on October 12, 1927, in Harrison at 82 years of age.

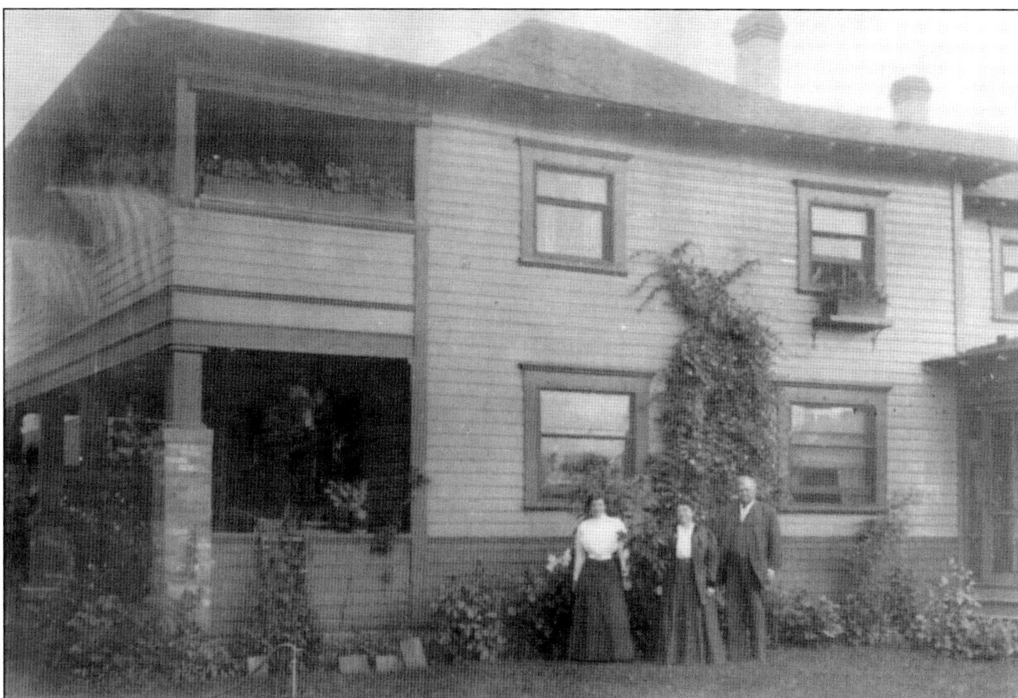

Crump Family House. The Crump family's journey to Arkansas started in 1624. Emigrating from England, the Crumps took residence in Virginia for several generations. John Gray Crump, born in 1796, moved his family to Arkansas in 1854. Many of his descendants lived and died in Harrison, marrying members of well-known Harrison families. Kirby, Garvin, Fitton, and Newton are just a few of those family names.

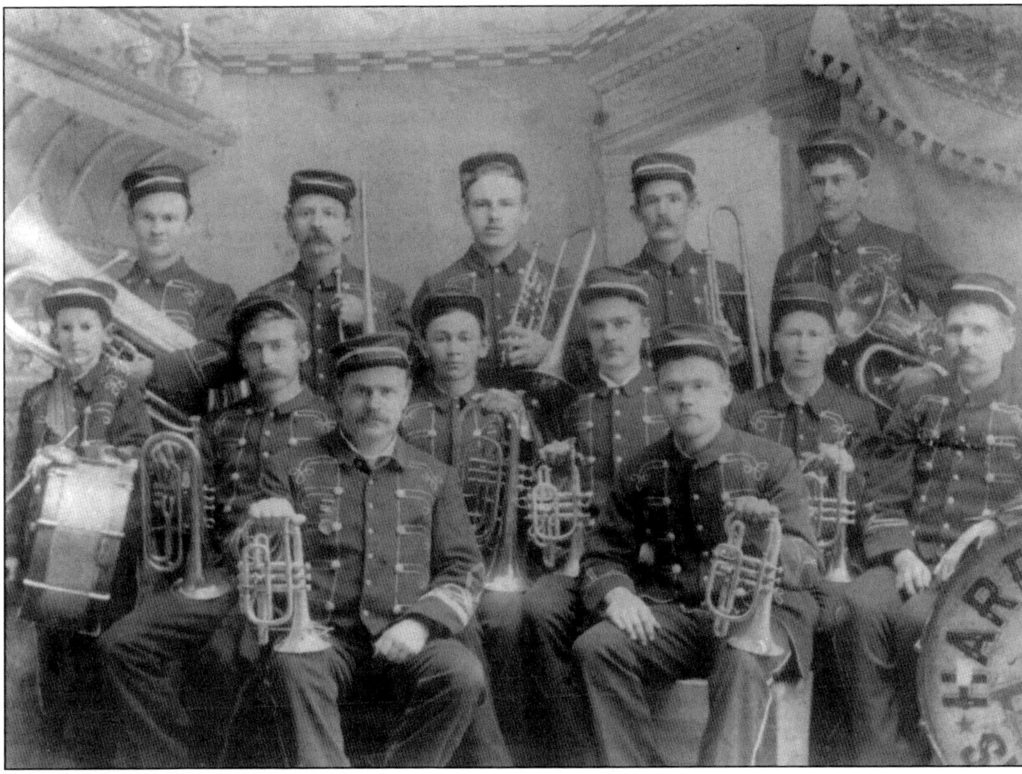

HARRISON SILVER CORNET BAND, 1895. This ensemble played on the bandstand on the courthouse square on weekends, holidays, and special occasions. It was also a marching band that played during parades. John R. Newman was the director and driving force behind the group. In those days, band music was scarce, and Newman had to write a lot of the music the band played.

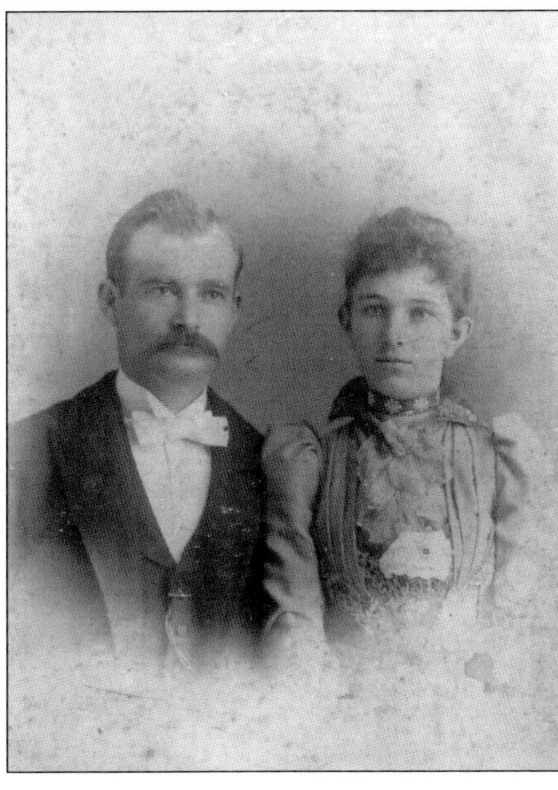

DR. E.L. AND NORA KIRBY EVANS. A Harrison native, Dr. Evans went to Marion Simms Medical College in St. Louis, Missouri, graduating in 1895. He returned to Harrison to practice medicine. He married Nora Kirby in 1897. She was a graduate of Christian College in Columbia, Missouri. Seeking a larger field to exercise his talents, Dr. Evans and his wife moved to Springfield, Missouri, in April 1906.

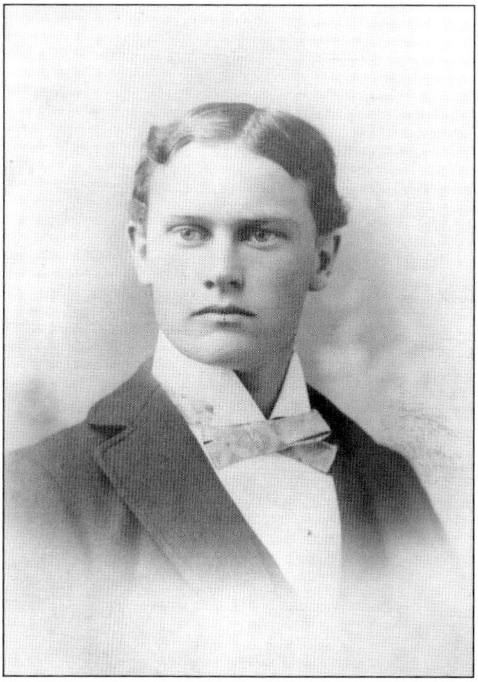

LEONIDAS "LONNIE" KIRBY JR. This photograph was taken prior to Kirby's departure for the Spanish-American War in 1898. He descended from a tough family of pioneers who first came to Virginia in the early 1600s and who fought in the American Revolution. The first Kirby to arrive in Boone County was his father, who walked from Dade County, Missouri, in 1871.

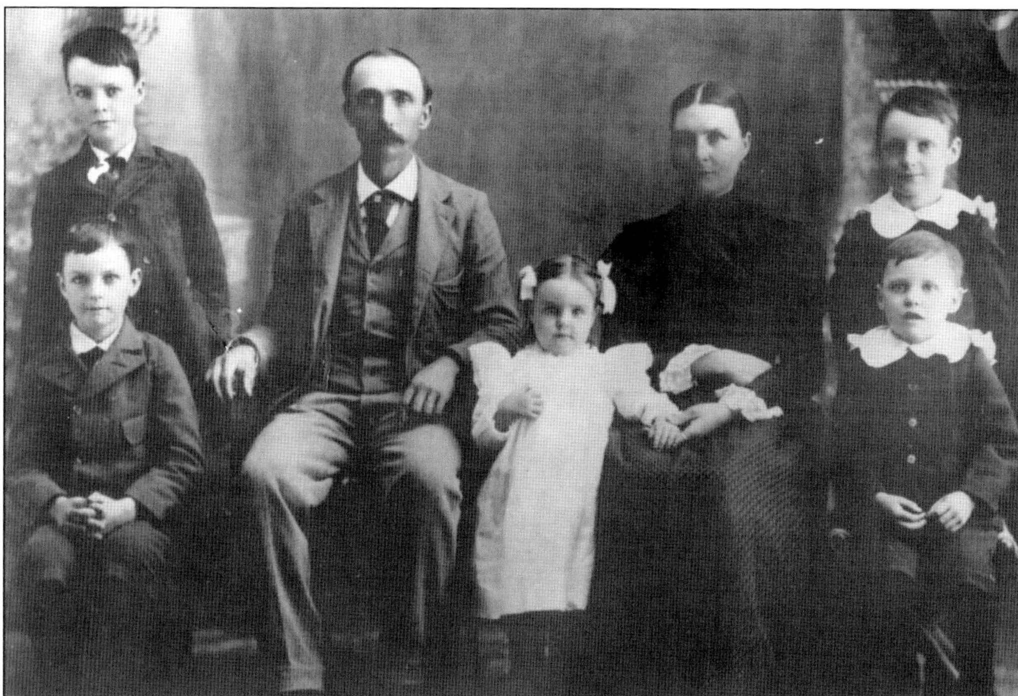

WESLEY WOOD HUDSON AND FAMILY, 1898. Born in 1861, Hudson suffered greatly during and after the Civil War. He served as Boone County treasurer from 1933 to 1939. The family members posing here are, from left to right, (first row) Coy Byrne Hudson, Hassie Hudson, and David D. Hudson; (second row) Clarence N. Hudson, Wesley W. Hudson, Ida Belle Eoff Hudson, and James Clio Hudson. Wesley died in 1951.

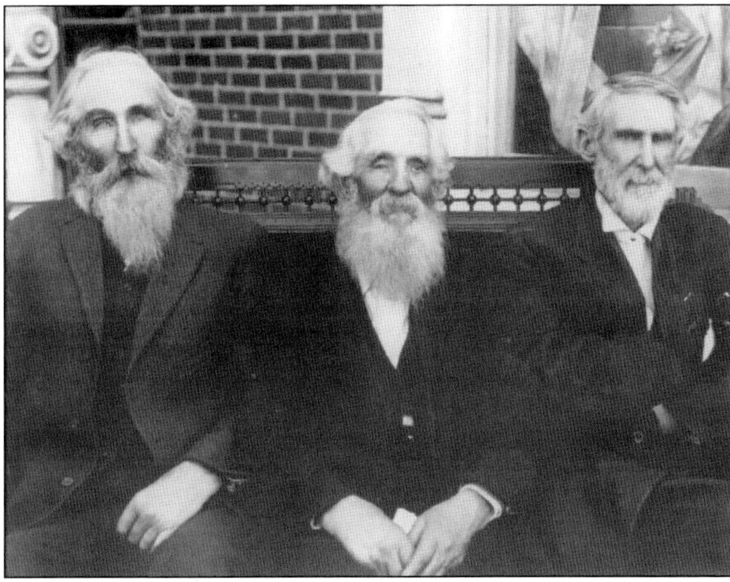

Civil War Veterans. Gillum Hopper (left), Joseph Holt Speer (center), and James Townsend "Town" Hopper, noted characters of the Civil War and Reconstruction, are seen in 1900. Hopper was instrumental in the founding and development of Boone County and Harrison. As Arkansas state senator, Hopper introduced a bill creating Boone County on April 9, 1869.

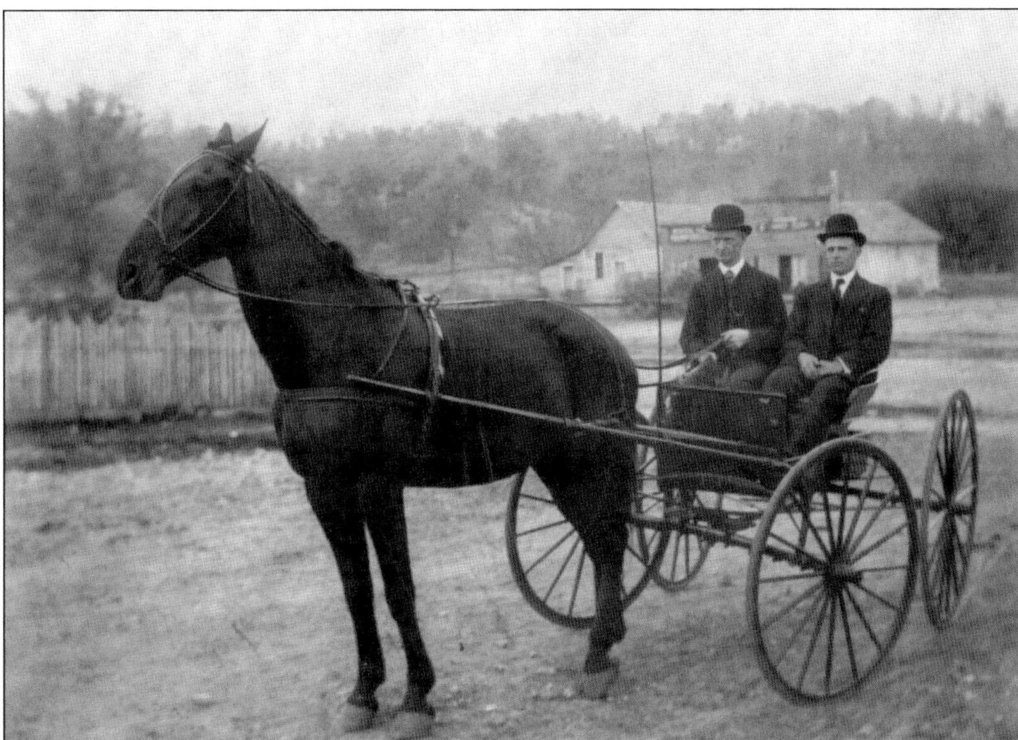

Herbert Bower and Dr. Frank Beverly Kirby. Bower (left) and Dr. Kirby are riding in a Bower buggy. Bower ran Bower Brothers Wagon Manufacturing Company, established in Harrison in 1888, with his father and brothers. Herbert Bower was in charge of the wood parts and paint. This photograph was taken about where the high school athletic field now stands.

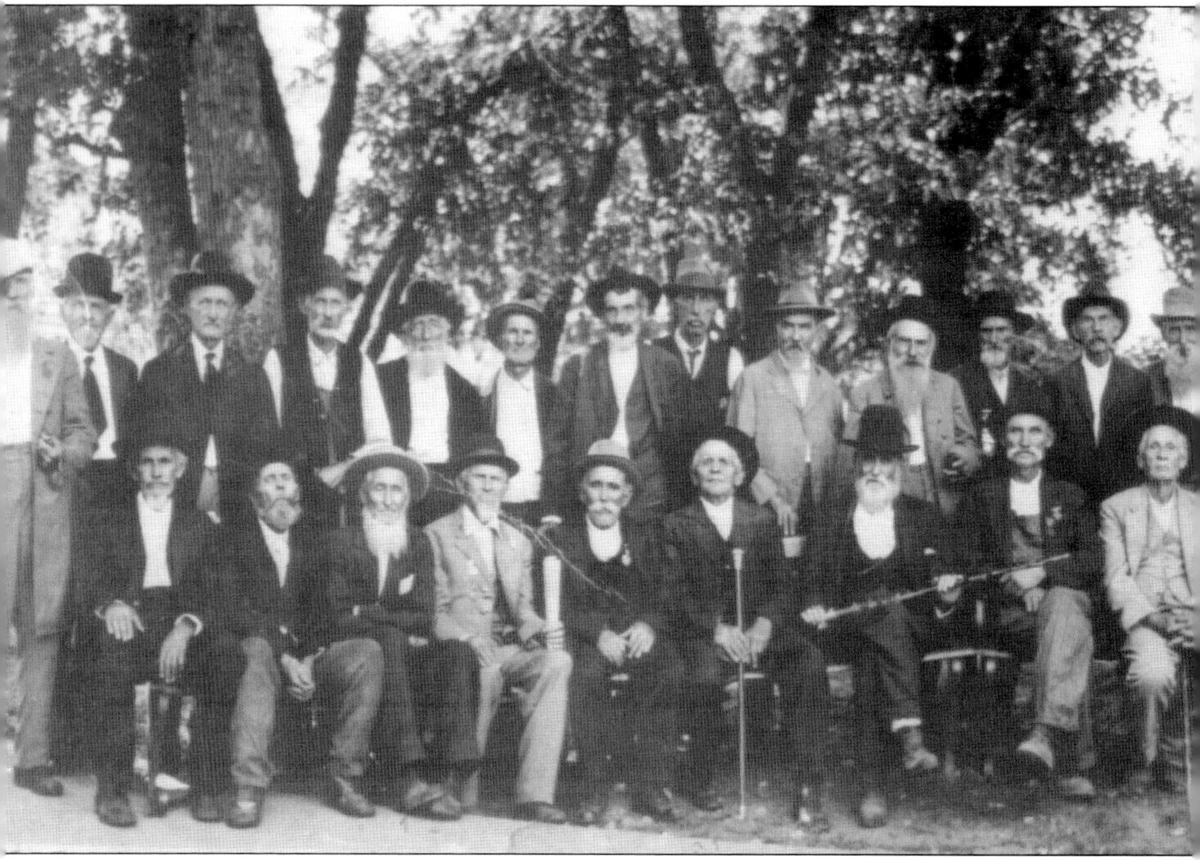

Confederate Veterans, 1900. For decades after the Civil War, veterans of the Confederacy and the Union were celebrated at parades and reunions. The camaraderie felt by Confederate veterans for one another was strong. During the war, their families back home suffered greatly. When these veterans finally returned from battle, many found their homes and land had been

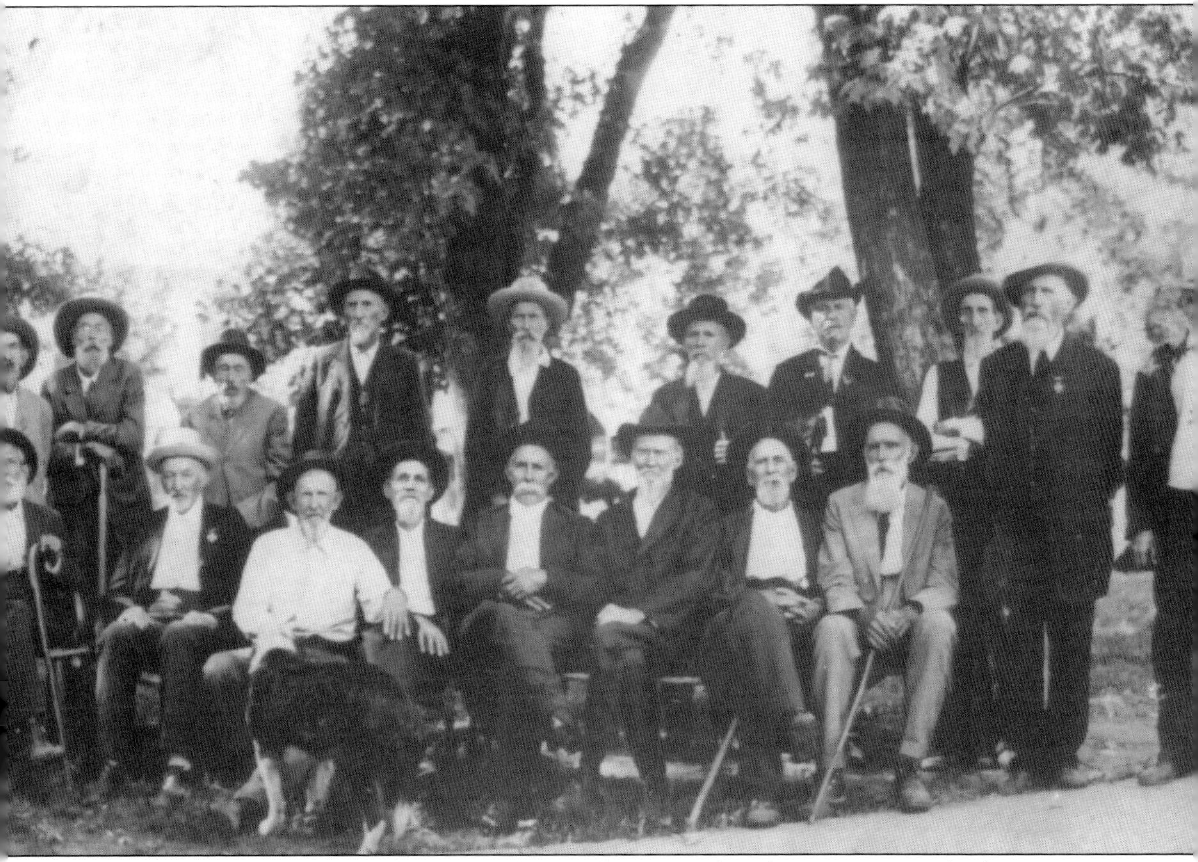

pillaged and destroyed. Many families in the Ozarks were reduced to an impoverished state in a region that was already challenging to live in. With limited resources, many families scraped by and had to rely on the kindness and generosity of their neighbors and the community at large. This cultural ethic remains to this day.

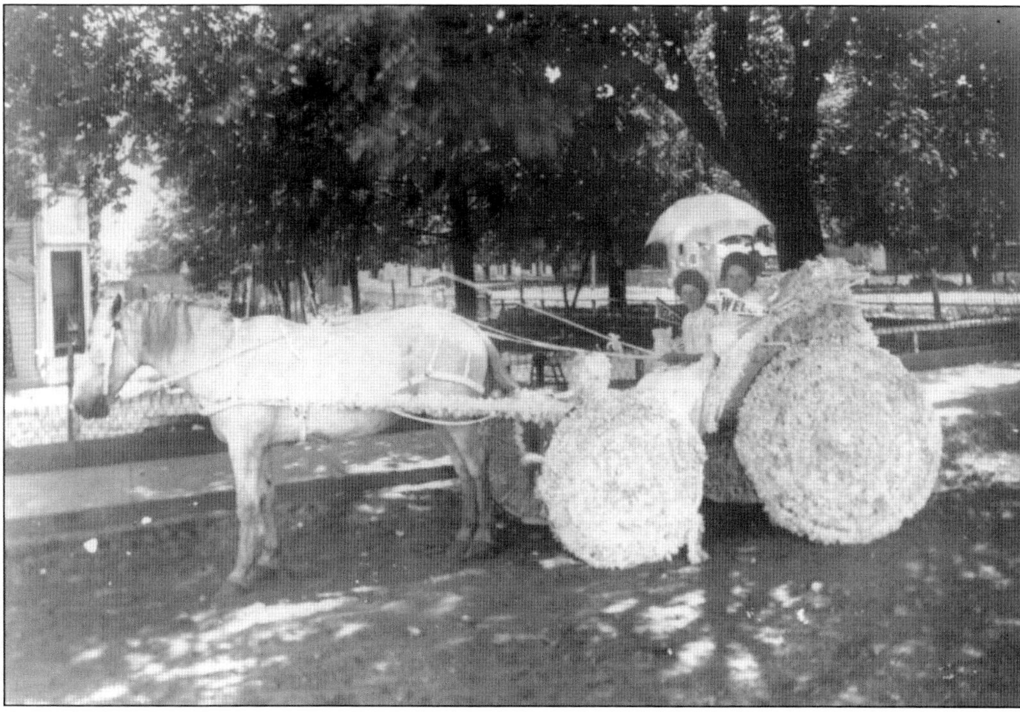

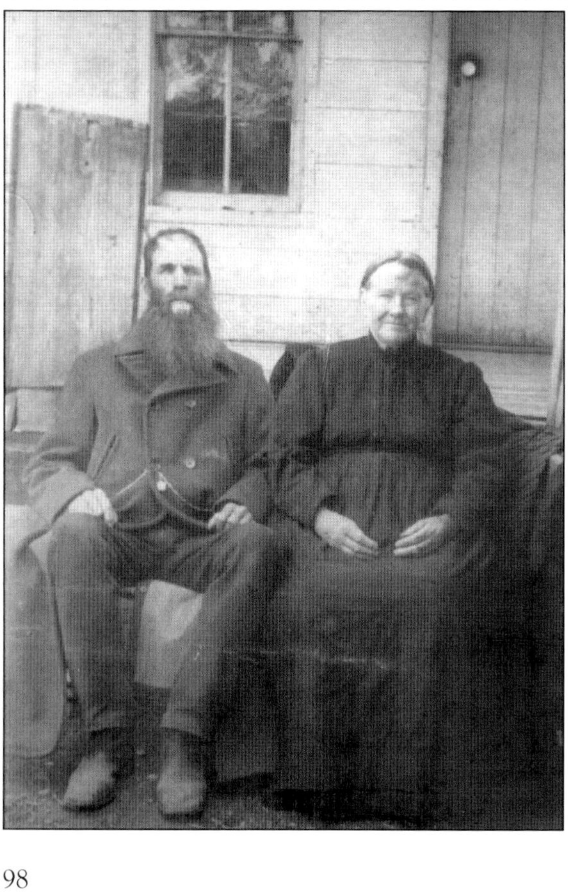

Fourth of July Parade, 1900. Seated in this horse buggy are Connie Myers (left) and Bess Godwin. According to the handwritten inscription on the back, this photograph was taken in 1900; however, Godwin was born in 1891 and would therefore be eight years old in 1900. She looks much older here, as does the residential area of Harrison in the background.

Dunlaps, 1901. David D. Dunlap (1837–1928) was a Civil War veteran. His first wife was Nancy Wyatt Buckley (1829–1910). Nancy's father, Walter W. Buckley, fought in the Civil War. Her paternal grandfather was a Revolutionary War soldier. When Nancy died, David married Nancy's sister Alabama.

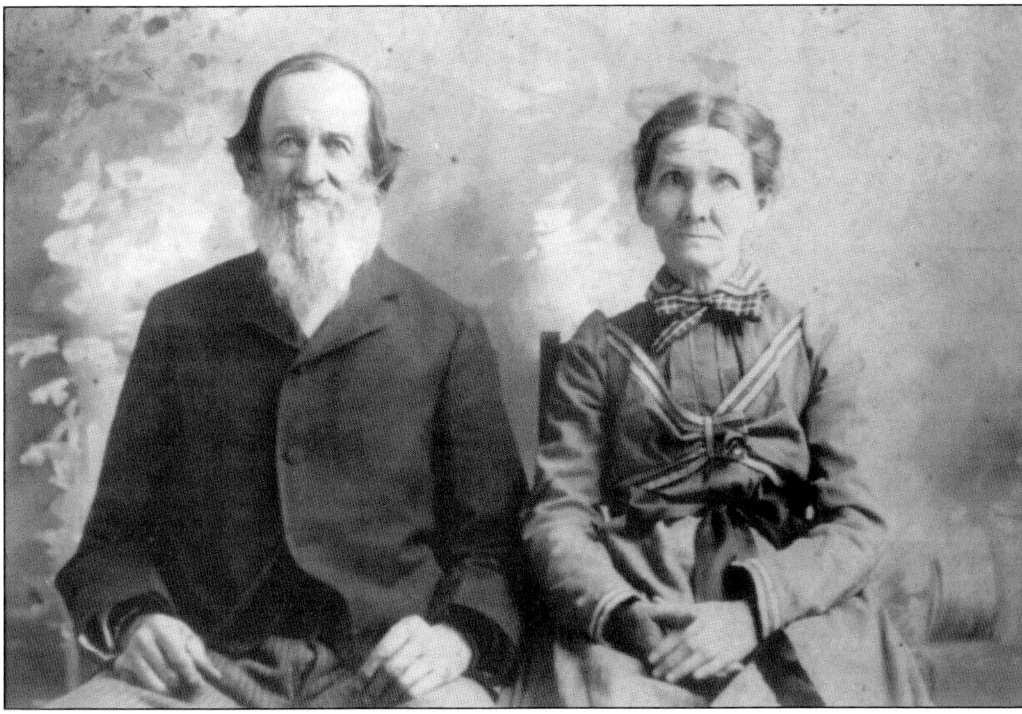

NICHOLSONS, OCTOBER 4, 1901. James Hargrove Nicholson was born in Alabama on November 4, 1824. After a stay in Tennessee, he went to Texas, where he got into trouble during a range war. He then moved north, settled in Harrison, and sometime in the 1850s married Mary Snelson. She was born on March 2, 1837. He fought for the Confederacy in the 19th Arkansas Infantry.

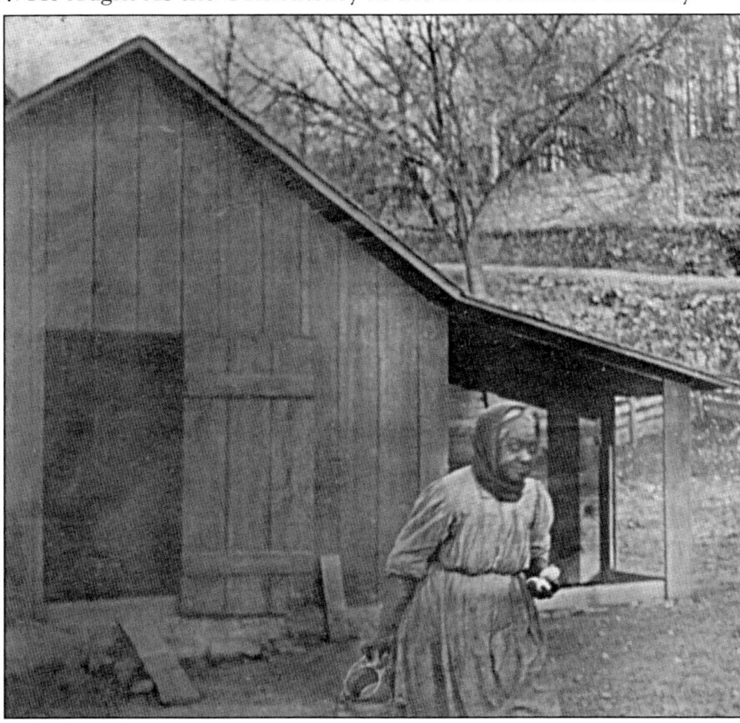

ALECTA CALEDONIA MELVINA SMITH. Known as "Aunt Vine," Smith was the last African American resident in Harrison after the Harrison Race Riots of 1905 and 1909. The census of 1900 revealed a black population close to 10 percent. This constituted a vibrant community that had a cohesive culture and deep roots. (Courtesy of Carolyn Cline and Marcille Lawrence.)

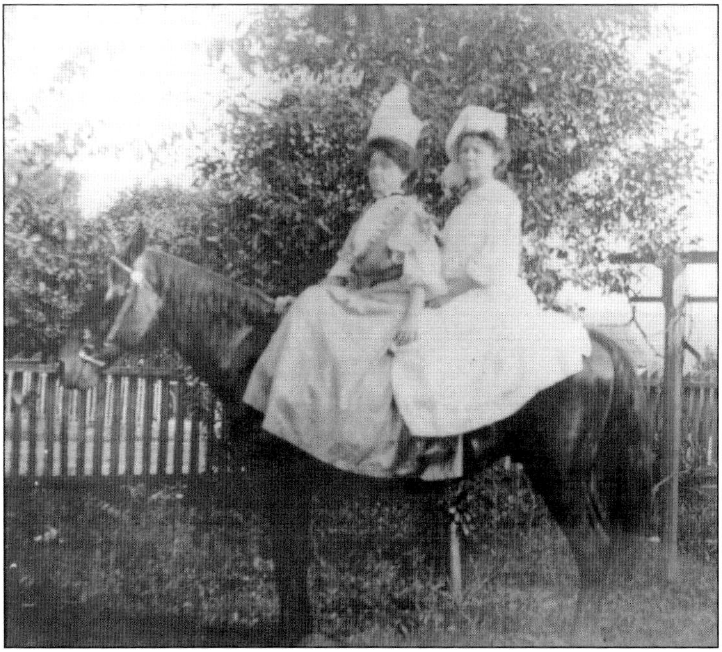

Goldie Worthington and Willard Worthington. These were the daughters of Judge John I. Worthington and Estella Leathers Worthington. Dr. Frank Beverly Kirby fell in love with Goldie (left) and proposed to her, though she refused to marry him until she was 18 years of age. She told her fiancé that she preferred a set of Haviland china to a diamond engagement ring. They were married in 1906.

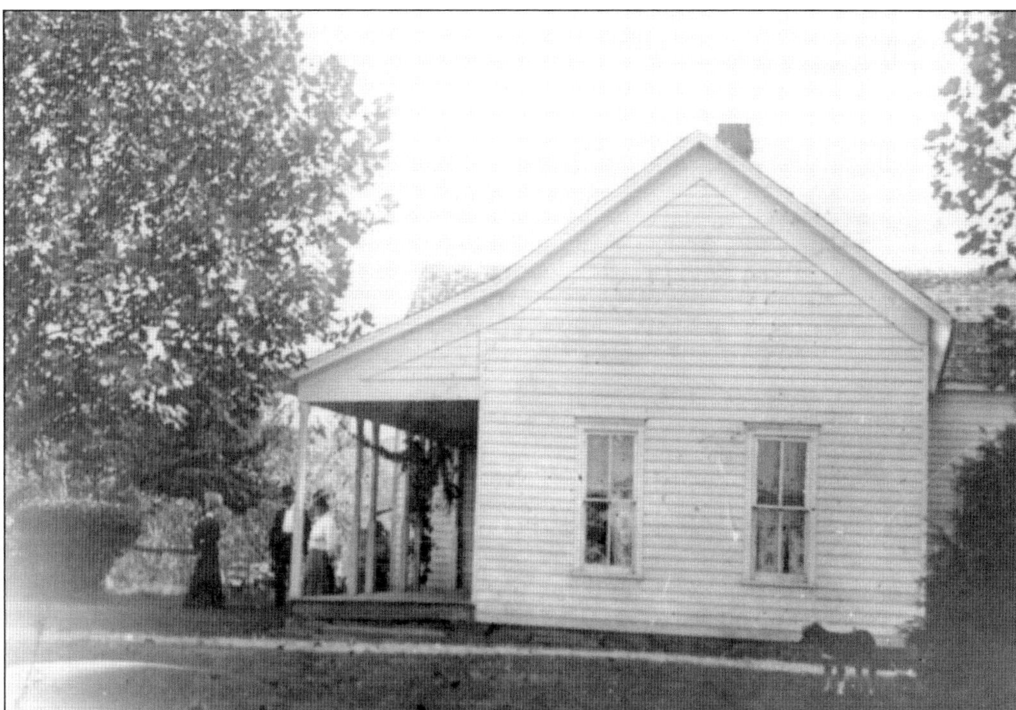

Ben Mason Estes House, October 4, 1907. Mason, a well-known figure in Harrison's early days, was a lieutenant colonel in the Confederacy and later became a prominent landowner and businessman in the area. He ran a 263-acre farm and had an additional 100 acres near Harrison. This home stood on Capps Road.

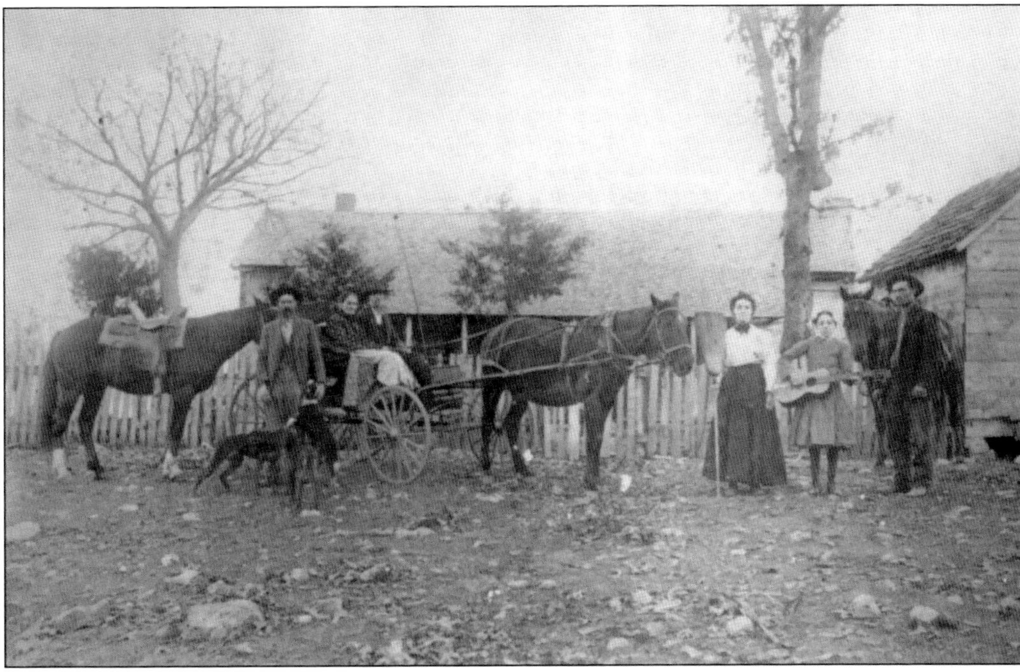

Jackson Home, 1910. The Jackson family settled in Boone County before it was officially established in 1869. Shown here are, from left to right, Albert Jackson with his dogs and horse, Harriet Ellingsworth Jackson and James Tolliver in the buggy, Ida Jackson Journigan holding the store-bought broom, Marie Journigan holding the guitar, and Thomas Jackson with his horse.

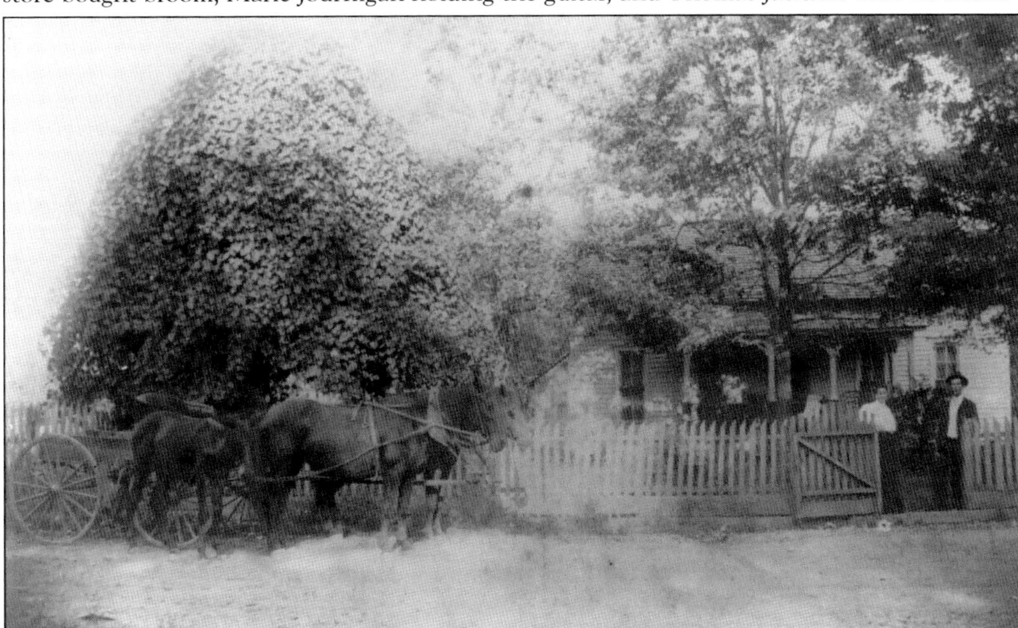

House on South Vine Street. This unidentified couple stands in front of their house. Their horse team and wagon are on the other side of the fence. This house was located not far from Crooked Creek and the mouth of Lake Harrison. The lake, created by a small man-made dam, is a popular area for the community, with parks, playgrounds, trails, and a live-music venue.

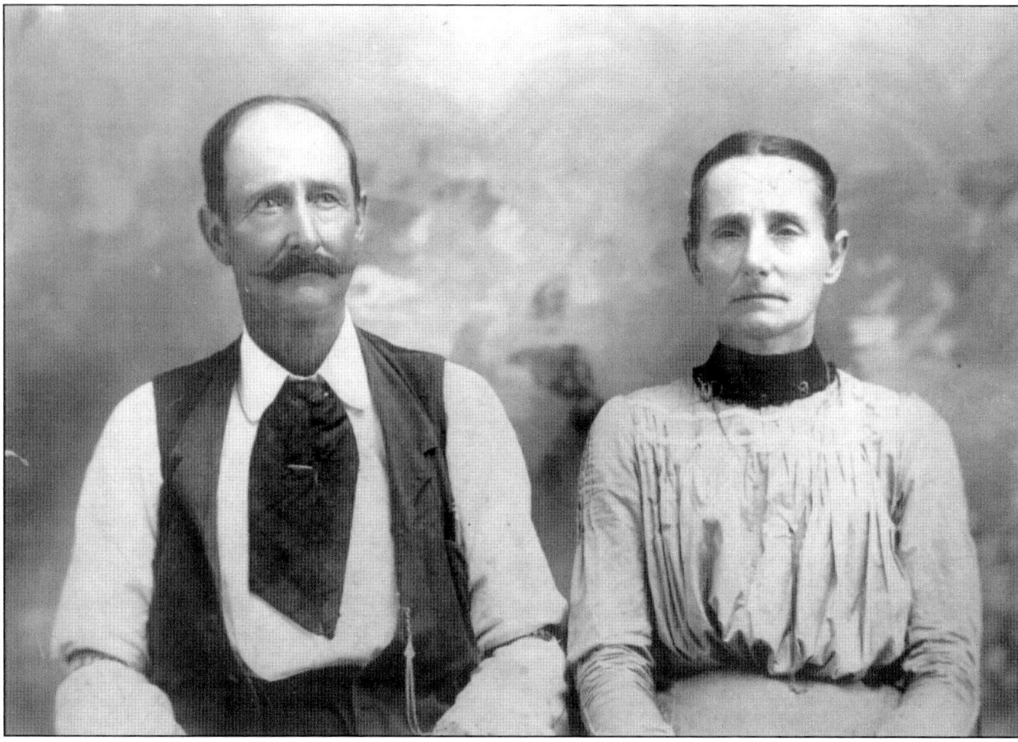

Marcus Lafayette Bevins and Sister. Born in March 1845, Bevins enlisted in the Union army in New York City on April 3, 1865, at the age of 18. He was a bugler for Company G of the 11th Regiment of the Missouri Cavalry during the Civil War. He died in 1917.

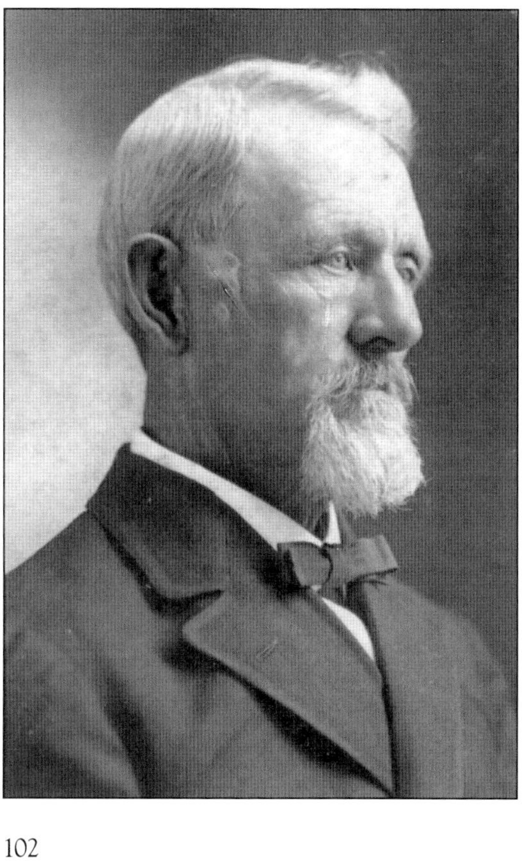

Ben Mason Estes, 1910. Born on September 23, 1844, Estes entered the Confederate army in 1861 at age 16. He served with Herrell's 2nd Battalion of the 27th Arkansas Infantry until 1865. Upon his return, he found his parents in a needy condition and helped them revive their farm. He became a successful carpenter, farmer, and tradesman and was representative of Boone County in 1910–1911. He died on August 13, 1934.

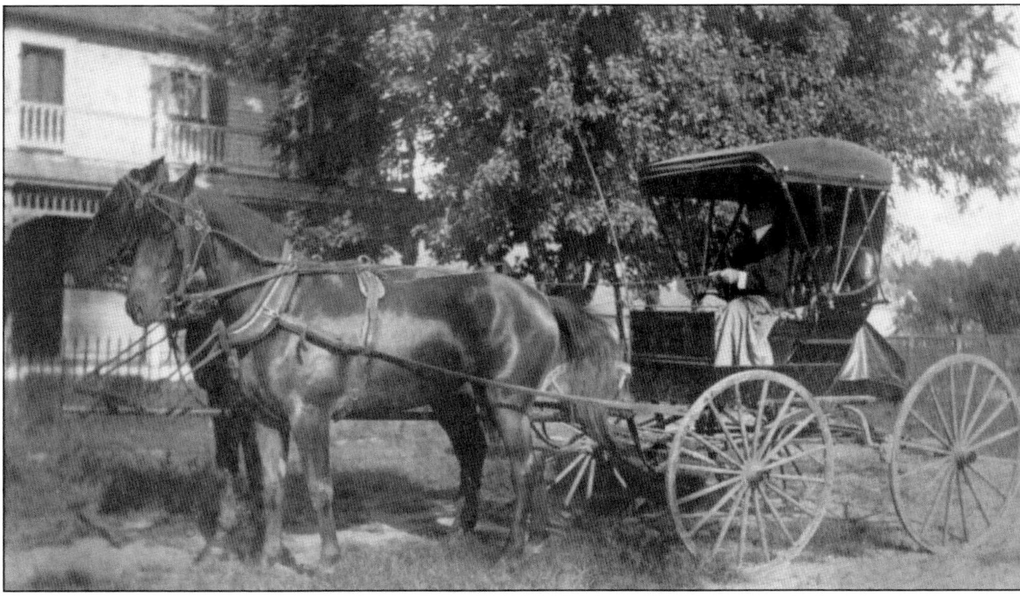

HORSE BUGGY AND HOUSE, 1910. Pictured here is Dr. Leonidas Kirby's buggy in front of his home. Dr. Henry Vance Kirby is driving the buggy. He is wearing a blanket over his trousers to protect them and keep them clean from the dirt the horses and buggy may kick up.

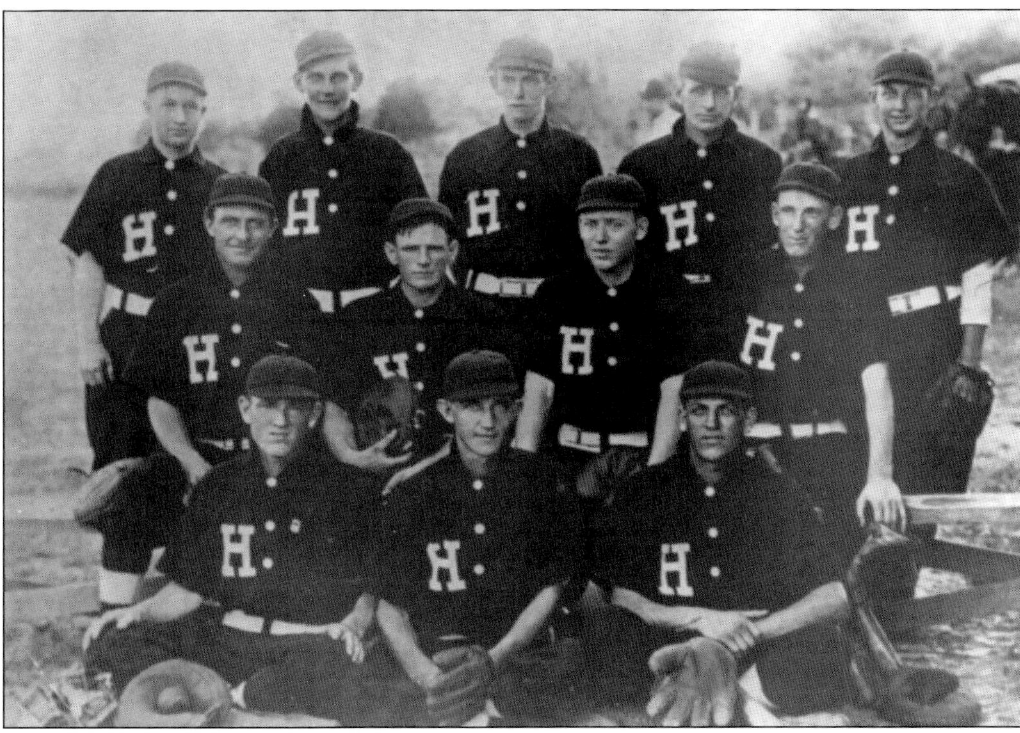

HARRISON BASEBALL TEAM, 1911. The team started using the Town Hopper pasture, now the site of Goblin Stadium, as the baseball diamond. Hopper collected rent for the use of his pasture as the park. Later, a small grandstand was constructed for the convenience of fans. When the team garnered enough money, the land was purchased from Hopper for the baseball park.

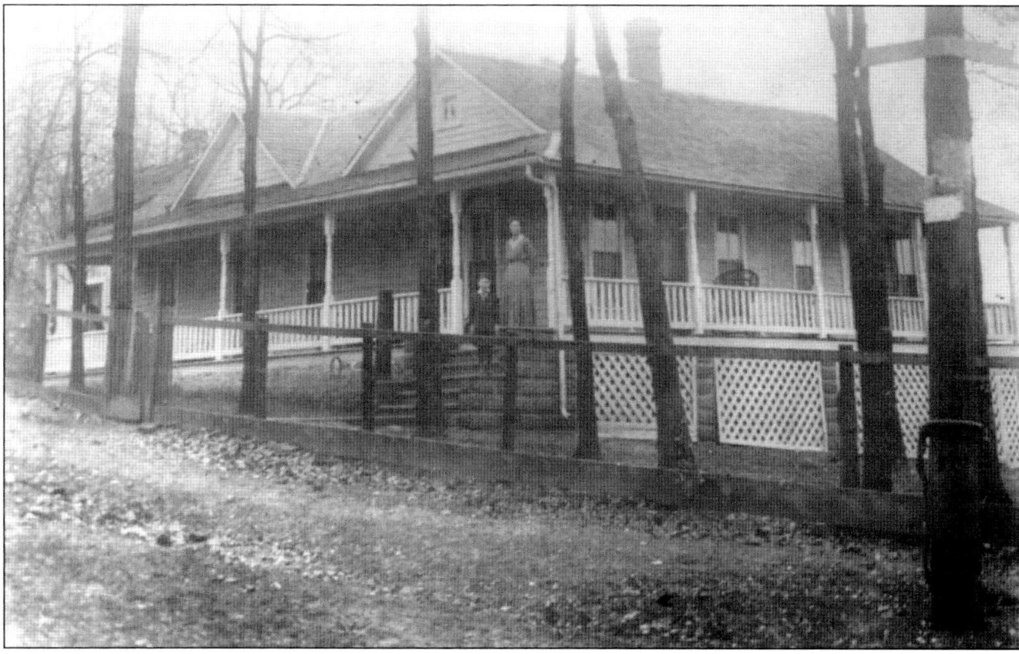

Dickey Home, 1912. Pictured here is the home of Frank and Eva Dickey, located at 224 South Maple Street. To this day, the house looks much the same, with the same wraparound porch and even the same wooden pillars in place. Among the main features no longer in place are the chimneys.

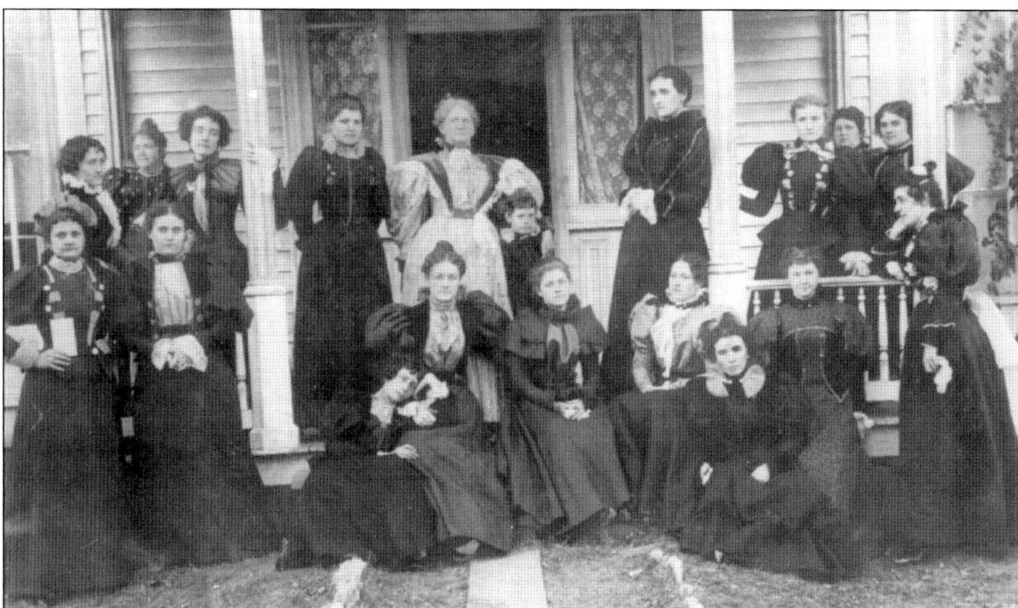

Women on Porch. These women, dressed in Victorian-era fashion, are, from left to right, (first row) Fannie Weaver Hearst, unidentified, Josie Crump Trimble, Walsie Weaver King, Annie Lewis George, Ada Pace Smith, Annie Cowdrey ? , Virgie Walters, and Arranah Morris Parr; (second row) unidentified, Lulu Vance Scott, unidentified, Zella Armitage Harper, Josephine B. Crump, unidentified, May Watkins Milum, unidentified, Mintie Crump Garvin, and unidentified.

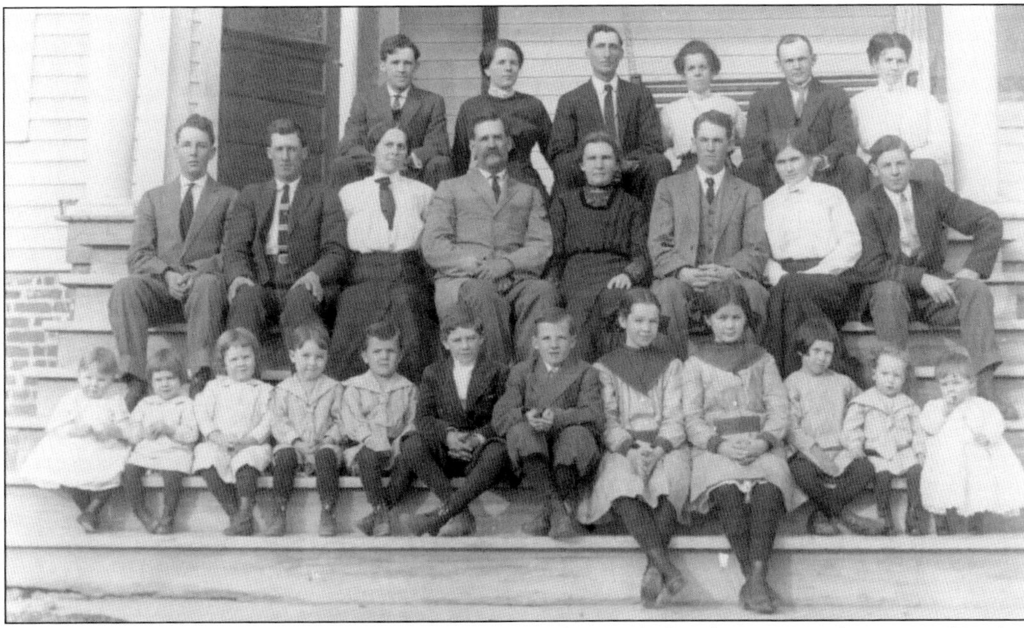

HOLT FAMILY, 1912. Members of the John Crittenden Holt family pose on the steps of Luther Clay Holt's home at 504 North Vine (Main) Street. J.C. Holt was born in Harrison in 1858. He is the man with the moustache in the second row, next to his wife, Fanny Ellen Johnson Holt (fourth from right). The most memorable events for the Holts were family dinners on holidays and birthdays. (Courtesy of Glenna Ragan.)

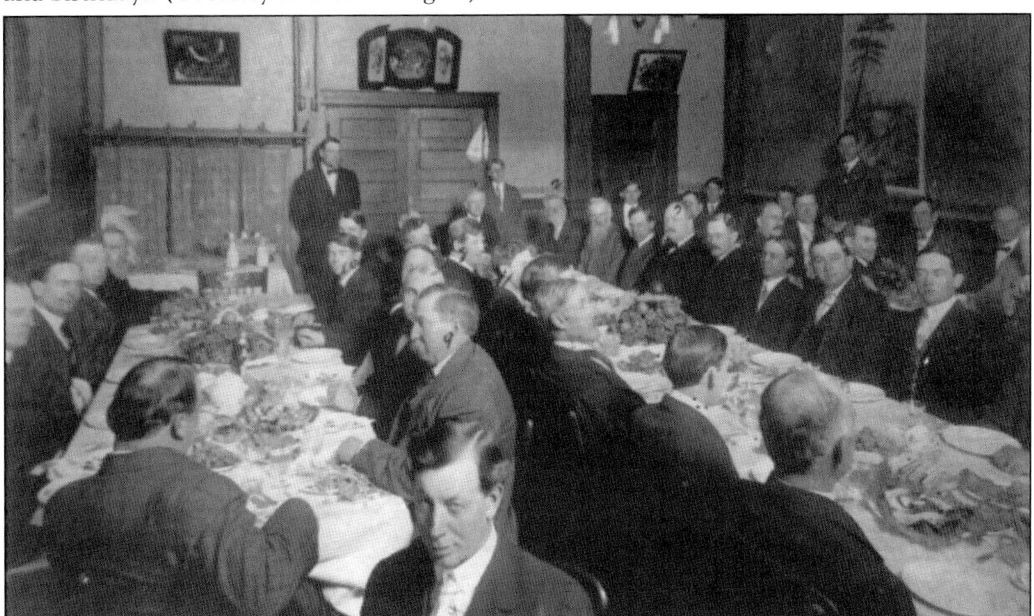

BANQUET, 1912. This banquet was held to honor Col. George J. Crump, who was moving from Harrison to Muskogee, Oklahoma. Crump, a lawyer and Confederate veteran, participated in the Brooks-Baxter War and later became an Arkansas legislator in the House of Representatives and Senate. He also served as a US marshal for the Western District of Arkansas in Fort Smith from 1893 to 1897.

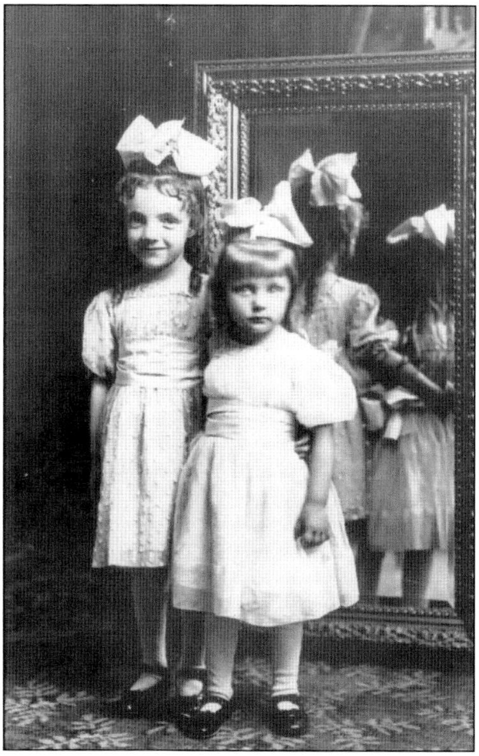

Hudson Children, 1913. Elva Clarence Hudson (left) was born on October 29, 1909. She married Henry Vance Kirby on June 21, 1936, and died on April 26, 1983, at age 73. Flora Modene Hudson (right) was born on August 14, 1911. She married Harold Eugene Sperry. Flora died on April 4, 1990, at age 78.

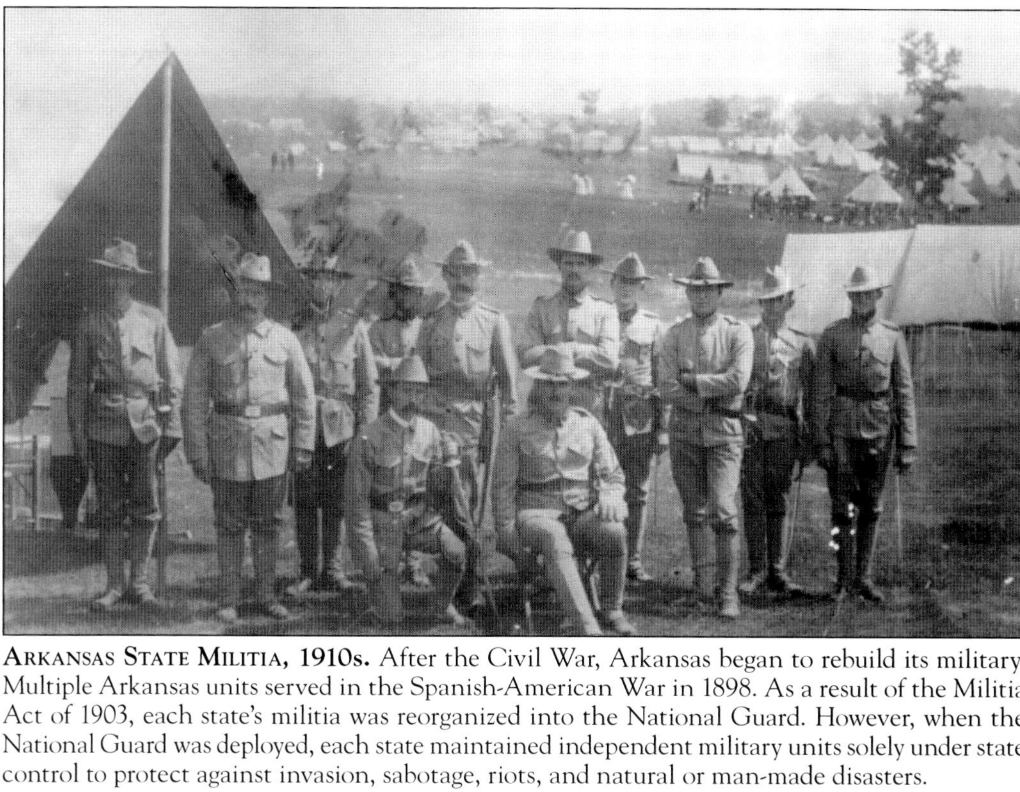

Arkansas State Militia, 1910s. After the Civil War, Arkansas began to rebuild its military. Multiple Arkansas units served in the Spanish-American War in 1898. As a result of the Militia Act of 1903, each state's militia was reorganized into the National Guard. However, when the National Guard was deployed, each state maintained independent military units solely under state control to protect against invasion, sabotage, riots, and natural or man-made disasters.

HOLT FAMILY, 1910S. Luther Clay (L.C.) Holt is in the driver's seat of his automobile, one of the first in Harrison. Behind him is his second wife, Ora Davis, and seated next to her is her sister Elizabeth. At right in the front seat is his son Sam. Holt, an entrepreneur, was elected mayor of Harrison in 1838, serving for six years. (Courtesy of Glenna Ragan.)

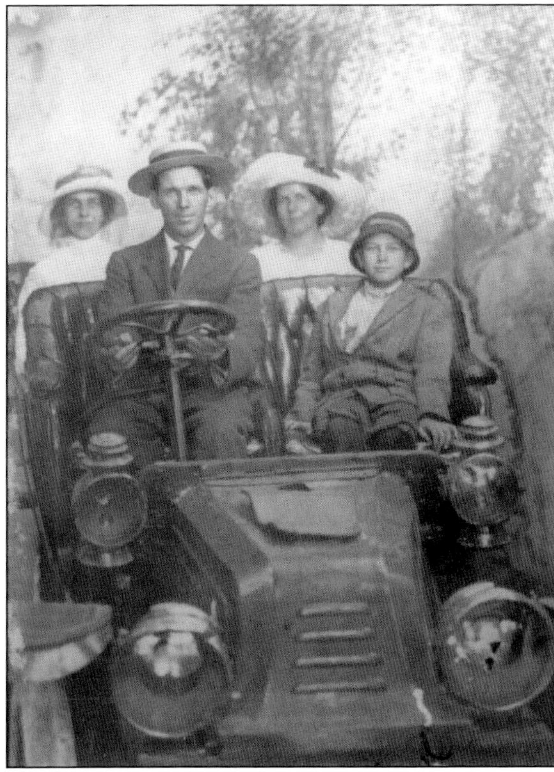

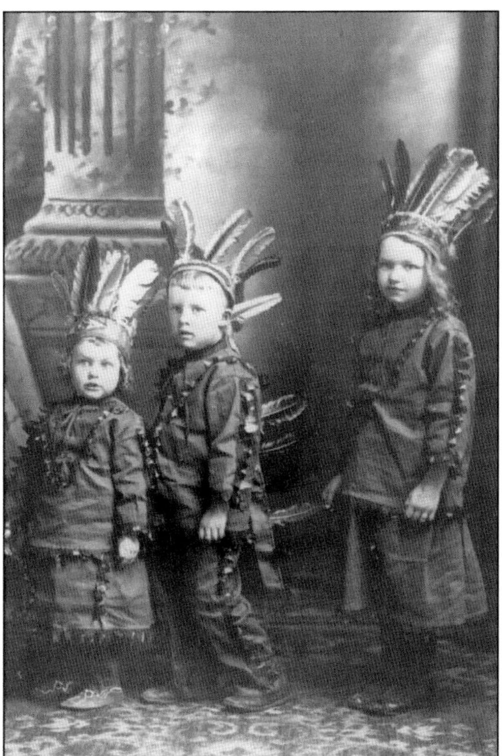

KIRBY CHILDREN, 1913. Posing here are Hazel Kirby (left), Henry Vance Kirby (center), and Lillian Kirby. Hazel married Herbert R. West, and Lillian married Robert Eugene Browning. Henry Vance became a prominent doctor in Harrison. The records pertaining to his medical practice were accepted into the University of Arkansas's Special Collections on July 26, 1989.

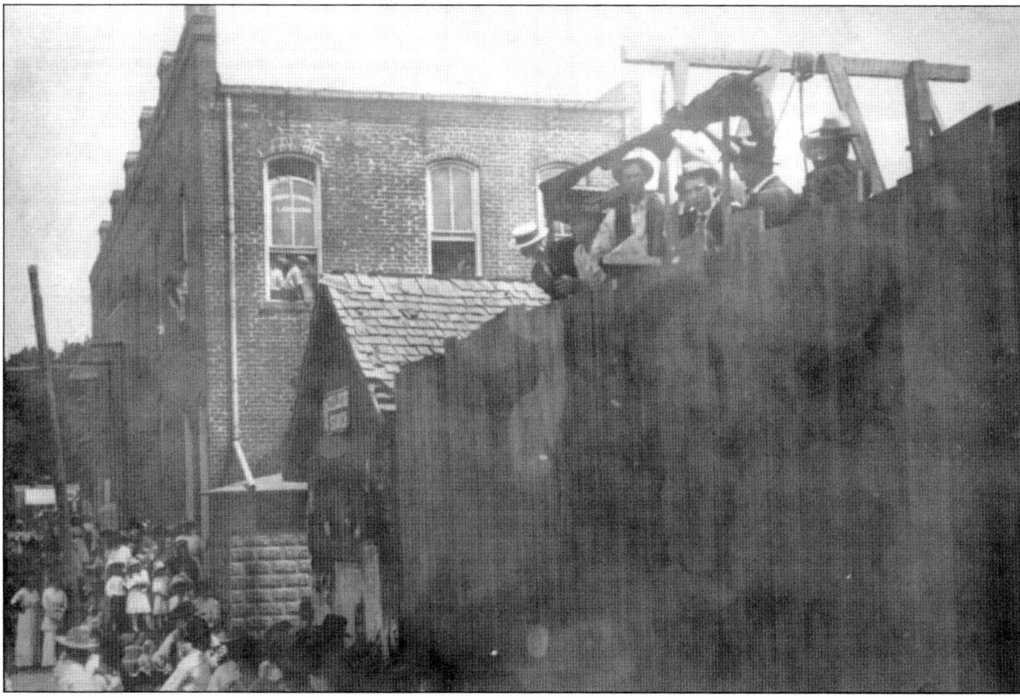

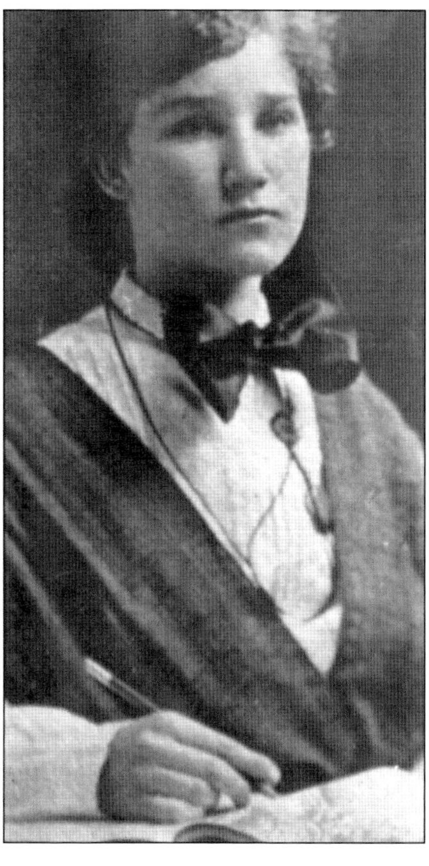

Hanging of Odus Davidson, August 1913. Davidson was convicted of the murder of Ella Lillian Ethel Barham. Davidson (fourth from left) can be seen looking over the fence at the crowd. He insisted to the end that he was not guilty. This photograph looks northeast. The scaffold is behind the old county jail, southwest of the town square at the rear of what is now First Federal Bank's loan building.

Ella Lillian Ethel Barham. Born on February 16, 1892, Barham was brutally murdered on November 21, 1912, at 20 years of age. Her body was found cut into seven pieces at the entrance to an old mine shaft on Crooked Creek. Her murder was devastating to her family and was a topic of conversation throughout their lives. To this day, controversy remains as to the identity of her killer.

ODUS DAVIDSON. Convicted of Ella Barham's murder, Davidson denied he was in love with Barham and maintained that he did not kill her. As to the person who did, it remains a mystery. Speculation includes his cousin Hargis and a man named Charley Martin. Years later, one of the two confessed to the murder.

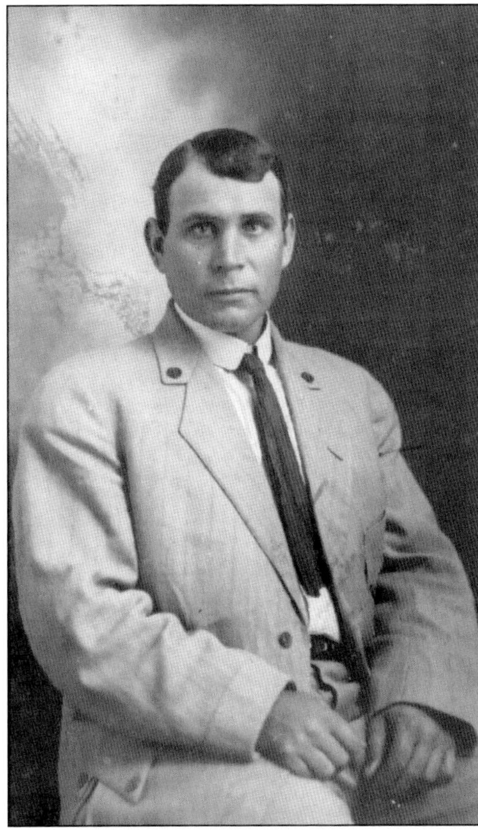

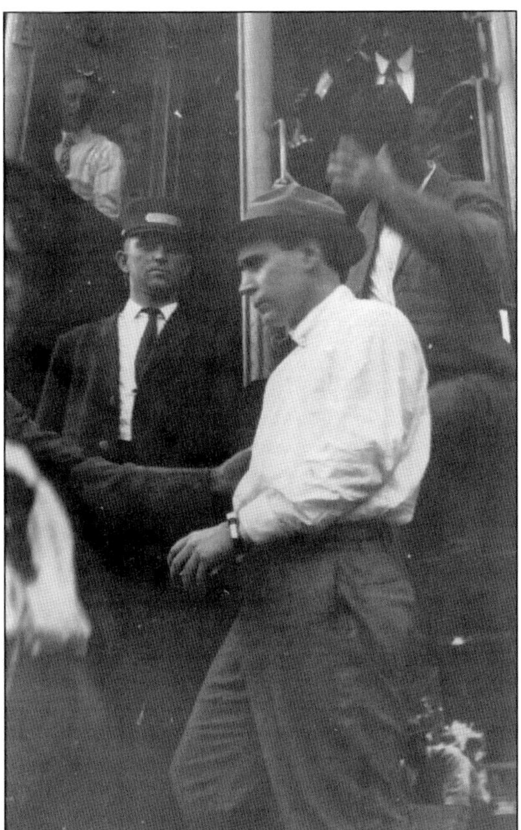

ODUS DAVIDSON ARRIVES FOR HANGING. Davidson, in handcuffs, is led off the train in Harrison. He maintained his innocence to the bitter end and had several supporters. Legend has it that the ghosts of Davidson and Ella Barham still haunt the area of the mine shaft where Barham was killed.

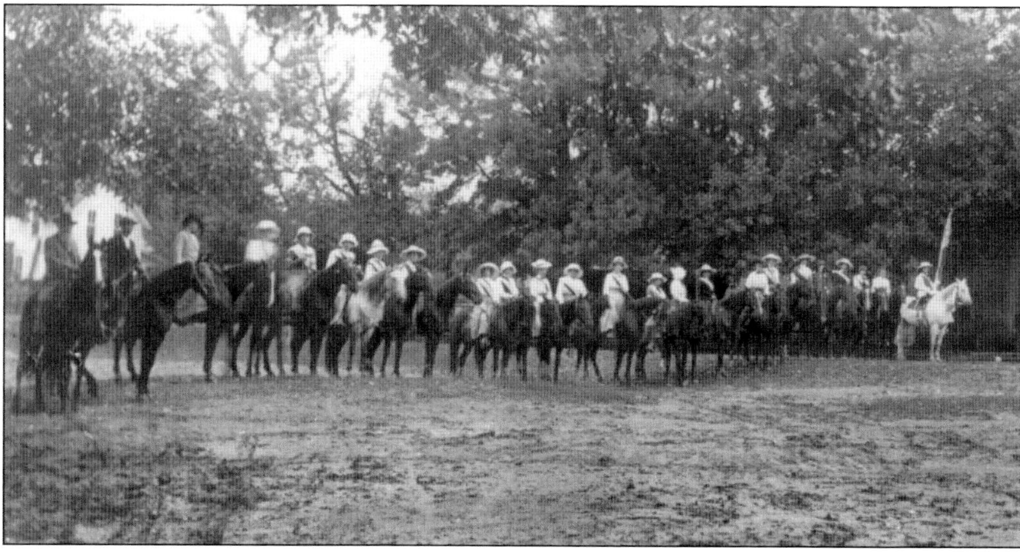

Parade on Horseback. These members of the United Daughters of the Confederacy ride sidesaddle, a technique developed in European countries in the Middle Ages as a way for women wearing skirts and fine clothing to ride a horse in a modest fashion. One objective of the organization was "to honor the memory of those who served and those who fell in the service of the Confederate States of America."

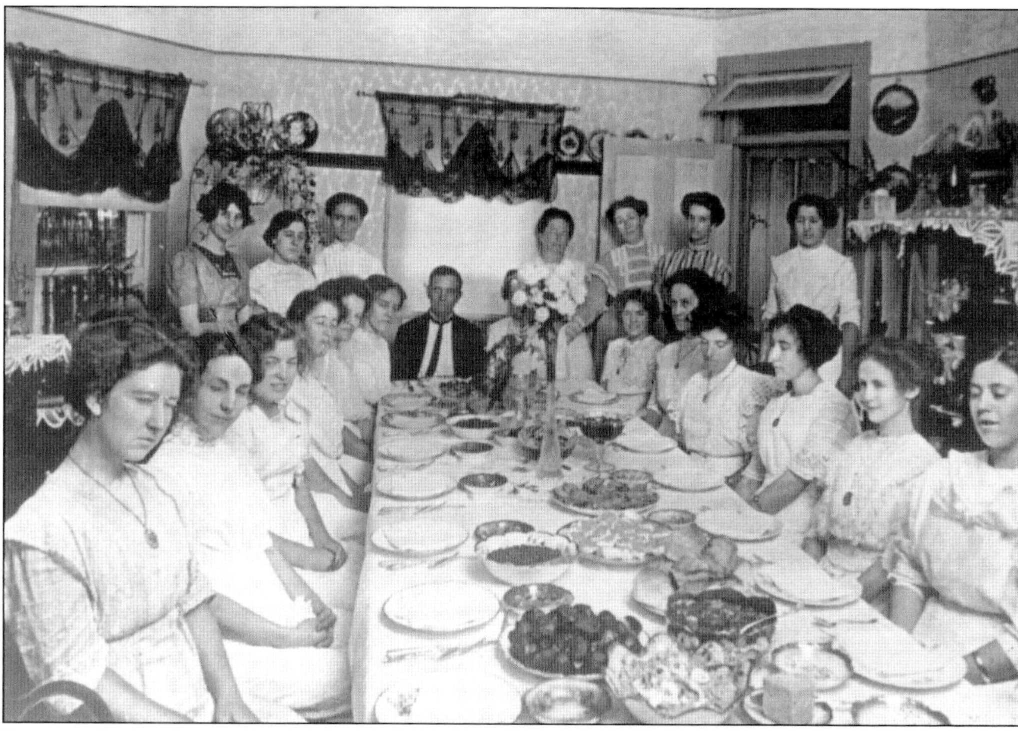

Dinner Party, William Harrison Cecil Home. Cecil, a successful dry-goods merchant, was, along with W.F. Gordon, J.R. Holt, and others, influential in raising the capital needed for getting the Missouri & North Arkansas Railroad shops moved to Harrison. Being a prominent man in local society, Cecil had the means to entertain at his home, as depicted here.

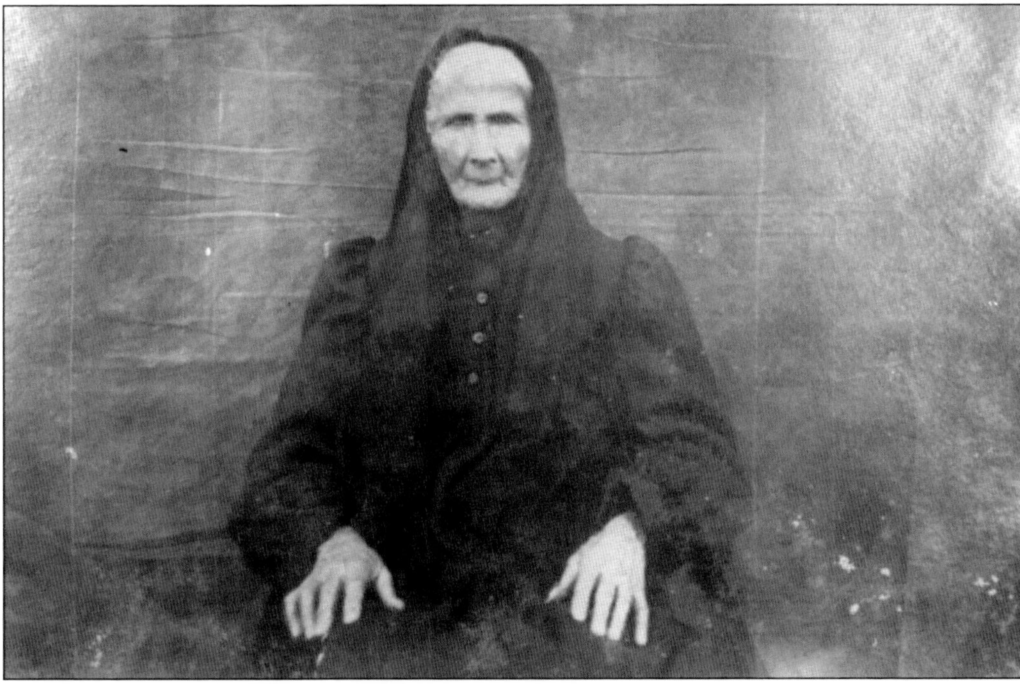

Elizabeth Dunlap Raley, Late 1910s. Born in 1836, Betty Raley helped rescue the children who survived the Mountain Meadows Massacre of 1857. With the efforts of family and friends in Arkansas, especially Col. William C. Mitchell, Raley was part of a rescue party that located and returned 17 children in 1859. She later became the second wife of William Raley. She died in 1917.

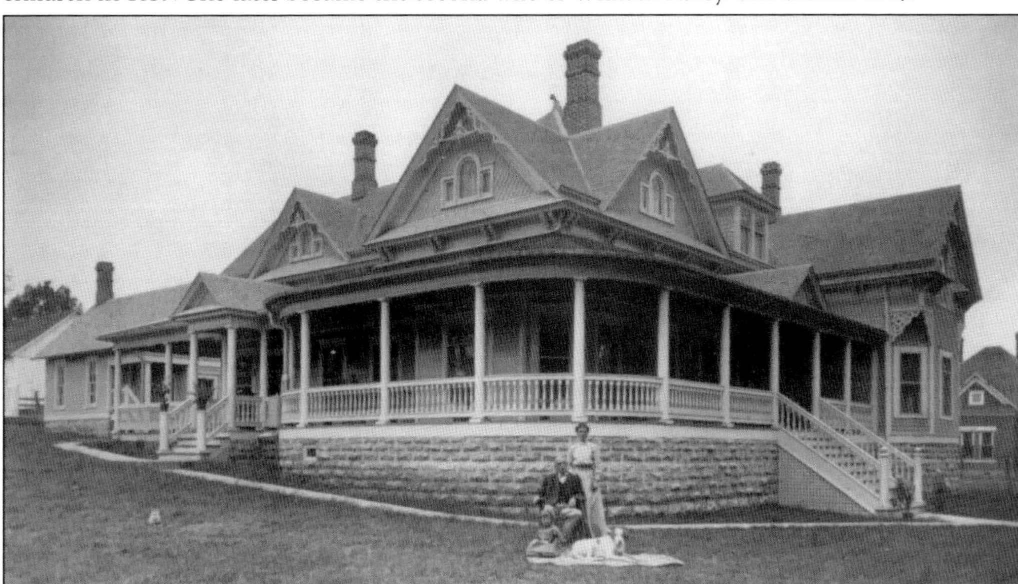

Czech Family Home. Charles W. Czech was the owner of Harrison Wheat and Flour Mill, which he operated from 1894 to 1915. It was located on Crooked Creek, where the parking lot for Harrison Junior High currently is. His mill was of vital importance to life in the early days, processing wheat and flour for city and county residents. His home, seen here, was located on South Pine Street.

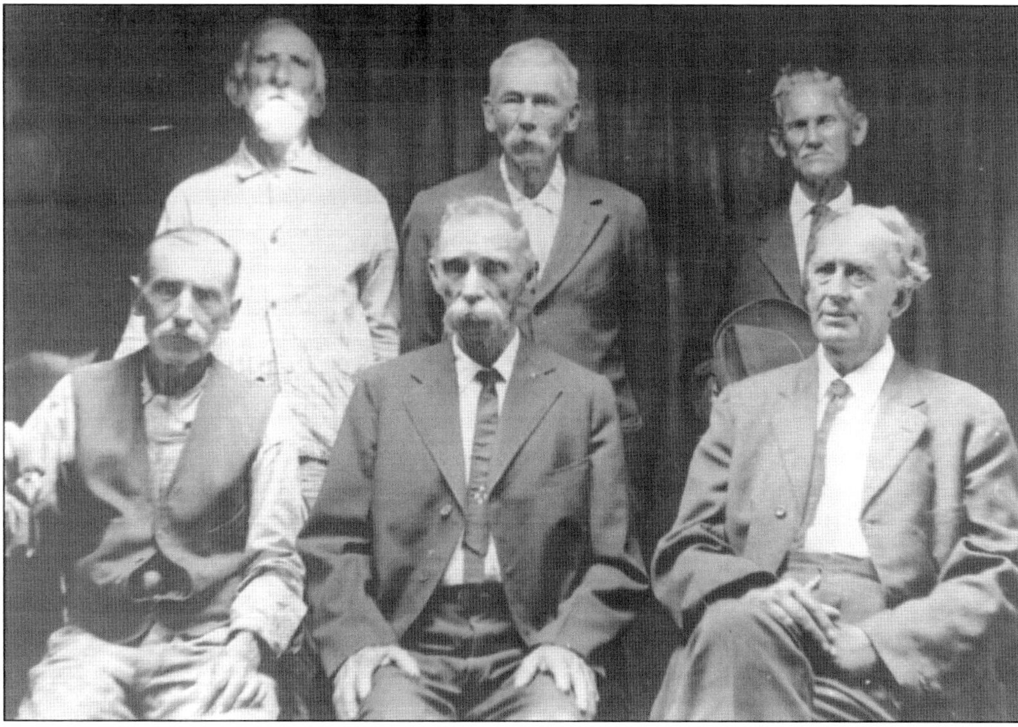

CONFEDERATE VETERANS GROUP. The only identified man in this photograph is James Morris Raley (second row, center). He married Mary Louvenia Starr on February 16, 1871. From Oklahoma, she was one-sixteenth Cherokee of the Ani'-Ga'tâge'wi (Kituah or Wild Potato) Clan. She was most likely related to notorious outlaws Belle Starr and Henry Starr.

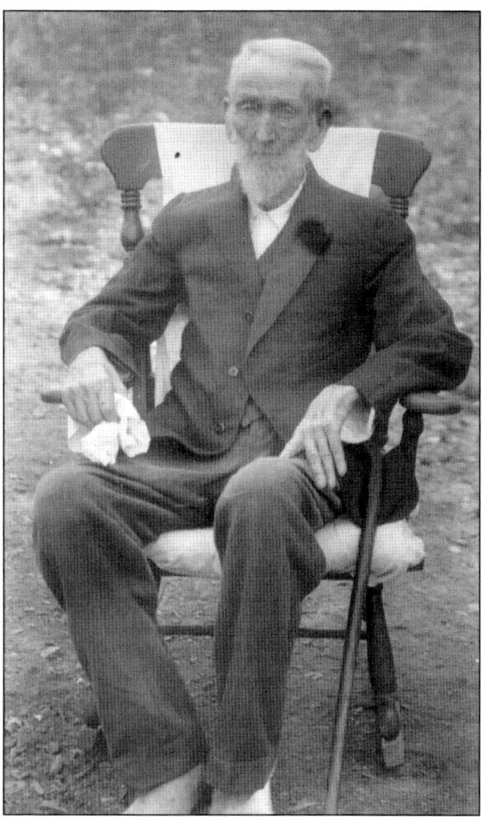

COL. ELI DODSON, 1910S. Dodson led the 14th Arkansas Infantry, a Confederate army regiment, during the Civil War. He commanded his regiment at the battle of Pea Ridge, where he was severely wounded in the hip and rendered unfit for duty for some time. After convalescing, he joined his troops in Memphis, Tennessee, just after the Battle of Shiloh. Dodson commanded his regiment until he resigned his commission in the fall of 1863.

REV. WILLIAM ANDREW DEES AND COL. ELI DODSON. After the Civil War, Dodson (right) practiced law from 1865 to 1881. In 1866, he was elected to the Arkansas State Legislature, serving until he was displaced during Reconstruction. After serving as county and probate judge for Marion County from 1878 to 1880, he was elected county and probate judge for Boone County in 1892. He lived from 1828 to 1921.

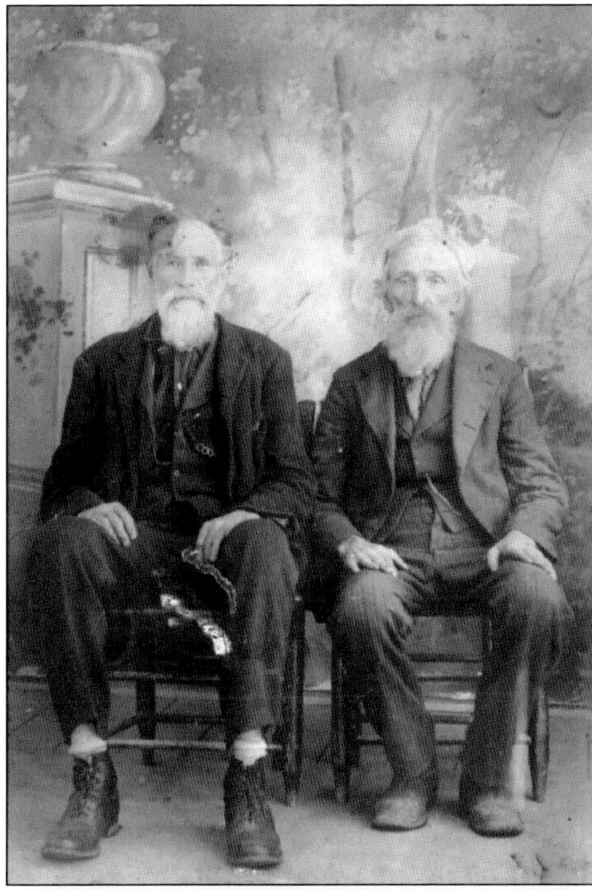

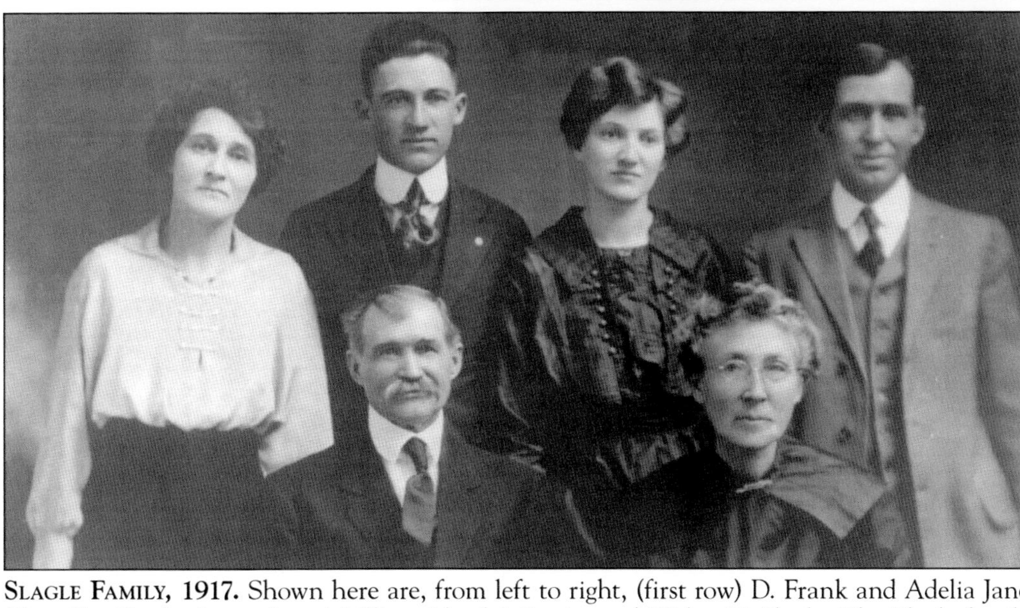

SLAGLE FAMILY, 1917. Shown here are, from left to right, (first row) D. Frank and Adelia Jane Chandler Slagle; (second row) Lillian, Lloyd, Minnie, and Walter T. Slagle. The Slagle family became prominent in Harrison, marrying into the Kirby and Hudson families.

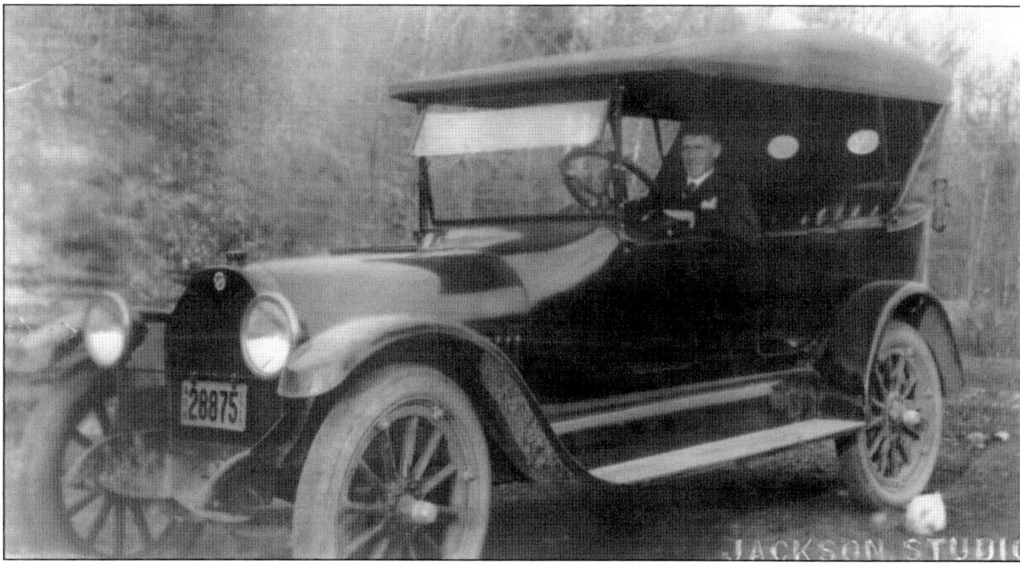

LAWSON MURRAY, 1918. Murray sits in the driver's seat of his Jeffery Touring Car. The Jeffery was an American automobile produced by the Thomas B. Jeffery Company in Kenosha, Wisconsin, from 1914 to 1917. Lawson was married to Myrtle Murray, and together they had one child, Martha Eugene, born on June 16, 1925.

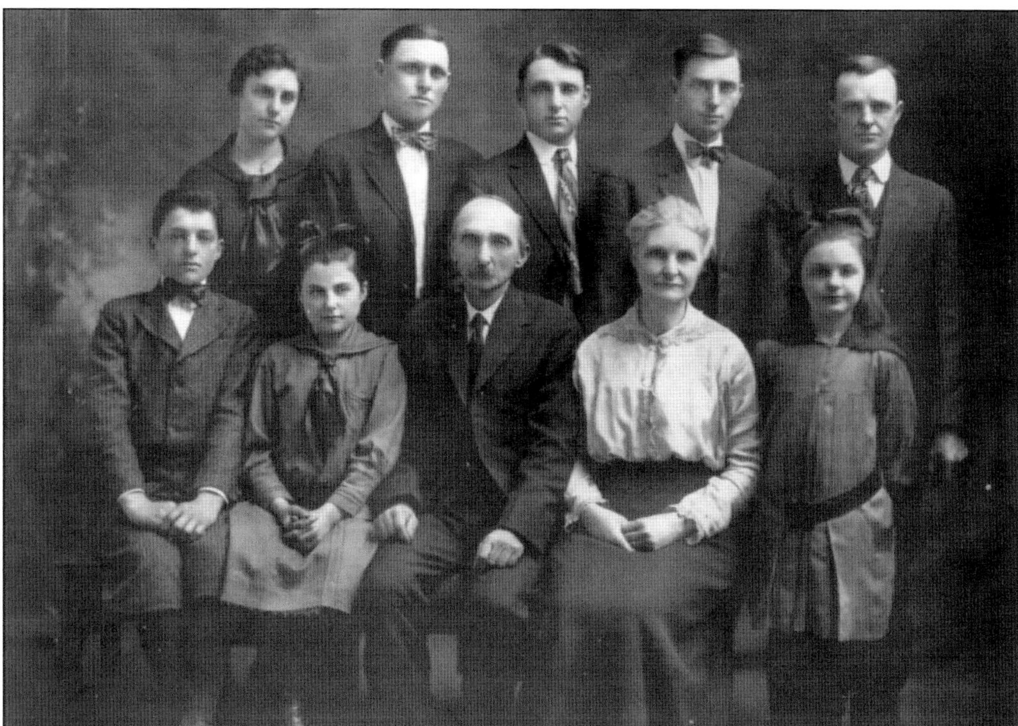

WESLEY WOOD HUDSON FAMILY, 1920. Family members posing here are, from left to right, (first row) Ralph Hudson, Neva Hudson Villines, Wesley Wood Hudson, Ida Belle Eoff Hudson, and Eva Jane Hudson Hickman; (second row) Hassie Leah Hudson Blackwood Phifer, David D. Hudson, James Clio Hudson, Coy Byrne Hudson, and Clarence Nichols Hudson.

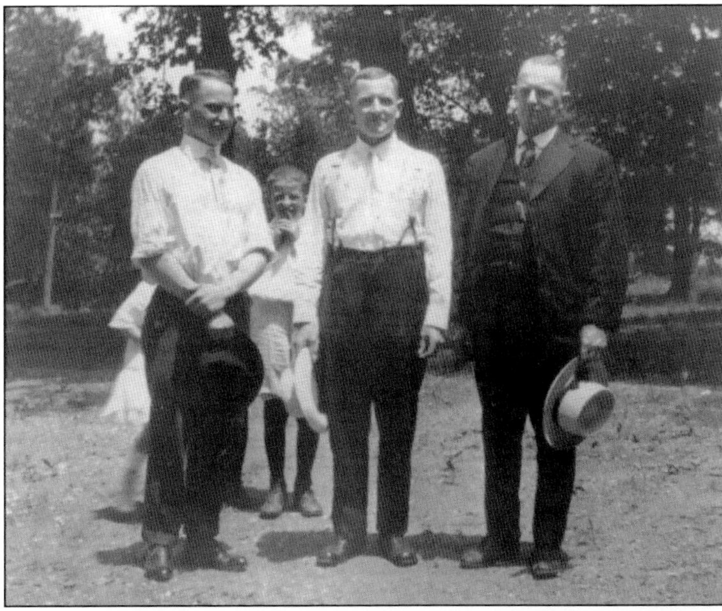

Kirby Brothers, 1920. Featured here are, from left to right, Dr. Alexander Crump Kirby, Dr. Henry Vance Kirby (as a boy), Leander Bender Kirby, and Dr. Frank Beverly Kirby. This photograph was taken in the yard of Leander Kirby's home. While his brothers were doctors, Leander was a pharmacist at the Kirby Drugstore.

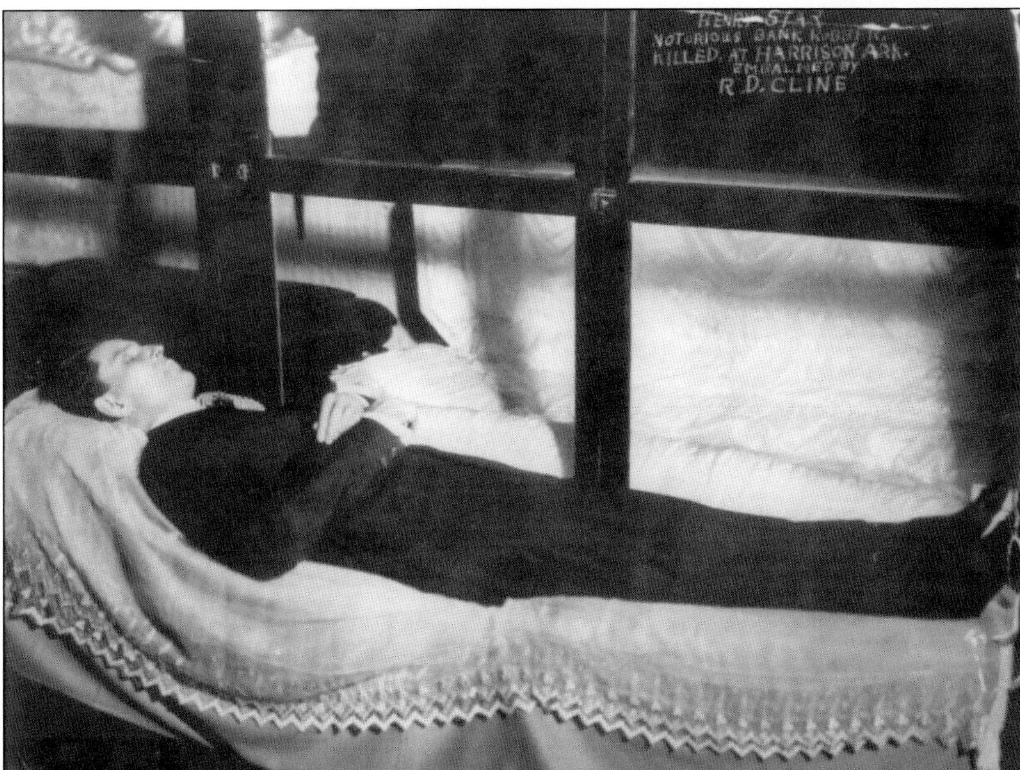

Henry Starr, 1921. During his 32 years in crime, Henry Starr robbed more banks than the James-Younger Gang and the Doolin-Dalton Gang put together. He started robbing banks on horseback in 1893 and conducted his last heist with an automobile in 1921. "The Cherokee Badman" netted over $60,000 from more than 21 bank robberies. He was shot and killed by William J. Myers in Harrison on February 18, 1921.

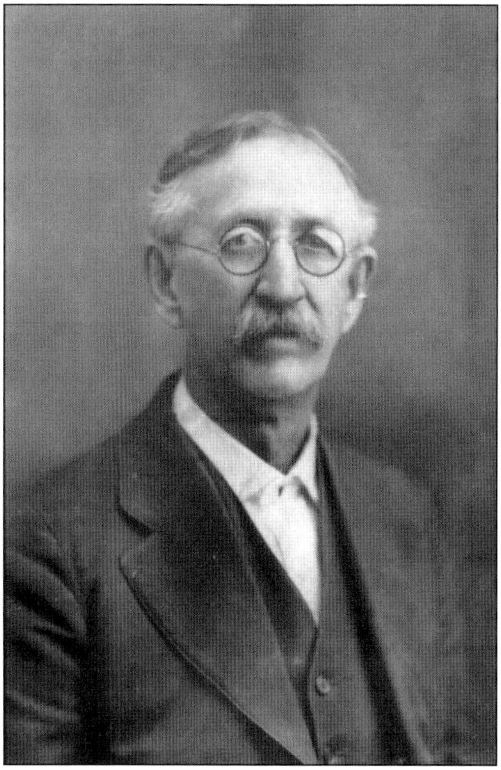

William J. Myers, 1921. Myers was the bank president in Harrison who gunned down notorious bank robber and horse thief Henry Starr on February 18, 1921. Myers shot Starr with a .38 caliber Winchester rifle, 1873 model, while Starr attempted to rob a Harrison bank. Starr was the first bank robber in the United States to use an automobile for getaways. Starr supporters targeted Myers and his family for decades.

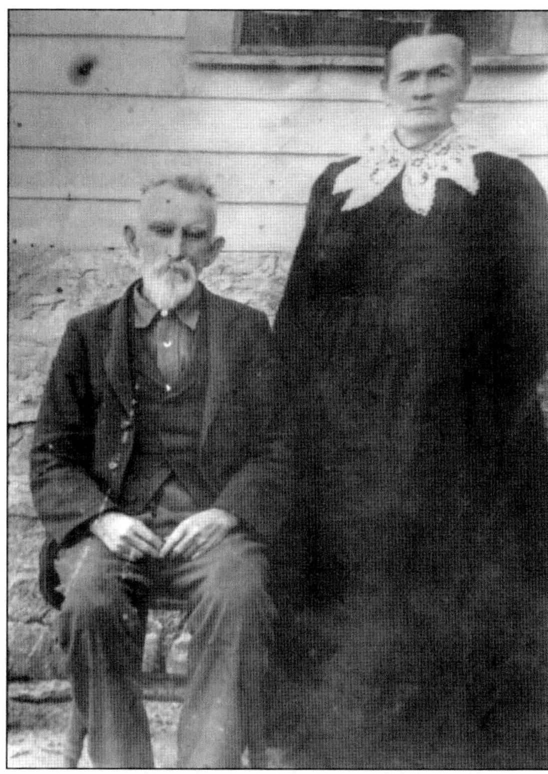

Pleasant Fowler and Mary Elizabeth Wilson, 1920s. Fowler served in the 14th Arkansas Infantry, Confederate States of America, rising to the rank of lieutenant colonel. At the surrender of Port Hudson, Louisiana, in July 1863, he was taken as a prisoner of war and sent to Ohio by his Union captors. After the war, he traveled a bit and then came back to the Ozarks to become a farmer.

Caswell T. Coffman. Coffman was a descendant of the Hugh White Coffman family, honored by North Arkansas Community College in 1981 as "Pioneer Family of the Year." Hugh White Coffman moved from Tennessee to the Harrison area in 1854, homesteading on 80 acres that he purchased from the government. Born in 1860, Caswell became an attorney in Little Rock and was elected county judge of Pulaski County.

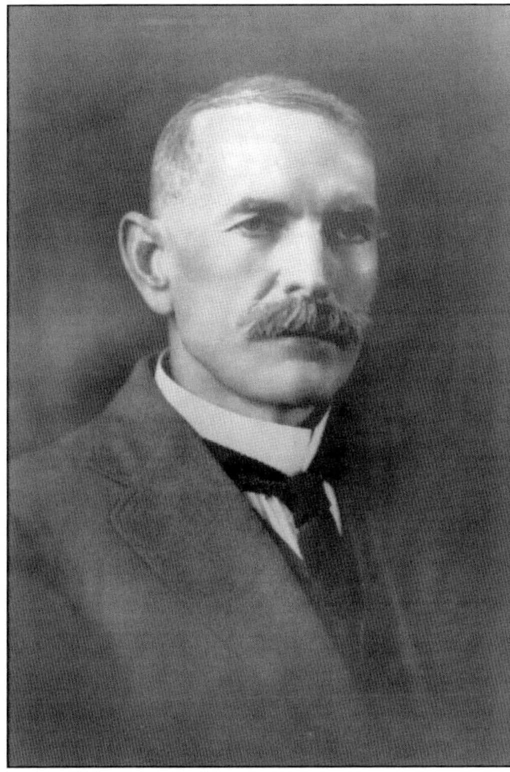

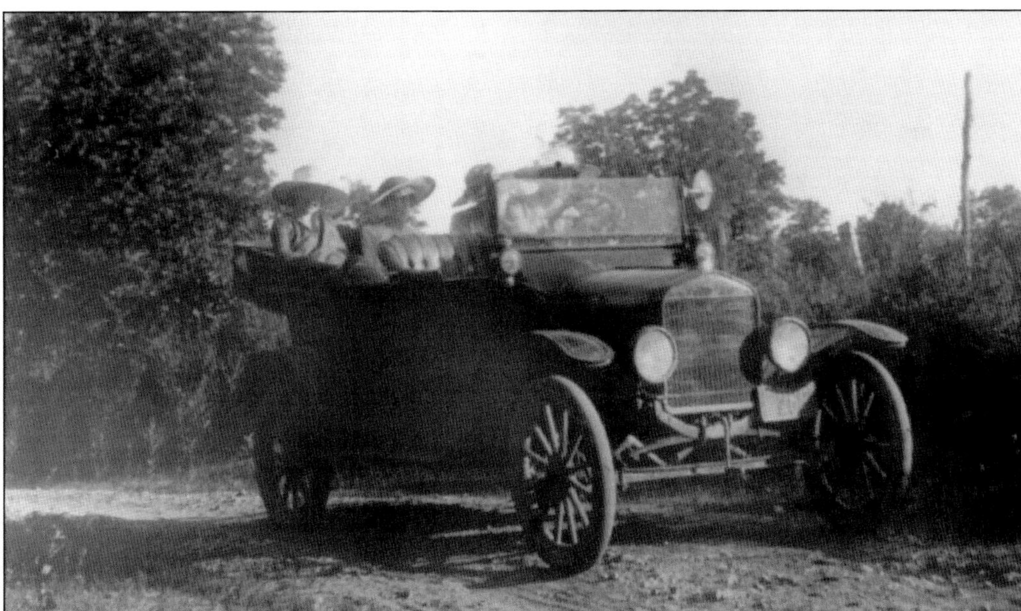

Women in a Model T. The Model T was produced by the Ford Motor Company from October 1, 1908, to May 26, 1927. It is generally regarded as the first affordable automobile, opening travel to middle-class Americans and becoming popular for the mass market. The price began at $825 but eventually fell to $360, becoming cheaper with time due to the efficiency of Ford's assembly-line system.

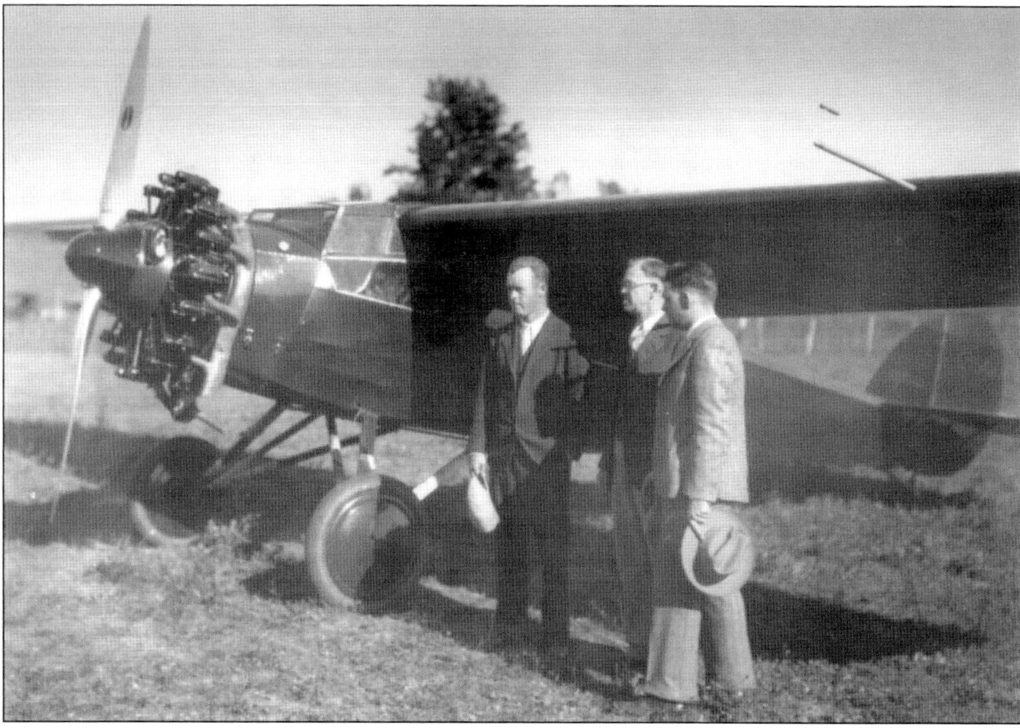

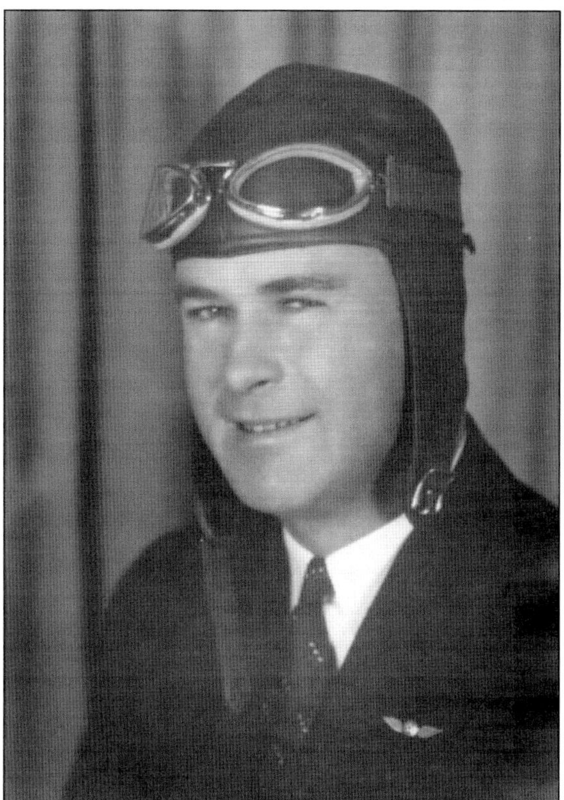

Earl Rowland, 1920s. Rowland was the first pilot to land at what is now Boone County Airport in 1921. In the photograph above, he stands at left beneath the wing of a 1920s Cessna. Rowland began flying in World War I at Kelly Field, Texas, in 1918. After the war, he was a test pilot for Cessna Aircraft from 1925 to 1940. In 1928, he won the Transcontinental Air Race, flying a Cessna monoplane from New York to California in five days. He won five National Air Races from 1928 to 1930. In 1930, he called for the building of an airport at Harrison. Rowland then flew with the US Air Transport Command from 1942 to 1945 during World War II. After the war, he became a helicopter and jet-aircraft pilot from 1946 to 1950. His last flight was at age 74. There is a memorial to Rowland at Boone County Airport in Harrison.

Group at Pilot's Knob. Located just past 4071 Pilot Knob Drive South, Pilot's Knob is a sought-after location for locals and visitors. Climbing the crags to the top of the rock formation is a popular activity. The views from the top offer expansive panoramas of the rolling hills that characterize the local topography.

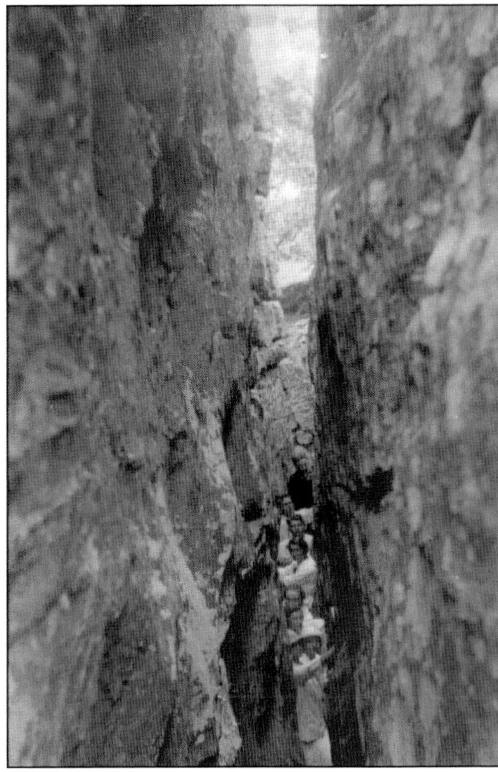

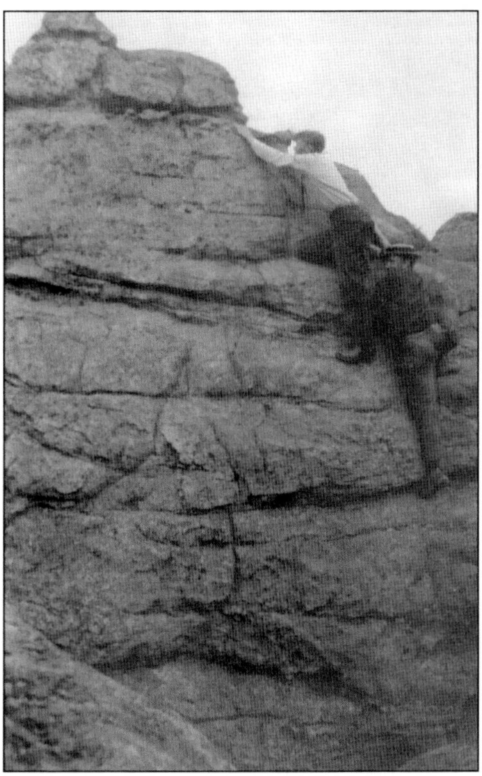

Climbing Pilot's Knob. Rock-climbing and bouldering is a popular sport in Arkansas, and some of the best climbing in the state can be found in the Harrison area. The hard sandstone rock typical of the Boston Mountains makes this sport an attraction for serious climbers of all levels and draws enthusiasts from all over the United States.

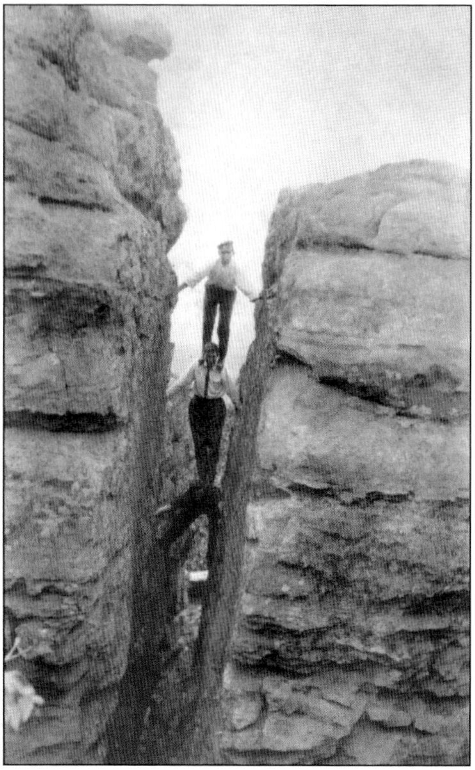

Pilot's Knob Climbers. While Pilot's Knob is located on privately owned land, the owner is happy to let visitors come and go as they please, as long as they leave just after sunset. On any given day, climbers can be seen free-climbing or top-roping. It has been a popular Harrison attraction for several decades.

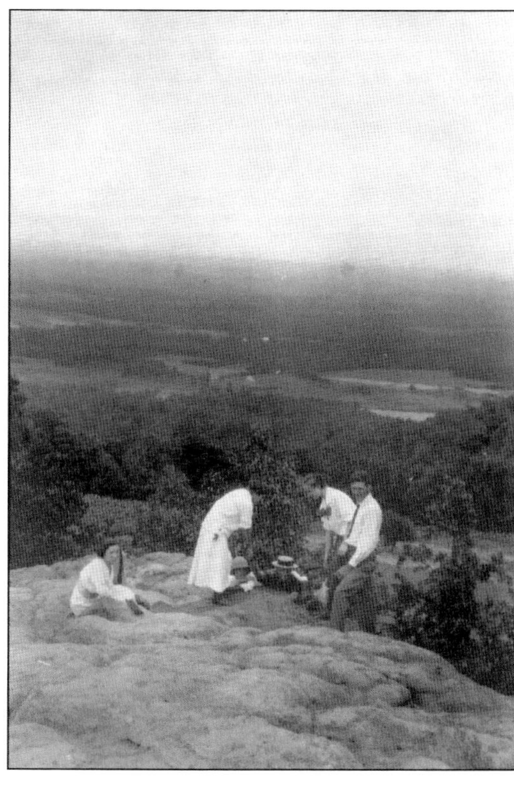

Top of Pilot's Knob. Located in the Boston Mountains of the southwestern part of the Ozark Plateau, the most-rugged and least-denuded section of the Ozarks, Pilot's Knob offers elevated views of Harrison and the surrounding landscape. While a great perch for enjoying 360-degree views of the area, visitors to this part of the state can catch views of bobcats, whitetail deer, great horned owls, and black bears.

J. Sam Rowland. Rowland (1874–1933), a prominent attorney in Harrison for much of his adult life, was also active in the community as a volunteer and philanthropist. He helped found the Rotary Club of Harrison on March 1, 1919, and served as its first president. He also served on the Harrison School Board for six years, from 1922 to 1928.

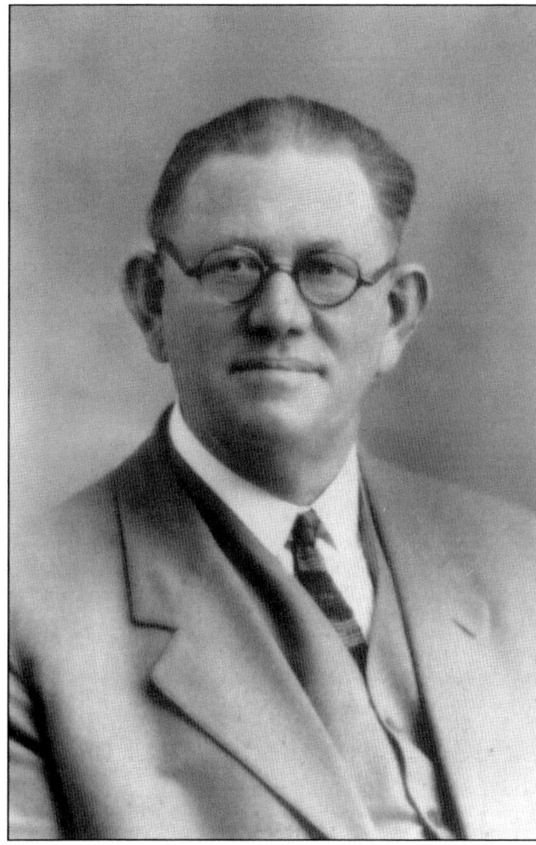

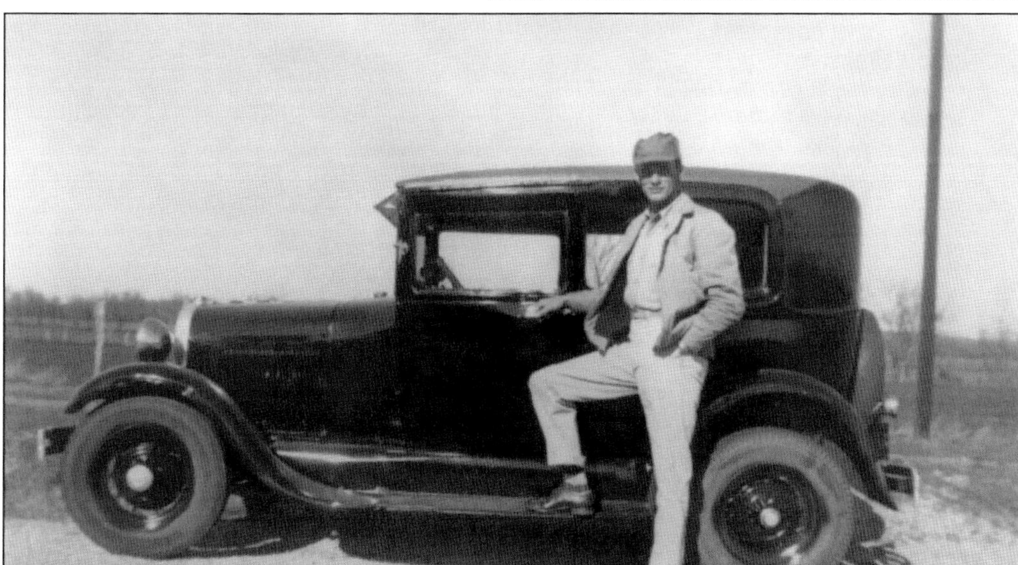

Willard Phillips and His Ford Model A. The Model A of 1928 to 1931 was another big success for the Ford Motor Company, following the Model T, which had been produced for 18 years. The price for the Model A ranged from $385 for a Roadster to $1,400 for a Town Car, and they came in four standard colors.

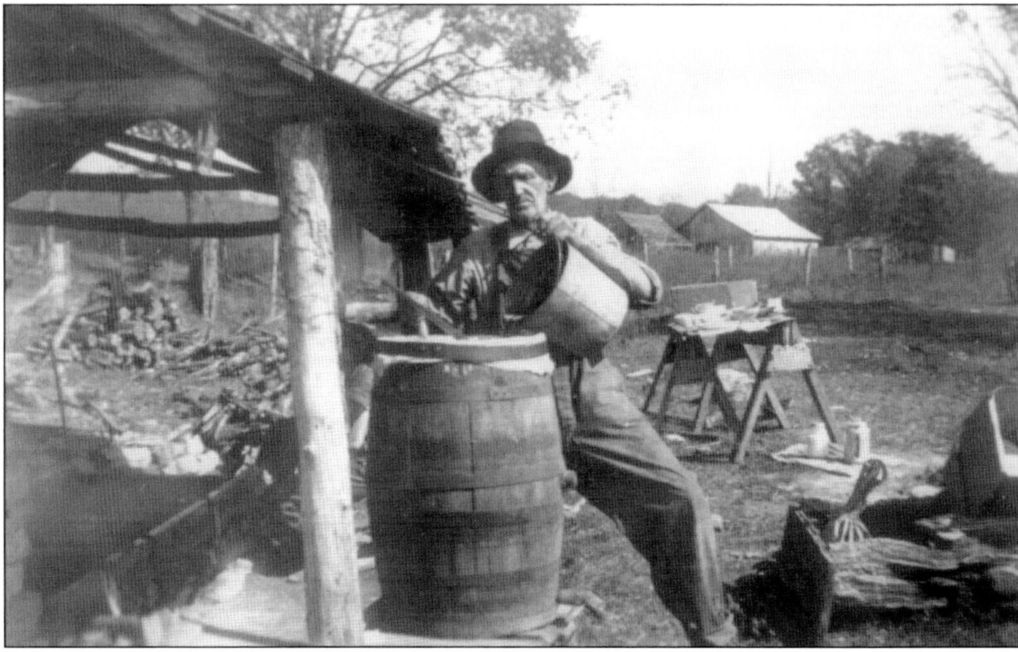

Making Sorghum Molasses, 1930s. Pictured here is Jesse L. Dees making sorghum molasses, an Ozarks staple for over 150 years. It was the main ingredient for sweetening foods. Sugar was expensive and difficult to get, and finding honey was too unreliable. Farmers could be more self-sufficient with something they grew on their own, like the sorghum cane crop.

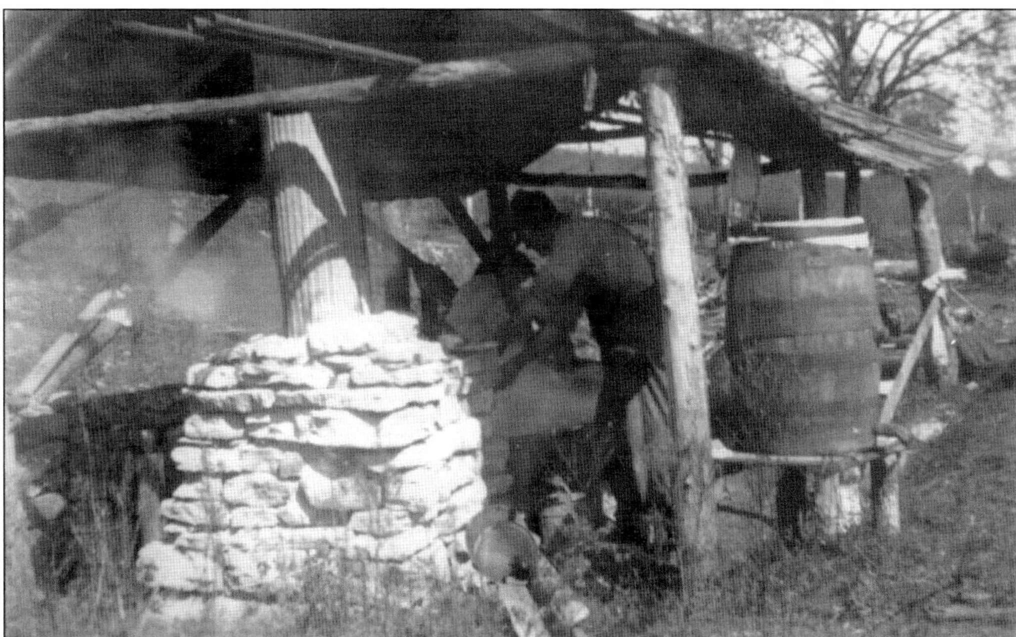

Jesse L. Dees Making Molasses, 1930s. It was very important to know what to do while growing, harvesting, and cooking sorghum cane for molasses. A poor growing season could produce an inferior crop. If the cane was not harvested and strained correctly, it would produce a bad batch of molasses. Making good molasses took training and was a rare skill.

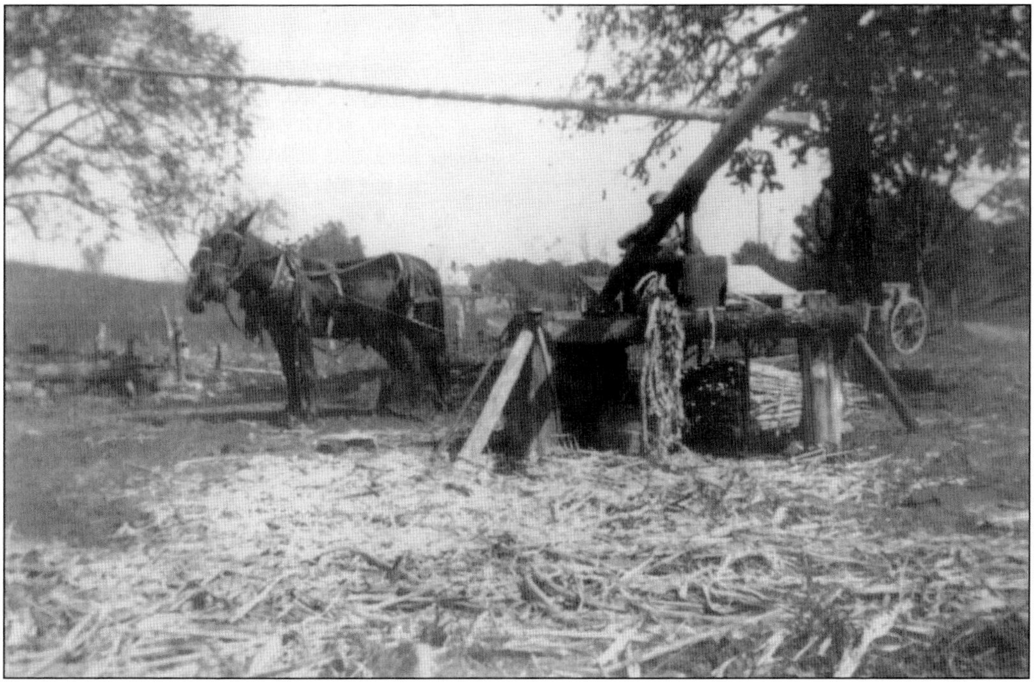

Extracting Sorghum Cane Juice, 1930s. Horses or mules were used to power mills that extracted juice from sorghum canes. Harnessed to a pole, the animals walked in circles. The pole was attached to gears, which turned the rollers of the mill. The animal was usually trained to start and stop on verbal commands, keeping a slow, steady pace. The mill was the first place to see what would soon become molasses.

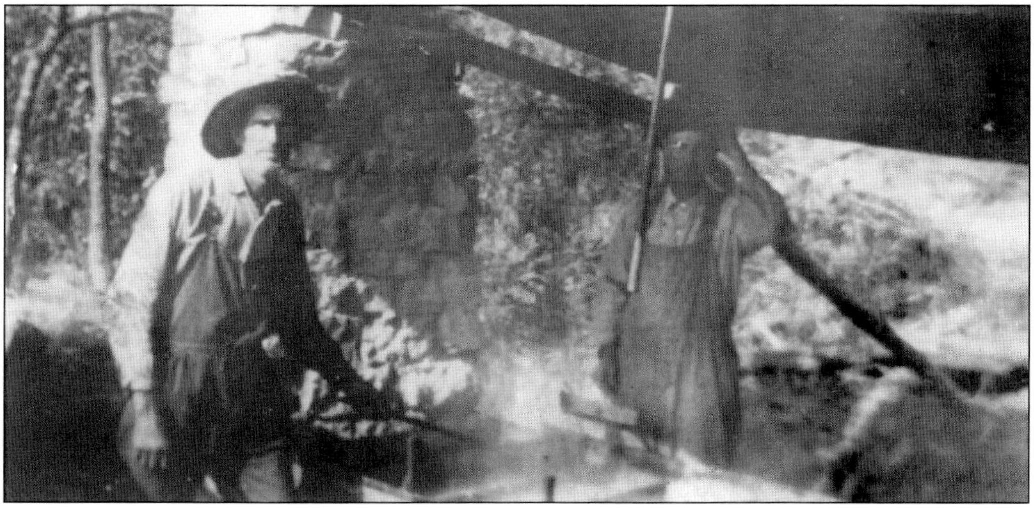

Cooking Molasses, 1930s. Making good molasses was a rare skill, and those who made it well were in demand. Molasses could be scorched from being cooked too fast, or it might be green from not enough cooking. It could be murky from dirty stalks or from improperly strained juice. It might be bitter from frosted cane or from improper handling during the harvest. Here, Jesse L. Dees (left) and Mittie Keeter engage in the process.

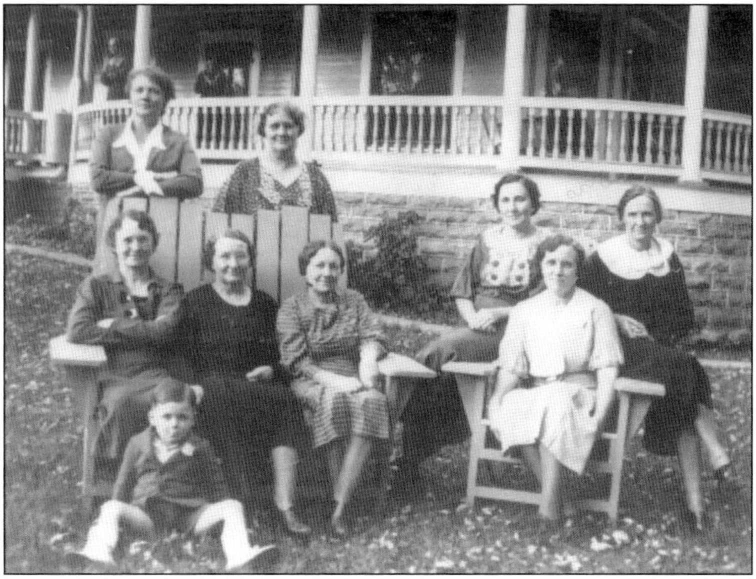

GLADDEN'S HOME, NOVEMBER 2, 1934. Dr. Gladden's home was located on South Pine Street. Posing here in no particular order are Bess Ruble, Bess Godwin, Willie Gladden, Pearl Olvey, Daisey Cecil, Mrs. Villines and grandson, Virginia Moore, and Flora Davis. The individuals on the porch in the background are unidentified.

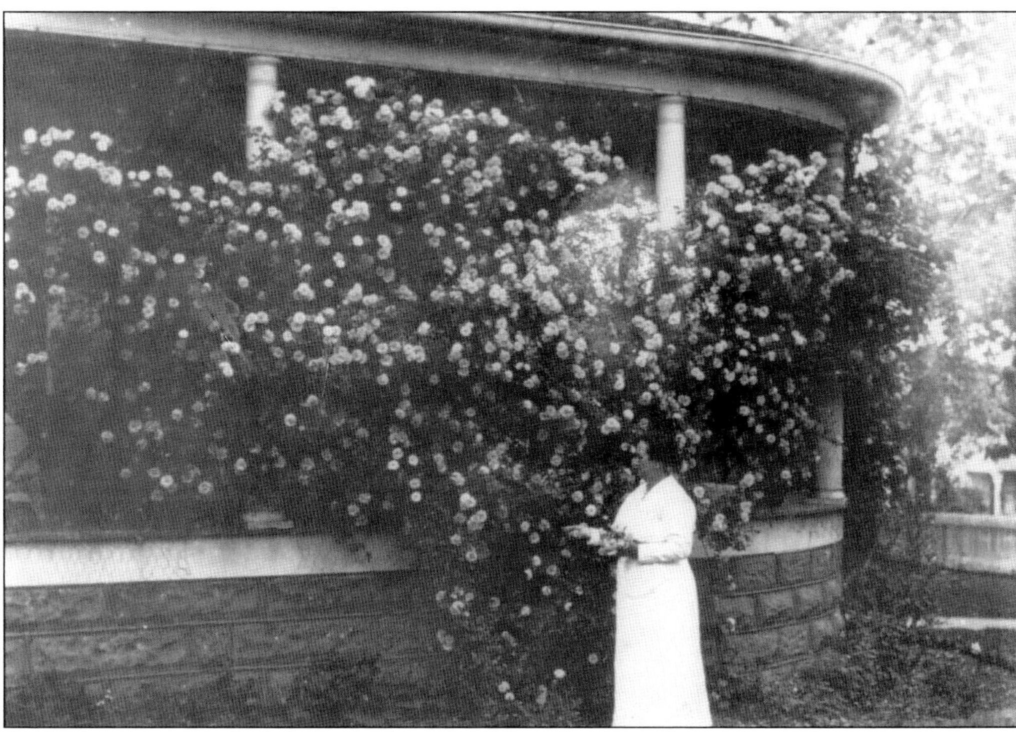

MARTHA HUDSON CAPPS. Born on April 7, 1863, Capps was the sister of Wesley Wood Hudson. She and Thomas Scott Capps were married on January 17, 1880, when she was 16. They had five children. Here, she stands outside her home on the corner of West College Avenue and South Cherry Street. She died on March 2, 1941.

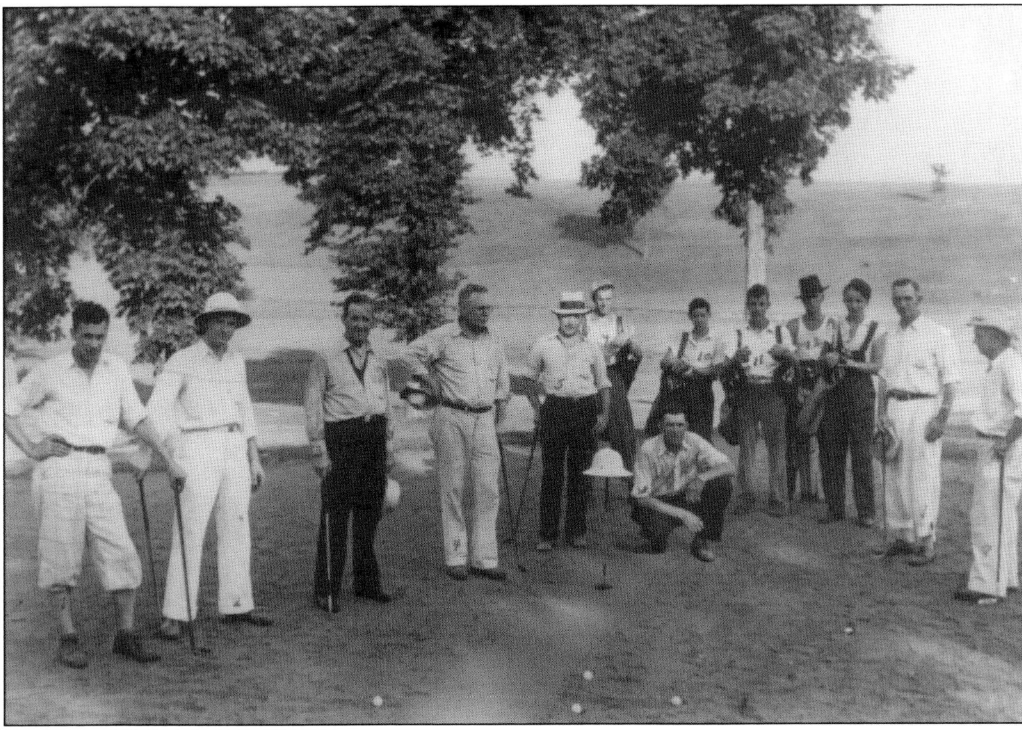

HARRISON COUNTRY CLUB, JULY 26, 1935. Established in 1924, the Harrison Country Club is one of the oldest golf courses in northern Arkansas. The golfers shown here are, from left to right, Web Newton, Arlis Milburn, Clay Holt, Homey Mitchell, Rex Worthington, Lex McAllister, Marvin Wagley, and Ed Fitton. The caddies are, from left to right, F.A. Cripps, David Fitton, M. Tippet, Ward Capps, and unidentified.

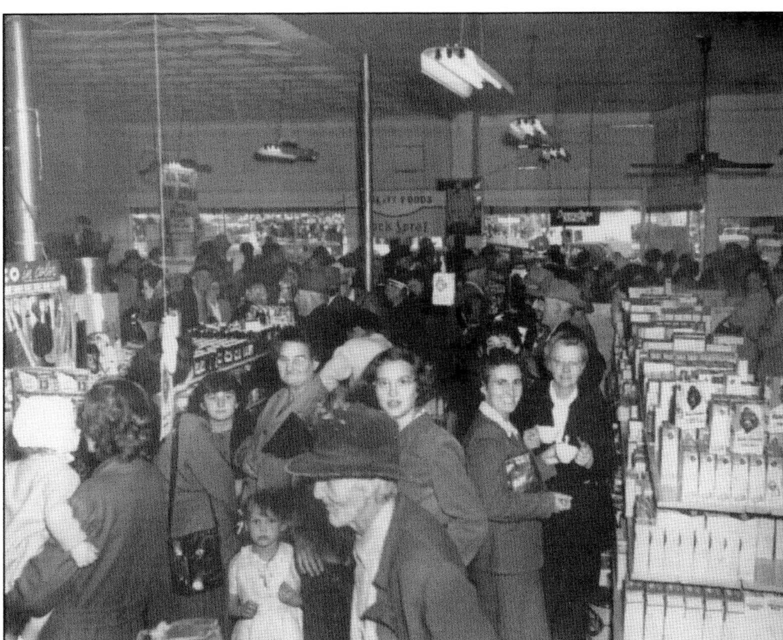

GROCERY STORE, LATE 1930S. Patrons in this grocery store appear quite happy about what is going on. It may be that Aunt Jemima Ready-Mix for Pancakes was new to the area. The pancake mix was one of a kind when it was introduced in 1889 in St. Joseph, Missouri. The Quaker Oats Company bought the brand in 1926; in a few years, the brand became a household name.

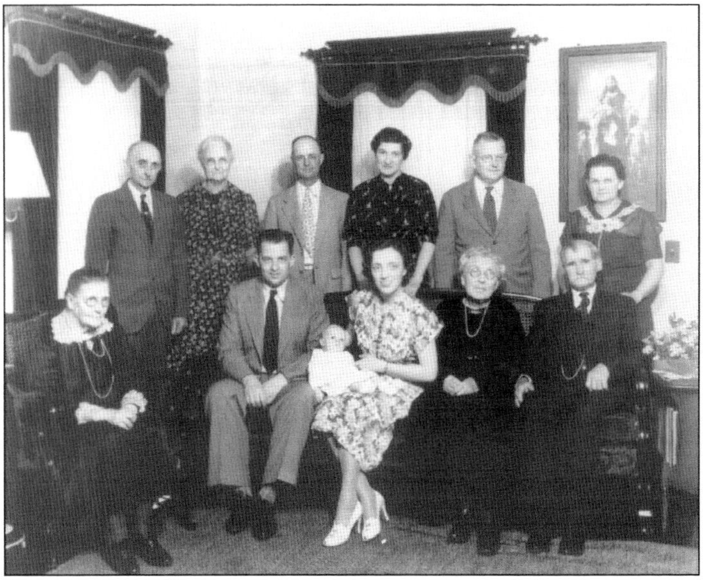

PROMINENT FAMILY OF HARRISON, 1938. Many of these names are still familiar in Harrison today. Shown here are, from left to right, (first row) Rhoda Virginia Kirby, Henry Vance Kirby, Henry Hudson Kirby, Elva Hudson Kirby, Adelia Jane Slagle, and D. Franklin Slagle; (second row) Wesley Wood Hudson, Ida Bell Eoff Hudson, Clarence Nicholson Hudson, Minnie Claire Slagle Hudson, Leander Bender Kirby, and Virgie May Kirby.

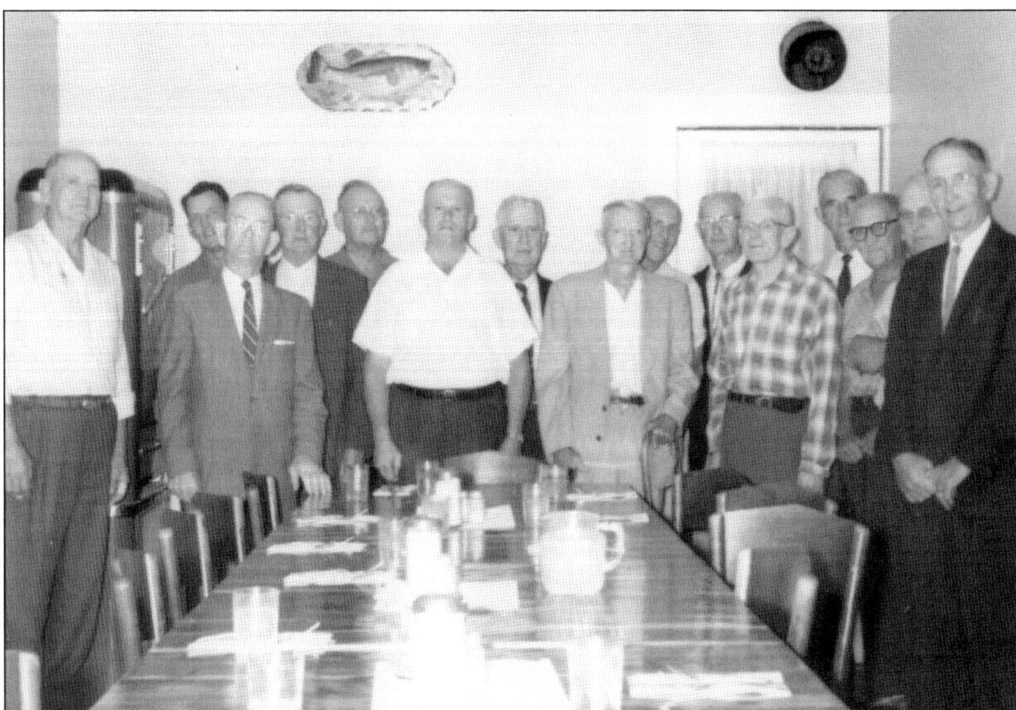

1911 HARRISON BASEBALL TEAM REUNION, 1962. Pictured here are members of the Harrison baseball team seen on page 103. The members are, from left to right, Clyde Middleton, Quinton Middleton, Ernest Cox, Sam Parrish, Roy Watkins, Otis Youngblood, Roy Milum, Tom Drive, Doc Keeter, Ernie Pruitt, Lonnie Gibson, Claude Alexander, John Roy Campbell, L.A. Watkins, and E.F. Cox.

INDEX